THAT PETER KAY BOOK

First published in Great Britain in 2006 by

André Deutsch
an imprint of the
Carlton Publishing Group
20 Mortimer Street
London W1T 3JW

A catalogue record for this book is available from the British Library

ISBN-13: 978-0-233-00180-7
ISBN-10: 0-233-00180-8

The publishers would like to thank the following sources for their kind
permission to reproduce the pictures in this book:

Page 1: Karen Peel (Top and bottom). Page 2: Karen Peel (T); Bolton Evening
News (B). Page 3: TopFoto.co.uk. Page 4: Retna Pictures Ltd. /MGM/
Photofest (T); Getty Images/Dave Benett (B). Page 5: Getty Images/Man Utd
(T); Rex Features/Mark Campbell (B). Page 6: Getty Images (T-L); Rex
Features/Mark Campbell (T-R); Rex Features/Richard Young (B).
Page 7: Retna Pictures Ltd. /Chris Finch (T-L); Rex Features/Brian Rasic;
(T-R); Empics/Yui Mok/PA (B). Page 8: Rex Features/Ken Mckay (T);
Empics/ Suzan/allactiondigital.com (B)

Every effort has been made to acknowledge correctly and contact the
source and/or copyright holder of each picture and Carlton Books
Limited apologises for any unintentional errors or omissions that will be
corrected in future editions of this book

Typeset by E-Type, Liverpool
Printed and bound in Great Britain by Mackays

THAT PETER KAY BOOK

THE STORY OF HOW PETER KAY BECAME BOLTON'S BIGGEST EXPORT

Johnny Dee

André Deutsch

To Kathy, Holly and Annie.
You are my sunshine.

Contents

'Imagination has given us the steam engine, the telephone, the talking-machine, and the automobile, for these things had to be dreamed of before they became realities. So I believe that dreams – daydreams, you know, with your eyes wide open and your brain machinery whizzing – are likely to lead to the betterment of the world. The imaginative child will become the imaginative man or woman most apt to invent, and therefore to foster, civilization.'

L. Frank Baum

'If you can talk with crowds and keep your virtue,
Or walk with kings – nor lose the common touch,
If neither foes nor loving friends can hurt you;
If all men count with you, but none too much,
If you can fill the unforgiving minute
With sixty seconds' worth of distance run,
Yours is the Earth and everything that's in it,
And – which is more – you'll be a Man, my son!'

Rudyard Kipling

'Garlic bread?'

Peter Kay

Introduction

It is 2 July 2002 and I am seated behind an enormous board table in a management office on Soho Square in the West End of London. I feel lonely. I haven't got an iPod or a newspaper to flick through and he's late. Outside, office workers are scattered around the small patch of grass in the middle of the square, motorcycle couriers dart in and out of traffic and I sit drumming my fingers waiting for him to arrive. I know he's in the building long before I see him – not because the building shakes as if he were King Kong or something, or because he's got a loud voice that bounces off the walls and makes you fall off your chair, but because I can hear people laughing. It's like a domino effect; a door opens somewhere in the building and a guffaw gushes out of it as if the room were filled with water. Then another person laughs, then another, I turn around and that's when I see him, perched on the edge of a secretary's desk holding an unfeasibly large chocolate birthday cake and asking her if she's all right, when she's going on her holidays, do her radiators need bleeding … finally he enters the room, puts the cake down and asks, 'Do you want a brew?'

He's a big man, but not as big as he looks on TV. They say telly adds 10 pounds. In his case it's more like 20. And he looks younger, too, especially as I'm used to seeing him in a grey wig wearing a BHS cardigan and drinking from a vase. His skin is as soft as a baby's arse, but his handshake is as firm as a bricklayer's. He tells me it's his 29th birthday. Do I want some cake? Go on, you know you want to.

I am here to interview him for *The Guide*, a pocket-sized supplement of entertainment wonder that's slipped inside the *Guardian* every Saturday. Because the first episode of the new series he has just made features a few famous TV soundtracks scattered through it (*Van Der Valk, Black Beauty, Minder*) they have hit upon the idea of basing the article around his all-time favourite themes. But before we talk about those there's other stuff I want to know, standard stuff, like how old he was when he first decided he wanted to be a comedian (seven), what he did before, what his mum's like, but also questions about his new series and in particular the scene at the family fun day involving a giant inflatable penis. His answers are brilliant and funny and so long that I begin looking at the tape wheezing inside my dictaphone and worrying it's about to die. The problem is that in most interviews, as you listen to rock stars and actors answer, you're thinking, 'This is boring' or 'I won't be able to print this' or even 'Please say something funny'. But every word that comes out of the mouth of the man in front of me is comedy gold. It's ridiculous. I could fill up two whole issues of *The Guide* with this stuff but I've got only a couple of pages.

Eventually we move on to discussing old TV shows and every time I mention a programme he starts singing the theme tune word for word, and not just ones we all know, such as *Minder*, but obscure, forgotten ones such as *The Fall Guy* – 'I never spent much time in school/But I taught ladies plenty'. As if this wasn't impressive enough, at the merest mention of a programme title he will not only tell me what channel it was on, but what day of the week, the time and what was on before and after it. Pushed, he'd probably go through the adverts and continuity announcements too but instead he tells me about his life around the time of the show's being broadcast – about his grandad baby-sitting and his dad buying fish and chips every Friday and his mum tripping over with a mug of tea in the middle of *Flambards*.

After we've spent two hours together, with the birthday cake demolished, he chucks me his *Live at the Top of the Tower* video across the table and we say our goodbyes – ignorantly, I hadn't even known he had a stand-up act. It's only later when I watch it at home that night and nearly die from laughing so much that it fully dawns on me how lucky I've been. I'm too young ever to have met Stan Laurel or Eric Morecambe or Les Dawson or Ronnie Barker, but I've met the next in that line of British comedy legends. Ladies and gentlemen, Peter Kay.

Chapter One

It was Much Better in Rehearsal

'If you're born a Catholic, you're not born in hospital, you're born in guilt.'

Peter Kay

'When I was a kid I used to pray for a new bike. Then I realised that the Lord doesn't work that way, so I stole one and asked Him to forgive me ... and I got it!'

Emo Phillips

Peter John Kay was born on Monday, 2 July 1973. According to the local newspaper, the weather that day was typical of British summertime: sunny intervals and scattered showers. Whether or not it was that fine rain that soaks you right through is unspecified. The rest of the afternoon edition of the *Bolton Evening News* – then still a tablecloth-sized broadsheet – was awash with incident: platform shoes 'on way out', screamed a front-page headline, while else-where there was the scoop that a blonde beauty queen from Ramsbottom had come second in the Miss Cinema Europe contest and that Denis Law had signed for his old club, Manchester City. Meanwhile, in Little Hulton, a two-year-old toddler had survived a 15-foot fall from a bedroom window with just a small scratch on his head. On TV the highlight of the evening was *The Two Ronnies* on BBC2 at 9.25 p.m. with special guests Lynsey De Paul, Georgie Fame and Alan Price.

Two days after his son was born Michael Kay visited the *Bolton Evening News* offices and placed an announcement in the Births, Marriages and Deaths section: 'On July 2 1973 at Bolton District Hospital to Deirdre (née O'Neil) and Michael, a son (Peter), brother for Julie Ann. Thanks to all concerned.'

Michael – the son of a driller – and Deirdre (who was born Margaret but dropped it in favour of her middle name), the daughter of a cable layer, were married, both aged 20, at St Peter and Paul's Roman Catholic Church in Pilkington Street, Bolton, on 22 June 1968. Julie was born just over a year later. Back then Michael was a maintenance fitter in a cotton mill, but by the time Peter was impressing the teachers at St Ethelbert's Primary School with his Frank Spencer impressions (his first school report noted 'Peter seems unable to resist trying to amuse') he was working as an engineer at the Daubhill Ropeworks, while Deirdre had left her job as a chiseller at a paper mill to stay at home and raise the family – motherhood rather than chiselling being her calling.

When he was in his twenties and he was asked what his father did, Peter answered: 'I dunno, bash metal, that's what dads do, isn't it?'

The Kay family lived in Daubhill – Peter used to tell people, 'You say it like wobble except with D instead of W at the front' – with Michael's parents, Stanley and Edith. Daubhill was an area with a large south Asian community a mile or so from the town centre, which consisted mainly of two-up, two-down back-to-back houses that easily reinforce dated southern stereotypes of grim northern towns populated by women with headscarves over their rollers scrubbing their front steps. Shortly after Peter's birth Michael and Deirdre moved one street north, staying in the same area.

The streets where Peter Kay grew up seem pretty unchanged by the ravages of time, the occasional abandoned fridge freezer notwithstanding – indeed, judging by the sunlight-faded mutant ninja turtles toys in the window of Kola's on St Helens Road, many of the shops still have the same stock.

Peter's father was a small man, just over five feet tall, but, like most of the men employed by the ropeworks, he had an unquenchable thirst for alcohol. He'd spread his custom over half a dozen locals as well as the Ellesmere Road Social Club and would sink a few pints before moving on to the whisky, or later in his life, white wine. He was a funny man who deployed bone-dry sarcasm and enjoyed telling jokes, especially the punchlines, which he'd repeat mercilessly until everyone got them – 'Are you having that?' Peter's mother, who was born in Coalisland in County Tyrone, Northern Ireland, was, he says, very different, 'a bit mad, more laugh out loud'. Neighbours say the couple were 'like chalk and cheese'; Deirdre wasn't a drinker, so they were seldom seen out together.

Like many a good God-fearing Catholic tyke, Peter Kay was an altar boy from the age of five. 'Whenever he does an impression of a creepy priest,' says schoolfriend Karen Peel, whose brother was also an altar boy at St Ethelbert's Church in Deane at that time, 'I just know he's doing an impression of Father Flatley.'

Yet Father Flatley was a good man, too. In 1994 a baby was abandoned on his doorstep and he took the girl under his wing. At his funeral in December 2001, Peter said: 'He had a great understanding and helped a lot of people. I knew him well. It is very sad.'

As a child, however, Peter worshipped in front of a different altar from the one Father Flatley would have preferred: a 24-inch oblong one that took pride of place in the Kay living room. Aged eight, he saw a vision, his first celebrity in the flesh, when the family walked out to Four Lane Ends in nearby Farnworth one wet Sunday April morning and watched Jimmy Savile jog by in the Bolton Marathon. To commemorate the occasion Peter bought a novelty soap-on-a-rope *Jim'll Fix It* medal.

Fortunately Karen Peel, who went to the adjoining St Ethelbert's Roman Catholic Junior School, was around to witness Peter Kay's debut public performance in a production of *The Wizard of Oz* in the spring of 1984 to celebrate the 50th anniversary of the school. 'He was the Mayor of Munchkinland and I do remember him stealing the show a bit,' she recalls. 'He played a very good, middle-aged, portly mayor, which at the age of 11 was quite a thing to carry off.'

This wasn't to be the last occasion on which Peter would follow the yellow brick road. The next time, rather like Dorothy's trip over the rainbow, it would be an event that would change the course of his life for ever. Until then, though, there are 562 episodes of *Coronation Street* to sit through, not to mention a couple of series of *The Gentle Touch*, six years of *'Allo 'Allo*, Kevin Keegan falling off his bike in *Superstars*, Five Star being called wankers in a phone-in on *Going Live*, and two rubber balls telling jokes in Irish accents on *Why Don't You?*. Then there's a lifetime of *Take Hart* with Tony Hart, *Top Cat*, *The Professionals*, *Loveboat*, *Dallas* and a couple of hundred chances for couples to win Bully's special prize on *Bullseye*.

> I can't go away with you on a rock climbing weekend,
> What if something's on TV and it's never shown again?
> > *The Lemonheads*, 'The Outdoor Type'

TV was not just an addiction for the young Peter Kay; it was much, much more than that. In 2001, when he appeared in the *I Love the 1970s* series of nostalgia shows, friends told him he must have been sent clips of the shows he commented on because he'd only have been a toddler when they were on.

'I wasn't, honest, people think I'm lying,' he says. 'In 1976 I was three but I remember what was on telly.'

'Television was so much a part of my life, I loved it,' he told me. 'A lot of my friends were out playing football and things like that, but TV was like a religion for me. You had to be in front of the telly when a programme started or you missed it.'

Where other kids' lives would be measured out by football fixtures or exams, Peter Kay's ran to the timetable supplied by the *Radio Times*.

'*Minder* always reminds me of Wednesday nights at nine o clock,' he says. 'Benny Hill would be on at eight. I'd go to bed at 8.30 and I'd always hear the *Minder* theme tune through the floor: "If you want to I'll change the situation ...". Then I'd hear the front door close and my dad going out and I knew where he'd be going; he'd send us to bed and then go and get fish and chips. He'd come back and I'd always come down and go, "I can't sleep ... ooooh fish and chips" ... and he'd go, "Ah, all right, you can have a butty." So I'd stay and watch a bit of *Minder*.'

Saturdays meant *The Pink Panther Show*, *Dr Who*, *Jim'll Fix It*, *3-2-1* and his dad's night to cook.

'We'd have breakfast at night-time, because it was all he knew how to make, so we'd have full English for tea.'

Peter's fear of missing something life-changing on TV abated in the early 1980s, when the Kays were among the first families on Willows Lane to buy a video recorder – a Ferguson Videostar top loader with a remote control on a lead. According to family legend, when Peter would press rewind on this primitive piece of hi-tech the whole house would shake. Soon Peter was matching his sister's obsession with filling a C-90 with the Top 40 chart rundown minus the 'this is Mike Read on 275 and 285' bits with an ambitious plan to videotape virtually everything. Soon his bedroom would be lined with entire runs of *'Allo 'Allo*, *Porridge* and his favourite in his early teenage years, a sit-com starring an alien from the planet Ork who once laid a giant egg from which his son emerged and enjoyed something of a romantic liaison with a puzzled young lady from Boulder, Colorado.

'I've got every episode of *Mork and Mindy* on video except the last one,' he says. 'There were ninety-five. The last f***ing episode of *Mork and Mindy*! I taped it religiously, because when I was a kid I loved it. I started taping them thinking there won't be that many ... I've got *Mork and Mindy* Volume 8, Volume 9 ... Every Wednesday I'd run home from school and tape them religiously. I carried on and I went to Spain in 1991 and it was the last episode of *Mork and Mindy* and I sent cards from Spain, I rang up from Spain saying, "Tape it, tape it." Did they tape it? Did they f***! It was on recently and the theme came on and I had this rush of being a child and my dad laughing so much at it.'

Peter's elder sister Julie also made full use of the new technology in the house and would hold regular Saturday movie afternoons for her pals where, unbeknown to Deirdre Kay, they'd watch 'video nasties' such as *Driller Killer* and *I Spit on Your Grave*. 'Mum'd be knocking on door going, "Your dinner's ready, are you coming or what?"' says Peter.

In years to come, of course, the Ferguson Videostar would feature in Peter's stand-up act when he recalled how his father would put a cushion over it whenever they left the house to prevent it being stolen. 'Nobody'd steal it,' jokes Peter. 'It were too bloody heavy.'

The video recorder also came in handy when, aged 13, he broke his ankle and spent a fortnight off school. With his son having to spend the entire time at home on the sofa, Michael Kay struck a cut-price deal with the local video shop – Take Two – if he agreed to hire two films a day. And so began Kay's love of films and, in particular, camp sci-fi musical *Flash Gordon*, which in turn led to an obsession with the band who had provided the soundtrack, Queen. Surprisingly, when you consider how often he is compared with Les Dawson and Eric Morecambe, the first comedians Peter Kay loved were Americans: Robin Williams (who starred as Mork), Steve Martin and master of the deadpan one-liner Steven Wright. His favourite movies were American too: Mel Brooks's *Blazing Saddles* and *The Producers* and the Zucker Brothers' brilliant parody of airborne disaster movies, *Airplane!*. He bought the stand-up records like Steven Wright's *I Have a Pony*, and soundtrack albums of all of them, and he would spend hours taping them and splicing them between strange vinyl oddities he found at the record store on Bolton Market and at Manchester discount stores, compiling what he called 'Crap Trax' on to cassette tapes for the amusement of his friends.

'They were brilliant,' remembers schoolfriend Michael Atherton. 'They'd have songs from Manhattan Transfer, Telly Savalas – Peter had all his albums and even wrote him a fan letter. There'd be "Theme from *Love, American Style*", John Inman from *Are You being Served* with a military brass band, I shit you not, Patrick Macnee and "Kinky Boots". Every track would be interspersed with blipvert clips from *Airplane!* like "Joey, have you ever been in a Turkish prison?" and various other things. I was really jealous of Peter's record collection.'

Mount St Joseph's in Hawthorne Road, Deane, opened in 1902 and was the first Roman Catholic secondary school in England to be built under the Balfour Education Act. Until 1979 it was a girls' grammar school, but in 1979 it became a co-educational secondary school. The school buildings were tagged on to a crumbling old convent, home to the authoritarian headmistress, Sister Barbara.

'She didn't like Peter,' remembers Karen Peel. 'But then I

don't think she liked me either. I don't think she liked children, full stop. She was an archetypal, stuck-up, prudish
Irish nun. She didn't like the idea of working-class boys
spoiling her school.'

'I don't think she ever got over the school switching from
all girls,' says Michael Atherton.

Despite the ominous presence of the nuns, Mount St
Joseph's wasn't what might be described today as a centre of
excellence. But what it lacked in academic prowess it made
up for in other ways. Peter joined in with all the school
holiday trips, to Wales and, most memorably, in 1987 to the
tiny nature reserve, the Isle of Rhum in the Inner Hebrides
of Scotland, the population of which doubled with the visit of
30-odd schoolkids from Bolton. Before the trip Peter told his
father he needed a proper coat, because they were going
walking and climbing. But Kay Senior's idea of what consti-
tuted a proper coat for a school trip differed somewhat from
his son's and he returned from town with a luminous yellow
jacket Peter described as the kind of thing people wear when
they're working on motorways. Embarrassed by his garish
jacket though he was, one day on the holiday it came in
handy when they explored the rugged Cuillin Mountains,
where they would be staying overnight in a remote and very
basic hostel building. For safety's sake the Mount St Joseph
kids were split into two, but then, disastrously, one of the
groups went missing.

'It was very emotional; they were missing for about four
hours, but it turned out they'd just gone down the wrong side
of the mountain and had to trek all the way round,' remembers Karen Peel. 'When they turned up there were hugs and
kisses. We thought they'd died.'

Peter Kay loved talking about this dramatic calamity and
in particular about the ferryman who appeared out of the
mist with a raised lantern like something out of John

Carpenter's *The Fog*, shouting 'Is everyone all right?', which ironically petrified half the schoolkids he was supposed to be rescuing.

'You'd never get away with school trips like that now, I suppose,' muses Karen Peel. 'We even had non-official trips organised by the teachers that had nothing to do with the school. Mount St Joseph's was quite old-fashioned in that it saw itself as part of the community,' she says. 'It had that family, community spirit thing where it didn't feel like you were at school sometimes. There was always some sort of club going on after school, dancing, drama or art, and Peter would always be there.'

Peter was a paper boy for Chris's News, a newsagent on his street, Willows Lane, from the age of 11 to 16 and was popular with both the old-age pensioners on his route (for whom he'd regularly do odd bits of shopping) and the small kids (one summer, he bought a whole box of giant ice pops from the shop and distributed them among the children on his round). After delivering the *Bolton Evening News* every afternoon he would rush back to Mount St Joseph's.

In the winter term of 1985, Peter's first year at the school, inspired by Band Aid, teacher Paul Abbott wrote a tune called 'Song for the Starving' and had 6,000 copies pressed on vinyl. During the recording Abbott scolded Peter for changing the lyrics and making the other singers laugh. 'Life's just a joke to you, Kay. Life's a joke,' he yelled. The line stayed with Peter throughout his school life and almost became his first catchphrase, as he would mockingly repeat it to himself behind the teachers' backs.

Peter also featured in a fashion show for CAFOD and in the annual talent contest held each year on St Joseph's Day, where he would sing or tell a few jokes. The majority of the school saw such activities as spectacularly uncool; not that this bothered Peter who, uncooler still, counted some of the staff among his friends, particularly art teacher John Clough.

'Him and John Clough were like two peas in a pod,' remembers Karen Peel. 'You'd walk into the room and they'd be chuckling about something. I'm sure he had a big influence on Peter's humour. He was a great bloke, not like a teacher at all really, he used to bring in cake.' Clough, whom Peter described as being 'the spitting image of Gorden Kaye in *'Allo 'Allo*' and 'really laid-back', also influenced his star pupil's music taste, making him cassettes of crusty rock artists such as Genesis and Dan Fogelberg. For someone who had grown up in a house with just five albums (*The Best of the Carpenters, The Best of the Beach Boys, The Best of Simon & Garfunkel, The Best of Tony Christie* and 'something Irish') it was a revelation. 'He showed films in art lessons and he used to get us to draw lyrics of Beatles songs,' remembers Peter. 'He made me see that art was not just in pictures in a frame, but also in film and cinematography – all around us. He made a big impression on my life.'

'Peter had this abstract way of seeing things,' John Clough, who still teaches at Mount St Joseph's, says. 'Even though he wouldn't really answer the question, he would say something even more interesting. Of course he was very popular with his classmates, being such an entertainer. But he was also a strangely calming influence.'

Kay's calming influence extended beyond the classroom into the playground. According to Michael Atherton there were some rough kids at the school, but they didn't spend long on Peter. 'He had a way of disarming people,' he recalls. 'But at the same time he'd be taking the piss out of them. He wasn't all that overweight at the time. Peter was picked on a bit, as was I for that matter, for being slightly filled out, which probably counted as fat to the street-hardened wastrels doing the picking.'

'I was bullied a bit, but it was only mild, nothing major,' remembers Peter himself. 'They called me fat and I'd just make a joke of it and say, "Yeah, I am, aren't I?" It was my own fault, I ate too much.'

'I just think most kids didn't know how to take him,' says Karen Peel. 'Most kids gave him a look of "I don't know what you're on about, you're just that strange kid who's a bit funny but I don't know why you're funny because I don't understand you". I used to hang out with Peter and Catherine, Michael and the Smith twins, Jane and Claire. He didn't really seem to have many male friends. He wasn't into football, he wasn't into the stuff average teenage boys were into; he was more interested in messing about with videos.'

Interviewed recently, Patrick McGuinness, who would be given his big acting break by Peter as a lecherous bouncer, pointed up the difference between himself and his friend: 'At school, although we were mates, we had different interests really. Peter was into sitting in his bedroom and listening to the words off songs and then writing them down, or taping stuff off the telly. I was just interested in getting my end away!'

It wasn't just his friends or John Clough's cake and Genesis albums that attracted Peter back into school when he could have been at home watching *Rentaghost*. There was the art and music lab which, as well as all the standard school paraphernalia, contained video editing equipment and a hand-held video camera. By virtue of the fact that he was the only person in the school who knew how to use it all, he became the school's unofficial cameraman. When nuns and priests from across Europe visited the school for Caring Church Week he was given the task, by Sister Barbara, of documenting the occasion. The nuns were happy with the results, but didn't know he'd made another copy, over which he'd dubbed the nuns and priests telling jokes. He was also using the equipment for video versions of his 'Crap Trax', to which he'd give titles like *Weasels* and copy for Michael Atherton and John Clough.

'Mentally scarred by football', he did have one hobby that took place outside the school gates. With two of his classmates (Warren Powell and Paul Coleman) he formed something of a comedy troupe cum prototype *Jackass*. Originally calling themselves the All Stars, they later became known as the Tree-ers (after the Irish pronunciation of the number three). The main *modus operandi* of this primi-tive comedy gang was to steal the school's video camera and take it into Bolton town centre, where they would film their skits: surfing shopping trolleys in Morrison's car park and re-creating the opening titles of *Dallas* on the corner of Trinity Street, outside Comet. The best idea of all, though, was interviewing old-age pensioners, bombarding them with a series of baffling, incoherent questions in order to film their puzzled reactions. In one compilation, 'They Flew by Night', Peter can be heard chuckling behind the camera while he asks a greying old biddy 'Whaddya-think-of-the-time-o-life-the-kinda-know?' and 'Is it prison of life?'

For comedy historians this tape alone would be evidence enough that Peter Kay was always destined for greatness. But there is another video, wobbly and out of focus though it is, that records the moment he became a star in waiting.

> Somewhere over the rainbow
> Skies are blue,
> And the dreams that you dare to dream
> Really do come true.
>
> > *E. Y. Harburg*, 'Somewhere Over the Rainbow'

Another of Peter Kay's duties was performing as the school DJ, although as Karen Peel is keen to stress, it 'was silly DJ-ing, not proper DJ-ing'.

'Let's just say he were no Judge Jules,' says another friend, Sonia Hurst, who witnessed Kay and his DJ partner in crime Michael Atherton on their hired wheels of steel together with flashing traffic light special effects. Pupils would bring in their records to be played at the irregular Friday-night events, scrawling their names on the sleeves, but Peter would sabotage the proceedings by splicing in the occasional piece of comedy dialogue from Leonard Rossiter in *Rising Damp*, Peter Cook and Dudley Moore's Derek and Clive comedy albums, Steve Martin's 'Grandpa bought a rubber' joke. Karen Peel also remembers Kay grabbing the microphone and impersonating the cheesy vocal stylings of a mobile DJ, interspersing songs with cries of 'shabba' and 'this one's for the laydeez'. Throughout, Sister Barbara would be prowling the floor to make sure there was no 'funny business'.

Peter would spend hours at home with his knackered double-deck ghetto blaster assembling the tapes he'd use to insert classic comedy TV moments between the hits of the day. He'd also include choice sections from the first record he ever purchased – a BBC Library sound effects album – speeding cars, canned laughter and explosions.

Even after he left school, Peter Kay still had a hand in the Friday-night discos, handing Michael Atherton, who was in the year below him, tapes together with long written-out lists as to when to insert the necessary between-song gag or clip. Michael kept two sheets of instructions for a fifth-form leavers' disco on 25 May 1990. Among the soundbite clips Peter Kay had assembled for his friend was Jimmy Cagney's classic 'Top of the world, Ma' line from *White Heat*, the *A Team* theme tune, a Radio One jingle and 'The Birdy Song'. Kay also included various snippets from James H. Reeves's late-night phone-in show, 'Nocturnal Emissions', on Manchester's Radio Piccadilly. Reeves was notorious for getting the sack from the station in 1981 for playing the

Queen song 'Killer Queen' after a news item about a 17-year-old student shooting blank bullets at the monarch during Trooping of the Colour. In the late 1980s Reeves played host to an expanding list of Mancunian eccentrics who would ring and share jokes such as 'Did you hear about that artist fellow with the dirty finger on one hand? That's right, he was called Picasso.' Among Reeves's own favourite japes was to read out car registration numbers of bad drivers and to attack mundane areas of British society such as the post office, government forms and Christmas TV. A cassette of these monologues, *Pocket Emissions*, was Peter's most cherished possession aged 13 as well as his own tapes of Reeves's 'Worst Records of the Year' show.

After they left school Peter and Michael earned some extra cash by DJ-ing at parties and even family weddings – all employing their trusted music and comedy cut-and-paste technique. 'Hi Ho Silver Lining' was followed by a James H. Reeves rant, 'Come On Eileen' with a sound effect of a horse clopping up a street.

'I do think the people at the weddings thought it was a bit odd,' says Michael. 'We were playing to a minority audience, really. It made us laugh.'

Peter, though, took the DJ-ing seriously and still counts among his proudest achievements keeping a wedding reception crowd in Clitheroe dancing for two solid hours. According to Catherine Hurst, who became Peter's first girlfriend when she asked him out at the age of 14, 'He always thought he'd end up being a wedding DJ.'

As well as being his girlfriend, Catherine – who had a dry, laid-back sense of humour – was also his comedy foil and when they were out the pair would often slip into character and start repeating lines from *Airplane!*. As a schoolboy Michael Atherton remembers that his friend was 'always on' and looking for comedy in everything – impersonating the teachers' vocal tics and movements. Whenever anyone mentioned the name of the metalwork teacher Mr Callan, Peter would stand up and mime swinging a light bulb like the scene in the title sequence of the *Callan* TV thriller series starring Edward Woodward. He'd also hear double meanings in the things people would say, where others might miss them. Once in the dining room somebody commented that the dried-out chips 'aren't that clever', to which Kay responded, 'What, chips trying to do algebra on the plate?' When anyone would ask 'Who's farted?' he would pantomime opening a giant ledger containing details of everyone who'd ever farted in the history of mankind.

'He'd also plant mental seeds in his audience to pay off on later, much as he and other stand-ups do today,' claims Michael Atherton. 'He suggested to everyone that a school roller blind featured a massive picture of [*North West Tonight* and *It's a Knockout* presenter] Stuart Hall. Consequently every time the teacher went to unfurl the blind Pavlovian sniggers of anticipation would be heard from the back.'

But despite his obvious intelligence, lessons held little interest for Peter Kay. 'He was always in the bottom class, but he'd doctor his reports before his mum saw them,' says Catherine Hurst. 'He was like you see him on telly, he never took anything seriously. He wasn't shy at all. He was very romantic; for my 16th birthday he bought me 16 presents and made me a tape with songs that had 16 in the title.'

It's true that Peter never shone academically – he once got 3 per cent in a maths exam – but through after-school activities he gained the self-confidence he didn't get from learning about ancient Greeks or logarithms. There was also his sense of humour. Karen Peel remembers that it went over the top of most people's heads: 'This was the 1980s and although his kind of observational humour is common now, back then people didn't get it half the time.'

Peter was very much the class clown but, more than this, he was, in the words of Michael Atherton, 'someone who was only comfortable as the centre of attention'. If his humour wasn't recognised by some of his schoolmates or the nuns (who Peter says were 'in and out of school like the hokey cokey'), at least some of the teachers got it. Art teacher John Clough recalls that he had a 'mischievous creativity'. 'He always had it,' he says, 'that natural funniness, but he wasn't sure how to channel it.'

That moment arrived when, after much nagging, he landed the part of the Cowardly Lion in the Mount St Joseph's production of *The Wizard of Oz*. This was a much bigger affair than the one at St Ethelbert's when he'd shone as the Mayor of Munchkinland. Far from being a small event, the musical was chosen as the moment to mark the end of the school's history on the current site – just a few weeks later the old school and convent was to be demolished, and when the new term year began pupils would switch to the new school in Greenland Road, Farnworth.

'We didn't do much drama at school,' remembers Peter. 'We'd do little plays in class, where we would all read out parts, but if you ever did it in a different voice, everyone would laugh hysterically – "What are you doing? Don't do a voice!" When I got the part of the Lion, teachers said it would be difficult with my exams coming up. Then I did fail most of my exams! I always just loved making people laugh. That's what I did. I was never an idiot. I was never brilliantly academic, I just wanted to make people laugh. When it got to exam time I just thought, "I don't know if I can be bothered."'

The Wizard Of Oz, felt the headmistress Sister Barbara, was all about new beginnings, and the new school site was to be their gleaming educational version of L. Frank Baum's Emerald City. *The Wizard of Oz* was also good, clean, wholesome family fun. For four nights from Wednesday, 19 April 1989 to Saturday, 22 April 1989 the school gym was taken over and various dignitaries – the local bishop, Father Flatley and the mayor of Bolton – were invited. The school art department spent months putting together an elaborate stage set to match the one Judy Garland journeyed across, while Mrs Jasmik, the head of needlework ('It was that kind of school!' says Michael), toiled away on the costumes. Peter's orangey fake fur lion suit will be familiar to anyone who's watched his career closely – its most recent appearance was in the 2005 Comic Relief video for '(Is This the Way to) Amarillo', in which he wore it flanked by Danny Baker as a scarecrow and Heather 'Mrs Paul McCartney' Mills as Dorothy, but he also wore it for his *Live at the Top of the Tower* video and it's also made fleeting appearances on various TV shows through the years. Decidedly less weather-worn than it is now, on the nights of *The Wizard of Oz* show it was topped off with face paint, a yellow smock top and Bermuda shorts with the words 'Grrr', 'Roar' and 'Growl' written across them in permanent marker. In a touch that was completely Peter's own the ensemble was topped off with a pair of Ray Ban sunglasses.

'The show was a really big deal,' remembers Karen Peel, who had the role of the Scarecrow. 'Sister Barbara was clucking around backstage. When the bishop came we were told that had to be the best night and to be sensible. Then on the final night we were told, "You've done a really good job, have fun, just relax, enjoy yourselves", which Peter took as his cue. We were all giddy anyway.'

Having studied Bert Lahr's performance, and particularly his southern drawl, in the 1939 musical, Peter Kay delivered his lines in a Texas accent that occasionally slipped into deepest Boltonian – the resulting scramble ended up sounding like Eric Morecambe in one of Ernie Wise's 'plays wot I wrote'. This alone was enough to have the audience in stitches, but there was more: Peter was virtually in a play on his own, ad-libbing and slipping out of character. 'That's not even a funny line,' he tells the audience who are laughing at his character's sincere fear of travelling to Oz to find some courage; 'it was much better in rehearsal.' Incredibly, he says all this deadpan and without cracking a smile or giggling at his nerve.

'When he was supposed to be onstage he'd be up and down the aisle swinging his tail or shouting "Hello mums",' remembers Karen Peel. 'He'd go and sit on people's laps or pull faces. At one point I could have crucified him because I was supposed to be dancing with him onstage and he just buggered off.'

This was during the jitterbug scene when Dorothy, the Lion, Scarecrow and Tin Man decide that the answer to their problems is to travel to see the all-knowing Grand Pooh-Bah of Oz in his impressive palace. But leaving his co-stars mid-jitterbug, Peter decided to go completely off script and do a solo wiggle to the back of the stage, where he cocked his leg and pretended to pee up against a tree (actually, in the grand tradition of British school plays where everyone gets a part, the tree was really a small girl from the second year). 'It was just complete, absolute chaos,' says Karen Peel. 'In the interval Sister Barbara grabbed hold of us backstage and gave us this massive lecture, saying she expected more of us, that the mayor was in the audience and we were letting the school down. We just ignored her and continued along similar lines. Peter wouldn't have paid any attention anyway; it was all water off a duck's back to him. No one took her very seriously.'

Sister Barbara should possibly have expected Peter's grandstanding, considering the fact that a few years earlier in the nativity, playing the innkeeper, he'd offered Mary and Joseph 'an en-suite with full English'.

The school video camera, set up on a tripod by Peter, captured all four performances of *The Wizard of Oz* and, in an early example of his meticulousness, he spent hours editing the best parts of all four of his performances for the final videotape which was copied for the cast. The tape also showed off his now customary cut-and-pasting skills, with a big-band version of '(Is This the Way to) Amarillo' and audience clapping from a sound effects album shoehorned on to the front and the final credits from *The Wizard of Oz* movie tacked on to the end.

Although time and technology haven't been kind to the copy of the video Karen Peel keeps tucked away at the back of a cupboard, it provides a brilliant insight into the young Peter Kay. The first thing that strikes you is that he's funny without even trying; just the sight of him makes the audience laugh. Despite everyone describing him as a fat kid, he wasn't all that overweight, but even then at age 15 he has the look of a middle-aged man – specifically Alf Roberts from *Coronation Street* – trapped inside a child's body.

The final five minutes of the *The Wizard of Oz* tape is taken up with another Peter Kay project. After school one warm sunny day, just weeks before it was due to be demolished, he filmed a tour of the school with a video camera mounted on a skateboard. There are also artistic pans of wire fences, the dinner hall and the school tuck shop, and in one flash of humour Kay himself dancing with a dinner lady while he smiles and winks hammily at the camera. Peter set the film to a soundtrack of Phil Collins's 'Take Me Home' from the *No Jacket Required* album and presented it to John Clough as a parting gift.

'I loved school so much that when I left I had a hard time really getting over it,' Peter reveals today. 'The problem was we left on the Friday and on the Saturday the bulldozers came in and demolished the school – it became a car park.' But Peter was lucky – the pupils at the relocated school not only mourned the loss of their old home, but also had to put up with the new one being treated like a brand-new sofa with the cellophane left on by the nuns. Every day they had to take two different pairs of shoes to school (indoor and outdoor).

Unlike many kids, who can't wait to leave school, Peter Kay dreaded it – as is borne out by his sentimental video for John Clough. 'He never used to talk about his home life,' says Karen Peel. 'Never mentioned his mum or his dad. I always thought he was a bit of a loner and I think a lot of the reason he used to hang around at school with the likes of John Clough was that he didn't want to go home.' In fact his home life was a happy one. At home he'd run errands for his nan, his father's mother Edith, who lived in their old house at 71 Croston Street. And between bouts of TV watching there would be family weddings, birthdays, trips to Northern Ireland and holidays to Wales, Butlin's in Minehead and a Warner's holiday camp in Burnham on Sea where Peter and his mum went to see Nik Kershaw perform live.

'And we'd go to Blackpool about six times a year,' he says. 'My mum would go, "I fancy a change. I know, let's go to Blackpool." It mentally scarred me, especially the B&B we stayed in; my dad got a 10 per cent discount at this really rough place that had a sign up near the door that said "Arrive as guests, leave as friends".'

As with much of Peter's life, the stories about Blackpool and his dad would be re-created in the future. 'They're all true,' he says. 'My dad really was obsessed with getting up early to make the most of the holiday. He'd leap out of bed at 6 a.m., go for a walk on the front, buy a newspaper and come back and insist on everyone getting up. We'd be going, "Ah, Dad, come on, it's only half past seven; we're on holiday." '

But trouble was brewing between his parents, and by the time Peter left Mount St Joseph's they had separated. The cause was his father's drinking, made worse by the fact that he had been forced into early retirement from the ropeworks with osteoporosis, a bone disease that can be brought on by alcoholism and hard manual labour. Michael's condition had one important effect on his son: he never went near a drop of alcohol. 'Because we were never the type of Bolton teenager who hangs around outside the offy drinking Thunderbird Peter being teetotal was never really an issue,' says Michael Atherton. 'Seeing his father the worse for drink most nights probably had something to do with it.' According to Catherine Hurst, Peter 'used to tell people he had an illness because he got fed up with people asking him why he didn't drink'.

At 16, with his father gone and his sister Julie living with her new husband, Kay found himself the chief breadwinner in the house following his parents' divorce, writing letters for his mother looking for new housing saying, 'I am a divorced mother of two seeking sheltered accommodation.' Instead, Peter and Deirdre moved back to 71 Croston Street while his grandad and nan moved out to a warden-controlled house a few streets away. Peter joked to Michael Atherton that it was particularly noisy in their house on Saturday mornings, a reference to the Sandi Toksvig-fronted kids' TV show *No. 73*.

In typical style Peter remembers the moment his mother and father announced their separation to him – it was halfway through an episode of *Mork and Mindy*. While it might be tempting to imagine Peter Kay was scarred by these events and that it shaped his comedy, it isn't the case. 'It's true he never talked much about his dad's problems or parents' divorce,' says Michael Atherton today. 'But then again we were a bunch of teenage lads, not the cast of *Thirtysomething*.' Pressed on the matter, Peter Kay will tell you that his parents' divorce was amicable. 'It wasn't that bad really,' he has said, adamant that there'll be 'none of that tears of a clown bollocks from me'.

His father went to live with another woman, Margaret Faulkner, and father and son saw each other regularly every weekend. If you are looking to find some misery behind the mirth of Peter Kay, then it is not here.

In August 1989, Michael Atherton arranged a week-long 'end of an era' holiday in his parents' caravan in the Lake District, inviting Peter and Catherine, Karen Peel, the Smith twins as well as teachers John Clough and Gerald Greathead, who taught history. 'I know that seems a little bizarre in hindsight but it seemed quite normal at the time,' laughs Michael Atherton. 'I know it's not the norm and people who went to other schools probably think it's a bit weird, but those teachers were like mates,' says Karen. 'Some people stayed in the caravan, some people camped, and we just had a farewell good laugh basically. We'd all been a bit of a gang, and after that Claire and Jane were going off to college in Wigan; it felt like the end of something.'

At the time Peter enjoyed giving complex things names – such as his beloved Leonard Maltin's *Movie Almanac*, which he called 'Bob' – and promptly dubbed the holiday 'Gareth'. Still high on his *Wizard of Oz* success, Peter and Michael used the holiday to impress the gang with their thespian skills and spent much of their time acting out a bleak improvised Harold Pinteresque play when pressed to do the washing up or fetch a Calor gas bottle.

'Go.'

'I'm going.'

'Go then.'

'Yes.'

'I'm gone.'

'I guess you had to be there,' chuckles Michael Atherton,

who soon afterwards dropped his acting aspirations and became a website designer. 'Peter was always funny. The problem was how to make a living out of it.'

If he'd been born to middle-class parents in west London rather than a working-class family from Lancashire, Peter Kay would no doubt have been directed to the nearest drama school, where he'd have ended up starring in *Grange Hill* or being cajoled on to the West End stage as one of Fagin's pickpocketing gang. Instead, it was the not so bright lights of the Bolton College on Manchester Road and, thinking that acting was his future, a BTEC in Performing Arts. At the interview he told the tutor simply, 'I'm a funny person.' It wasn't a happy time. 'It was a bit hard,' he says, looking back. 'It was the first year they'd done it. We started off as 20 and at the end there was just three of us. I really went off the thought of acting or doing drama after I left there in 1991; I more or less decided that being creative wasn't for me. I was really despondent after that.'

Adding to his unhappiness was the death of his grandad, to whom he was very close.

'His grandad was a source of comedy inspiration, too,' says Michael Atherton. 'He was forever shouting "Rub-yed!", a somewhat inexplicable cry related to rubbing your head.' This was a sad time for Peter, but as Michael Atherton explains, even in his darkest time he was still looking for comedy. 'There were times when the laughter stopped,' says Michael. 'There were times when Peter was quick to anger, or hard on people. But aren't we all like that at times? The notable thing was that he always managed to eventually find some levity in the situation, and I think use that to work through the hard times, such as his parents' divorce or his grandad's death.'

Despite thoughts of forgetting all ideas about a future in entertainment and harbouring reservations about acting,

Peter continued to keep his hand in by joining the Bolton Octagon Youth Theatre and working in the box office. The Octagon job was one of many part-time positions Peter Kay would hold between 1990 and 1998. With his father and sister no longer at home, he needed them to help out there, but he hated every single one of them. The jobs, however, gave him something that no Performing Arts course ever could: material.

Chapter Two
Eye Level is Buy Level

'The trouble with the rat race is that even if you win, you're still a rat.'

Lily Tomlin

'He who laughs most, learns best.'

John Cleese

In 1990, aged 17, Marc Rowlands, an A-level student who would later go on to be a journalist for Manchester listings magazine *City Life* and later the *Guardian*, went to a party at his friend Marcus Hulme's house. Marcus was taking advantage of his parents being away on a caravanning holiday to throw open his doors for the youth of Bolton.

'A few of us were sat upstairs listening to Massive Attack's *Blue Lines*, drinking booze we were too young for, when a lad came in, crying with laughter,' Rowlands remembers. 'He insisted that we follow him back downstairs and there, in the front room, was this stocky kid with a really broad Bolton accent entertaining 20 or so people with these stories about his job and his mum and dad. He was hysterical. That was the first time I met him.'

After this Marc would often run into Peter Kay at parties around town. He would always see him around 2 a.m. – the only sober person there – with a huge crowd of kids around him, just laughing their heads off. 'Peter was a popular lad, really well liked; people had heard of him all over Bolton. It's mad, I know, but the things he was saying weren't all that different to the stuff that made it into his stand-up show years later,' says Marc. 'For example, I remember him doing impressions of his mum with an Irish accent and about her buying shit cola from the Spar when he really wanted Coke. A lot of his stuff was a bit more blue than he'd do today, though.'

Kay also had another party trick up his sleeve. For years he'd been filling an E-180 videotape with the opening titles of his favourite and not so favourite TV shows – just the opening titles, relentlessly, one after the other – everything from crime shows such as *The Professionals* to the long-forgotten drama set on board a North Sea ferry, *Triangle*. 'You probably think that's sad, don't you?' he asked me in 2002. 'But when you put that tape on at two in the morning, when everyone's pissed, people love it.'

As well as the opening titles tape he had another with just adverts and even one dedicated to closedowns – hard to imagine now but TV stations didn't broadcast for 24 hours until the era of Sky and home shopping. ' "That's it from Granada. Whatever you're doing tonight don't forget to have a nice night," ' he says, imitating the continuity announcers of his youth. ' "Don't forget, your local radio stations are still on air and don't forget to unplug your set from the wall." And then the screen would turn black or they'd play the National Anthem. What were you supposed to do? Stand to attention? Sing along? And then there'd be a zzzzzzz and you had to wake up in case you got some brain thing.'

Missing school and his role as class clown, the teenage Peter Kay found a new outlet for his humour when in the summer of 1990 he took a part-time job working the 6-to-10 p.m. shift at the Majestic Garage, an Esso petrol station on St Helens Road, the main road between Daubhill and Bolton town centre. The best thing about it was that his friends were allowed to hang out there with him as he worked the till and, thanks to the management's liberal attitude to stocktaking, could eat as many packets of crisps and drink as much free pop (and not that Rola Cola either, proper stuff like Lilt) as they wanted.

'We were his audience, basically,' says Michael Atherton who, along with Marc Rowlands – whose friend Marcus Hulme also had a shift at the garage – and a few other ex-Mount St Joseph lads, would spend their evenings at the Majestic. 'From the minute somebody would arrive on the forecourt he'd do this running commentary on them for the benefit of his mates in the shop with him,' remembers Marc Rowlands. 'By the time they got to the door of the shop he'd told their whole life story, and the customers couldn't understand why the moment they walked through the door they'd be faced with these kids hiding behind the counter giggling into their hands.'

Among his other favourite things to do at the garage was abusing his access to the Tannoy system by yelling 'boo' to scare people innocently filling up their Ford Fiestas with £10 of unleaded or announcing non-existent special offers to an empty forecourt. He also particularly enjoyed visits from the feral kids from the nearby estate whose missions to steal Twixes and Yorkie bars he would thwart by adopting the mannerisms of a 1950s shopkeeper, roughing up their hair and playfully yanking at their cheeks until they'd disappear out of sheer embarrassment. Another one of his pastimes, remembers Michael Atherton, was to wave off customers with DJ catchphrases: ' "Don't go changing", he'd tell them as they left the shop, or "Keep your feet on the ground and keep reaching for the stars".'

The garage was also the venue for one of Peter's first comic creations: Derek Bollock, a twisted, bitter character who'd threaten to put children on a spike, 'and I don't mean Jeffrey Holland in *Hi-De-Hi*', if they dared cross him.

As well as his friends, there was another visitor to the Majestic Garage who would have a far-reaching effect on Kay's comedy synapses. He was an eccentric gentleman in his early fifties who, according to Michael Atherton, looked like a cross between 'Martin Jarvis and Derek Jacobi with a voice approaching Duncan Norvelle'. (Norvelle, in case you have forgotten, was a comic of the old-school pre-alternative comedy era whose catchphrase was camply to witter 'Oooh chase me, chase me'. This type of thing was strangely popular in the early 1980s, and Norvelle was a regular on ITV game shows such as *Celebrity Squares* and *Bullseye*.) The man's name was Leonard, and years later he'd be immortalised as Bolton's longest-serving paper boy in an episode of *That Peter Kay Thing*.

The real Leonard wasn't a paper boy and he didn't carry a giant cross around the town centre, but like his fictionalised namesake he was a religious man and his house had a small fairy light-covered cross in the front living-room window with a bright pink Robin Reliant parked outside. He would wear socks and sandals, even in winter, and a maroon sweater with Jesus Loves You emblazoned across it.

'I'm not sure if he was mentally unstable or anything but he was a nice chap,' says Marc Rowlands. 'All the local kids used to hang out at his house drinking cider and smoking cigarettes. I suppose he was the sort of person mums and dads would worry about being a bit dodgy, but he was totally harmless.'

For most of the kids, who were too young for pubs and too old for playgrounds, Leonard's house was somewhere to go. But for Marcus and Peter it was different. 'He wasn't very well and they looked after him a bit,' says Marc. 'They'd ask if he needed any shopping doing and stuff.'

Leonard was a regular visitor to the garage and, whenever he was there, Peter would tape their conversations together – a habit that had started several years previously when he recorded the family chit-chat over a Christmas dinner. 'Peter used to create situations to push Leonard's comedy buttons,' says Michael Atherton. 'I remember once he did a word association game, during which Peter called out ' "Brian Cant", to which the slightly deaf Leonard replied, "Hitler's book".' Asked what fascinated him about Leonard, Peter Kay replies: 'He had a lust for life. Everyone used to think, "Keep your kids away from him", but he were nothing like that. It taught me not to judge a book by its cover.'

The last time Peter and Marcus saw Leonard he was rescuing a cat from a tree. The next day he died. He had always told them how he had loads and loads of friends, but when they attended his funeral a few days later, they were the only ones there.

For the next seven years Peter would be in and out of 14 other part-time jobs ('I was never a full-time person') but his evening shift at the garage would remain a constant. He emptied bins for the local council; worked behind the bars at the Blur Boar pub and Yates's Wine Lodge; priced up tins of beans with mini-meatballs ('4p a can') and worked the tills at budget supermarkets Aldi and Netto. When he revealed the latter to a journalist from the *Scotsman* in 1998 she asked: 'An Italian comedy duo?' 'Nah, they're supermarkets for poor people. Really sad places.'

His employment history followed a familiar pattern. He'd stay for four months then either leave at the end of his probation period or get sacked for slacking or having a laugh when he should have been working. At Take Two Video, the small video rental store behind the Spar store in Deane, he once changed the labels on a kids' movie and swapped it with a porn film.

His other employment misdemeanours are the work of comedic licence. At Netto he says he was fired after he'd called his supervisor 'a dyslexic bitch' but he only told people this to set up the punchline that she'd misspelt her report to the Human Resources department; he lost his job at the Bolton Octagon box office for telling a customer he couldn't come in wearing white jeans: 'I was only joking'. Of course it didn't help that the customer was Phil Middlemiss, who played Des Barnes in *Coronation Street*; and at Yates's he got the boot for attempting to put a head on a pint of lager.

The reality, of course, was a bit more ordinary. He was disciplined for mucking about. 'I just spent more time eavesdropping or listening to people than I did really getting involved in the job,' Kay admits. 'Whereas other people would be having an eye on the supervisor's job or seeing how much they could do in a day, how much stock they could shift. I wasn't lazy, I was just interested in having a laugh and not taking it too seriously.'

At work Peter felt like an outsider, as if he wasn't really supposed to be there, but his detachment from wanting to join the rat race was countered by a fascination with the people who did and the mad characters who populated every workplace.

Peter's first job was in the autumn of 1989, when he spent four months working at F. H. Lee's, the toilet paper processing plant known locally as Franny's because it was owned by the former Manchester City footballer. Franny's, which was only a few hundred yards from Peter's home, employed about 120 people, among them plenty of eccentrics. Maddest of all was a stocky chap in his thirties who favoured enormous turn-ups and was nicknamed Disco (due to his part-time mobile DJ business) who once put the forks of his stacker truck through a 22-gallon tub of glue and who at a works 21st birthday party tried to incorporate fire eating into his act but ended up causing thousands of pounds' worth of damage when he sneezed mid-performance. Once, attempting to put a spin on the old pub trick of tossing peanuts in the air and catching them in his mouth, Disco tried to do the same with money and ended up swallowing 10p. There was also an elderly gentleman called Cliff who owned three wigs – one for work, one for Saturday mornings when his job was to clean the machines, and one for Friday night out. His extravagance on hairpieces didn't extend to footwear – despite the pain, he used to wear a pair of shoes that were two sizes too small because he got them cheap in a sale. Looming over everybody, though, was the boss, Francis Lee's older brother Arthur. 'He just loved shouting at people,' says Mick Hall, who worked at F. H. Lee's for 24 years before switching to social work. 'It was all about production. If he caught you sitting down you were in big trouble. He caught me sitting on a couple of logs of paper in the back of the machine once and for that I was transferred to Manchester for three-and-a-half years. Mind you, I was sat there with my feet up having a brew and reading the paper.' Arthur Lee's favourite term of endearment was 'cocker', a word the workers would invariably hear as he guided a new recruit around the factory on their first day: 'Follow me, cocker, follow me.'

Peter's job was a simple one. He was one of the four workers who would wrap, glue and pack the toilet rolls as they emerged from the log-cutting machine. The three middle-aged women he worked with, who would talk openly all shift about their relationships and families, made up for the mundane nature of the job. For Peter it was comedy gold dust, and he'd rush home at the end of his shift and jot down all the conversations. Sometimes the things he heard were so good he'd sneak off and scribble them down on bits of cardboard – taking notes was a hobby. Women, he believed, were much funnier than men, who'd just talk about cars, football, shagging and getting pissed. 'Women are uninhibited; they tell you how they feel. The women at Franny's would talk about what they dreamt about one minute then operations the next.'

How Peter ended his time at Franny Lee's is unknown. Sometimes he says he was sacked, other times that he left when they shifted to continental shifts at Christmas – and he refused to wear a sombrero! 'He wouldn't have been sacked,' argues Mick Hall. 'If you worked at Franny's you were there for two weeks or the rest of your life. It was that sort of place.' Sombreros it must have been then. And toilet roll packing's loss was to be British comedy's gain.

After Franny's Peter moved on to Booker Cash and Carry on the Stonehill industrial estate in Farnworth, where he'd work in the afternoons a couple of times a week and then all day at the weekends. He was a favourite with the women in the cash office, Julie and Pat, and the ladies on the tills – Moira, Gina, Miriam and Sonia Hurst, who was known to him as the boyfriend of her sister-in-law Catherine Hurst. Their relationship lasted for three years after school but fizzled out when Catherine started dating someone else.

'I'd known Peter since he was about 14; he used to baby-sit my son, he were always a character,' says Sonia. 'He even DJ-ed at my wedding – well, if you call it DJ-ing – and he did my son's second birthday party, which was a joint do with Catherine's dad's 50th. Peter always told me he was going to be on television,' she says. 'When he made it nobody at the Cash and Carry would have been surprised; he had us in stitches. Whenever anything different came in, like bonsai trees, he'd always have some comment that would crack everybody up.'

Everybody, that is, apart from the Farnworth branch

manager, Brian Shacklady – a man in his late fifties preoccupied with his thinning hair and, far more importantly, shelf-stacking techniques. Peter would impersonate customers, particularly the women, but his most successful impersonation was of Mr Shacklady, who would endlessly repeat phrases such as 'if you've got time to lean you've got time to clean' at his more idle staff. 'He was one of those people who would terrify you,' says Sonia Hurst. 'But he was a character and all. If you were shelf stacking he'd come up to you and say, "That's a good seller that, put it at eye level. Eye level is buy level."' Despite most of the staff being scared of their boss, Peter didn't take him seriously, repeating Mr Shacklady's 'eye level is buy level' mantra whenever he was out of earshot.

Peter Kay's time at the Cash and Carry marks the only time in his life when he experimented with his hair. He tried to grow it long, but instead of growing downwards it grew up, resulting in a horrific Curtis Stigers-style mullet. According to Sonia, 'It gave him right grief; we said, "Get it cut, for God's sake."' She also remembers how Peter would get into trouble occasionally. 'He'd make light of everything,' she says. 'It would never be enough to get a written warning. Sometimes I don't think he realised the boundaries.'

This was more than evident when Booker's became the venue of some real drama one Thursday evening, when armed burglars raided the store. Customers scurried under pallets and staff lay flat on the floor with their hands behind their backs. Meanwhile, Kay was pricing up some tuna in brine with another employee, Kevin Broughton, on the other side of the store when he suspected something was up from the panicky voices blurting out of the Tannoy. 'We ran round the corner and they were in front of us with these sawn-off shotguns,' he told Michael Parkinson in October 2002. 'It's delayed shock isn't it; two days later I was sobbing in the

middle of *Tomorrow's World*. They said, "You two, get down."
And I swear I went, "What, like dance? Get down, eh Kev?" I
thought we were all going to be on *Crimewatch* and this'd be
my big break into telly, but it was an inside job. Then I got
bollocked for putting in the time book – 4 p.m. to raid.'

After completing his Performing Arts BTEC at Bolton
College, Peter was supposed to return there to study for his
A-levels and, because he came from a low-income household, was given a small grant. However, despite starting
them he didn't see the course through, opting instead to
spend his grant cash on a coat and do a college open video
course for one afternoon a week. But when his friends
announced their plans to continue student life and go to
distant universities he began to wonder whether he was
wasting his life away. Not wanting to be left out or one to let
his situation get him down, Peter enlisted the help of his
friend's forgery skills and a borrowed *Roget's Thesaurus* and
spent an evening at the Esso garage applying for courses.
He'd asked his tutors for references but they'd declined, so
he decided to do his own. On the UCCA and PCAS forms he
wrote that he had A-levels in psychology and English literature and five GCSEs. The reality, of course, was that he
had just one GCSE, in art. He applied for a BA course in
Drama, Theatre Studies and English Literature at
Liverpool John Moores University and to his amazement
got an interview and then, after they failed to check his
credentials, a place on the course.

Liverpool University posed several problems for the 20-
year-old. First, new digs on the campus 38 miles from home
represented the first time, apart from holidays, he had spent
away from his parents. Hours after his mum and dad had
dropped him off at the university, he was back in Bolton
watching telly with his tea on his lap. His first lecture wasn't

for a week and he didn't see the point of hanging around when he could have been at home. The second problem, as befitted a student who had no qualifications and 'apart from *Charlie and the Chocolate Factory* and *Ferris Bueller's Day Off* on my holidays' hadn't read any books, was that he was hopelessly out of his depth. After floundering for the bulk of the first year, he made the decision to downgrade to a more hands-on Performing Arts Higher National Diploma (HND) course at the Adelphi College in Salford. The location meant it was nearer to home, but another feature of the HND course had caught his imagination: a 10-week module in stand-up comedy. After attending an interview and completing the task of writing a review and writing and performing a short sketch, he got the news that he'd been accepted for the term beginning September 1994.

It had taken a long time for Peter to admit that he could maybe make a living out of being funny – taking the carrot of the stand-up comedy module at Salford was the accept-ance of it. As he would explain many years later: 'I always wanted to be a comedian. You're naturally funny and there's a lot of egotism around that people go, "Oh so you think you're funny do you?" If you're a good mechanic or a good carpenter people accept it, but if you go, "I'm funny", people go, "Oh ay, Mr Big Head." I'm just good at making people laugh, I always have been, and I didn't want to be a 70-year-old sat in front of the telly going, "I could have done that. I'm funnier than that." '

In between leaving Liverpool and starting at Salford Peter would have to endure what he soon labelled 'the worst job of my life'. The summer of 1994 was memorable for two reasons. First, Wet Wet Wet were at number one for all 15 weeks of it with 'Love is All Around' from the soundtrack of *Four Weddings and a Funeral*. Second, it was one of the warmest ever. Not that Peter Kay noticed; he spent the entire length of it inside a windowless shrine to gambling, geriatric style – or, as he put it, 'I spent the summer with the cast of *Cocoon*'. He worked every day at the Top Rank Bingo Hall opposite the market in Bolton from 8 a.m. to 11 p.m. behind the bar, as a runner checking winning calls and as general dogsbody. Each day he'd leave his house in Croston Street and walk down the hill into Bolton listening to the James album *Laid* on his personal stereo – it was his habit to borrow cassettes from the library and he liked this one so much he renewed it over and over again and it'd become a ritual that he'd turn the corner to start each day with it. He didn't enjoy the work, but the mundane obsession of the bingo players, who'd dab their number grids with giant marker pens, and the blinkered worldview of some of the staff tickled him. Among them was head caller and manager Tom Henderson, a bingo veteran in his late forties who would make his arrival onstage to Tina Turner's 'Simply the Best'. He loved the tricks some of the old people had, like asking for a glass of water then topping it up with orange squash from bottles they'd later sneak out of their handbags under the tables. Peter was fascinated: 'I soon began to learn that bingo was a world unto itself, that it was much more than just a game. People would change when they came into the place, they would become aggressive and territorial, and we're not talking young ones, we're talking about the fragile and elderly members of our society. They were addicts. They were hooked. I remember one woman collapsed, she keeled over in the morning, they sent for an ambulance, they took her away to the infirmary, they gave her some tests, she woke up, discharged herself and was back in the bingo hall later that night in time for the National. That's how bad it was.'

The National was a game in which customers would buy special cards for a nightly bingo session where the whole of the Top Rank chain would link up to play one big game for a pooled prize fund. This was the hall's big money spinner and the bosses demanded complete silence from the staff, as the numbers would be broadcast by telephone over the Tannoy from the host hall in Wigan or Liverpool, a system many of the bingo players struggled to hear. One night Peter Kay found himself in trouble when he made too much noise stacking glasses, and towards the end of the all-important game he was called into the management's office for a telling-off about his slack attitude. The caller Tom Henderson asked him what his plans were in life. Aghast when Peter told him he was about to do a degree in Performing Arts, the caller allegedly replied, 'Have you no ambition? Don't you want to be a caller?' To which Kay replied, 'F*** off, it's bingo.' The pair continued talking while Kay kept one eye on the clock, mindful that arguing the toss was more fun than actually doing any work. 'Why do we keep on having to go through this?' asked Henderson. 'Because I've not clocked off yet,' replied his cheeky employee. 'That's another £1.25 you owe me.' When he emerged from the meeting he told his fellow staff waiting in the staffroom: 'I've just had an internal examination.'

That summer he also began a job with a brilliant perk – free cinema tickets – when he took a Sunday job as usher at the ABC cinema on Bradshawgate in the heart of Bolton town centre. In a previous incarnation it had been known as the Lido Casino and had been opened in a grand ceremony by *Coronation Street* actress Pat Phoenix, but in 1994 its glamour days had long gone and it was affectionately known locally as the flea pit, with good reason. Its down-at-heel nattiness didn't worry Peter Kay; he liked the fact that it was decaying and clinging on in the era of out-of-town multi-plexes. At one point there had been 21 cinemas in Bolton; now there was only one. He loved everything about it, from telling his mates the endings of movies as they walked in to the local urchins who attempted to run away with a life-sized Gene Hackman standee just for a giggle, to eavesdropping on the ladies who worked behind the confectionery stand and cleaned the toilets.

'One day,' he recalls, 'Pamela was working in box office while Marie was changing roller towel in loo, so she said to a customer, "I'll tear your ticket here because Marie's upstairs changing her towel." And this chap looked disgusted and said, "That's more information than I needed, thank you." You couldn't write that, could you?'

After a summer spent almost entirely in the dark – dispensing free cups of water to the bingo ladies and watching *Forrest Gump* eight times in succession – Peter Kay emerged into the bright late summer sunshine of the Adelphi College building at Salford University. Contrary to popular opinion, the sun does occasionally shine in Greater Manchester.

'I'm not sure if it was the stand-up comedy element that caught his eye,' says Salford lecturer Lloyd Peters, who ran the module Peter Kay chose to incorporate into his two-year diploma. 'I know he was looking to get away from Liverpool. At the time it was getting a lot of publicity; I did quite a lot of interviews on the radio about it, although Radio Five got it into their heads that this was all we did, that students would spend their whole university life telling jokes to each other.'

As if! In fact a much greater part of the course was theatrical production, stagecraft and acting, and prior to his stint on Lloyd Peters's much-hyped module he appeared in several plays, including Euripides' Greek tragedy. *Electra*, where he played Tutelus, and, most notably, Nikolai Gogol's parody of Russian corruption *The Government Inspector*, in which he was given the lead role as the Mayor in three performances at the Adelphi Studio Theatre.

'He was wonderful,' says Lloyd Peters, who directed the Gogol piece. 'In fact Maureen Lipman, who was a visiting professor at the time, came to see a rehearsal and she picked him out. He did a lot of improvising around the script, which threw some of the less quick-witted members. I encouraged him to extemporise, which he grasped immediately.'

When it came to teaching stand-up comedy, Lloyd Peters was convinced that Peter Kay had done it before and was dumbfounded to discover that his only performance had been a best man's speech the previous summer.

'You didn't have to teach Peter much at all,' he says. 'I suppose another reason the module was quite attractive to him was that he knew he wouldn't have to study to get a good mark. A lot of the things I told the group – like keeping a notebook of jokes and ideas – he'd been doing for years. It involved a lot of homework, writing material, but Peter didn't need to, he'd have it all written already. In fact he was always helping other people with their acts.'

Peter was popular, but in a different way to how he'd been at school or at the Esso garage. Rather than fêted as the class clown or as someone who could blag you endless supplies of KP crisps, he was sought out because, according to Lloyd Peters, 'people recognised his talent'. Secretly though, the Peter Kay comedy recorder was still switched to 'on' and the middle-class students, especially those with artistic pretensions, fascinated him as much as the ladies on the assembly line at the toilet roll factory had done a few years previously. He noticed the limp way they smoked, their hand gestures and their liberal name-dropping. Like everyone Peter had spent time with, they too would find themselves incorporated into his comedy in the future.

Not that he spent much of his spare time at university indulging in the standard student pastimes of binge drinking, watching *Betty Blue* and experimenting with joint-rolling techniques. Peter Kay was far too busy working, and in his second year at Salford took on yet another part-time job: working Thursday nights as a steward at the newly opened Manchester Nynex Arena (later to be known as the Manchester Evening News or MEN Arena). On his first night there – Torvill and Dean's 'Face the Music' tour – the supervisor neglected to have a badge made up with his name on, so he had to wear one that read Mohammed instead. The day of his 22nd birthday in 1995 lived long in his memory, because prior to the show that evening the stewarding team staged a mock evacuation of the arena. And the music playing over the speaker system as they shooshed fake concertgoers from a venue they were supposed to imagine was ablaze? 'Burning Down the House' by Talking Heads. You couldn't make it up! All this was brilliant potential material for his first stabs at stand-up comedy; rather than make stuff up, he'd recount tales from the cinema and the arena, including the seminar he had to go on where two long-in-the-teeth security guards warned them of the dangers of flash photography and that 'men should search men and women should search women', to which one shady, bearded wannabe steward eagerly enquired: 'Can we frisk kids?'

On the stand-up course they would study other comedians, master microphone technique and write 'improvised' responses to heckles – Peter's was 'A penny for your thoughts. Sell! Sell!' Peter was interested in comedy history and fascinated by Peters's story about the time Danny Kaye had performed at the London Palladium and during the interval had remained onstage drinking a cup of tea and chatting to the audience instead of disappearing into his dressing room.

Sessions would begin with Lloyd Peters asking them to read a newspaper and pick something out to make a joke about. 'Reading a newspaper was quite a novelty for some of them! I'd tell them, if you can make a joke about the

European Community you can make a joke about anything.' He would also get them to open up about their lives at home, about being bullied at school or about their parents. Some found it hard, but for Peter it would all come tumbling out. He was on home ground; he'd been talking about this stuff for years.

'For such a young lad he had amazing observational skills,' says Lloyd. 'I think it was his working-class roots that gave him this maturity that I didn't see in the other students. The things the rest would dismiss – such as the price of pop they were selling at Netto, where he'd worked – he saw as comedy fodder.'

Kay was no less enthusiastic, later telling people that for the first time in his life he'd found something that he loved, that he was good at. Kay's tutor was also struck by his knowledge of TV and by the fact that he knew about TV shows someone his age really had no right to. When he discovered Peters had a collection of 1960s TV theme tunes he nagged him to lend them to him then incorporated them into his act.

Part of the course was developing what Peters calls 'a comedy persona' – either a character or a heightened version of themselves. But despite this he believes that with Kay there was less of a dividing line between the onstage Peter and the offstage. Indeed, later on in his life Peter would insist that he was more himself on a stage than off it. 'All this theory and practice we did,' says Lloyd. 'With Peter? He just went up there and did it.'

The culmination of the course was a show in the function room at the Pint Pot pub in Salford, a regular comedy venue near the university, where each of Lloyd Peters's students would perform a ten-minute set and be marked accordingly. Peter Kay came away with a Distinction, but it wasn't the top mark. 'He actually got a D minus minus, which he was really disappointed about. There was a guy who got a D, which is a higher mark, who was hopeless for eight weeks but then suddenly found his voice and was absolutely hilarious.'

Thinking he was the star of the pack, Lloyd Peters gave Peter Kay headline billing, but he ended up penalising him because rather than perform the statutory 10-minute set, his routine lasted closer to 45. He was also marked down for a slow start, Peters having taught him the importance of making an early impact.

After leaving with his diploma Peter toyed with taking up the offer of joining the final two years of the BA course, but with Lloyd Peters's advice to get an agent ringing in his ears he declined the chance and in the words of his mentor 'got out there and did it'. In his teacher's mind at least there was no doubt that Peter Kay was going to become a star. 'It comes along so rarely that when it does come along you know it.'

Kay himself was less confident, and he fell back into his old routine of working at the garage and the cinema. But he did keep his hand in at the theatre, and Sue Reddish of the Bolton Octagon Youth Theatre, aware of the achievements of a former member, asked Peter if he would adapt and direct the group's summer production based on *The Year My Voice Broke*, an Australian film about a boy watching his first love bloom into womanhood and fall for the charms of an older, insensitive brute instead of him. Because the play was for a cast of just four characters and there were about 25 kids in the youth group, Peter created a party scene so that everyone could have a part. It was like the film with a bit of *Home and Away* tagged on. Because they were all kids a box-office employee was roped in to play the lead character's father.

The play, staged on 23 and 24 August 1996, was successful with both performances selling out. When Peter Kay, Reddish and the box-office team went out to celebrate a day later – at Peter's suggestion to the karaoke evening at the nearby

Wagon and Horses pub – they found themselves there at the same time as an engagement party. Eyeing up the party's buffet bar, Peter managed to negotiate a deal where he would do some stand-up in return for some of the buffet. Impressed with his cheek, the young bride and groom to be agreed and, in return for a sausage roll, a couple of vol-au-vents and a pile of Skips, Peter Kay performed his first gig in Bolton.

Move Forward Eight Spaces

'To get a job where the only thing you have to do in your career is to make people laugh – well, it's the best job in the world.'

Ronnie Barker

'I'd like to apologise to viewers in the north. It must be awful for them.'

Continuity announcer, Victoria Wood: As Seen on TV

Peter Kay's stand-up routine in exchange for a plate full of buffet wouldn't be his last professional engagement. After graduating from Salford University and spurred on by his friends at the garage, he telephoned a middle-aged gentleman known as Agraman for advice. Ten years earlier Agraman, whose real name is John Marshall, had ambitions to become a comedian himself and, not knowing quite how to go about it, started his own club in the function room of the Southern Hotel in the Manchester suburb of Chorlton-cum-Hardy. A lover of puns, Agraman (an anagram of anagram) named it the Buzz Club to complement the *double entendre* possibilities of the suburb's name. Numerous big names had been through the Buzz – Caroline Aherne, Steve Coogan, Eddie Izzard, Harry Hill, Jack Dee and Alan Davies had all played there early in their careers – with Agraman as the resident compère. Over the years Marshall had become something of a local comedy legend, a man who had been there at the start of the stand-up comedy explosion. He was also regarded as one of the nicest men in the business. Comedians, every one of them – even in the north, where we imagine comics to be take-me-as-you-find-me, unruffled sorts – are a self-doubting, suspicious bunch, but the niceness of Agraman was something they could all agree on. Even if his puns did make you groan – 'Shakespeare walks into a pub. The barman says, "You're bard." '

On 5 August 1996 the Buzz was due to host a heat of the coveted City Life Comedy Awards. Marshall suggested, on the phone to the young Boltonian, that he enter – all he needed to do was send in a cassette of his performance and if he thought it was up to scratch he'd be in. Such was the boom in local comedy that the alternative, waiting for an open-mic slot at the Buzz – amateur comics' usual route into the club – would take about seven months. Without any proper gigs to his name, Peter Kay decided instead to put his dictaphone down in a pub and record his conversation with his friends. Despite the unusual approach, Marshall was impressed enough to call him up.

'It was funny but there was a little bit of choice language and stuff like that,' he says. 'I rang him up and said, "If you do this sort of laddish stuff in the competition it's not going to go down very well".'

On the night of the show Peter Kay got the number 22 bus from Bolton to Chorlton and arrived at the venue jangling with nerves. 'It were a bit intimidating because I'd never done it before. And all the other comics who were there were like, "How long have you been doing this, son?" And I told them it was my first time and they said, "I don't think you should be here." But I had a go, like.'

'His name was randomly selected to go first,' remembers John Marshall. 'He went onstage and he was just about the Peter Kay we know today, an absolute natural; he won it by a mile. I've never come across that before or since: someone so fully formed at such an early stage in his or her career. I'd had people like Eddie Izzard and there were signs of what they would become, but no one was as natural or near the finished article as Peter Kay. And I'd never seen anyone come on first and win; that in itself was remarkable.'

In its six-year existence the City Life Comedy Awards had grown in stature in the north west, not because of its prize of £200 and a £20 HMV voucher, but as a stepping stone to greater things. The 1991 winner, Dave Spikey, who would compère the final at the Levenshulme Palace nightclub, had appeared and narrowly lost out in Jonathan Ross's prime-time *Big Big Talent Show* and landed a slot as the presenter of a daytime quiz show *Chain Letters*. But the real star to emerge from the contest was the 1990 winner, Caroline Aherne, who had appeared then as the foul-mouthed nun Sister Mary Immaculate ('How many Protestants does it take to put in a light bulb? None. They live in eternal darkness'). It was, though, another of Aherne's creations that had turned her into the most acclaimed comedienne of her generation. Disguised as the lovely elderly lady Mrs Merton, Aherne hosted her own chat show. Behind her blue-rinse wig, Aherne was as sharp as a tack and managed to touch the raw nerves of her guests with far greater success than TV veterans such as Michael Parkinson and Terry Wogan with their cosy knee touching. It signalled the end of the chat show, but it was hysterically funny, and for added effect her entire studio audience would be full of pensioners who were too old to know who half of the celebrities were and spoke their minds without brakes. Famously, Mrs Merton once asked wittering magician Paul Daniels's wife Debbie McGee: 'What was it that first attracted you to millionaire Paul Daniels?' And to feminist Germaine Greer she said, 'You were a right old slapper in the seventies, weren't you?' While Bernard Manning was simply asked, 'Are you a racist?' To which he replied: 'Yes.' Afterwards he claimed it was a trick answer!

Mrs Merton was Peter Kay's favourite programme in 1996, so he was somewhat alarmed to find her creator sat amid the faded glory of the Levenshulme Palace. Like everyone else in the swelteringly hot venue on Wednesday, 25 September 1996, Caroline Aherne was there to witness what was considered a foregone conclusion: the crowning of a spectacularly over-weight comic from St Helens called Michael Pennington whose *alter ego* Johnny Vegas was causing huge excitement in Lancashire with a comedy routine that somehow incorporated a potter's wheel, masturbation and an audience rendition of the Frank Sinatra standard 'New York, New York'. Further stiff competition came in the form of Jenny Ross, who was fresh from sharing the first prize BBC New Comedy Award at the Edinburgh Festival with Marcus Brigstocke.

'Johnny Vegas was just brilliant,' says John Marshall. 'The audience loved him, but it was a long evening.'

'There were ten acts and Peter went on last when the audience was very, very tired and very pissed,' says Dave Spikey. 'He always reminds me that just before I introduced him I said, "It's all right, ladies and gentlemen, there's only one left." Then he came on and blew them away. Stormed it.'

'I was one of the judges in the final that year,' says Agraman *alter ego* John Marshall, who joined last year's winner Chris Addison and Palace owner Lawrence Hennigan on the panel. 'It was very difficult to decide between Peter and Johnny. They were both fantastic.'

'I got involved in the judging because they didn't know what to do,' says Dave Spikey. 'I couldn't understand what the problem was – there could only be one winner.'

'There were a lot of shocked people there,' says Marshall. 'Those that hadn't seen Peter in the heat thought it was a foregone conclusion that Johnny would walk it.'

The next day the *Bolton Evening News* reported their local lad's triumph under the headline 'Peter Becomes a Master of Mirth'. 'With members of the audience flagging as the night approached its conclusion,' they reported, 'Peter woke them up with his incredible fast and furious routine mixing quick-fire gags, hilarious observations and ad-libbing, feeding off a raw nervous energy. There was enough material in his 20 minute set for at least three performances, such was the speed of his delivery.'

Gauging the mood of the audience, Peter Kay had completely changed his style for the City Life final. In his three or four previous attempts at performing in front of a live audience he'd attempted a dry, slow style. That was now gone for ever.

'I just wanted to wake the audience up, so I speeded things up,' he told the local paper. 'I'm still a bit bewildered by it all. I couldn't believe it when I was announced as the winner, because I was up against some people who had been on the circuit for six or seven years.'

Immediately Peter Kay's world was turned on its head, and adding to his jobs at the garage and the cinema he now had a run of comedy gigs to keep him busy. Within a week of winning the City Life Award he appeared at the Manchester Boardwalk, the Frog and Bucket in Manchester and the Rubber Chicken Comedy Club at King George's Hall in Blackburn. Winning meant that he went from a nobody to a known act at an unprecedented rate. 'It was like move forward eight spaces,' he says.

'I was absolutely blown away by him,' says John Marshall, who since giving up the Buzz Club now books acts for dozens of venues in the north of England. 'Aware of how good he was, I gave him some one-man shows at a place called the Dancehouse Theatre in Manchester. People said, "Peter Kay? Never heard of him." And it was a real struggle to begin with. I barely got it half full, but by the time he'd been on twice we put him on again and sold out. I was happy in the knowledge that I had a real winner on my hands with Peter. He was brilliant value; you knew he'd bring in the customers and his sets would just carry on. He'd do the work of two comics and you'd only pay the one fee.'

Kay, though, couldn't believe the money he was earning: 'I remember being at my nana's after the City Life Award and being told on the phone, "I can give you £30", and me thinking, 'Bloody hell! £30 for 20 minutes. I used to work all week at the cinema for £42.50." '

It was at the cinema that Peter met Susan Gargan, a Boots cashier from the neighbourhood of Deane. A pretty red-haired girl a couple of years his junior, she'd been to Mount St Joseph's too, although the bulk of her time was spent at the new building. They got chatting and she decided to go and watch him play a gig at the Jabez Clegg in Manchester. The next night the pair went on a date to Blackburn Ice Arena, but they ended up spending the bulk of the evening in the Casualty Department of Blackburn Royal Infirmary after Peter slipped on the ice and broke his arm. 'Thankfully it didn't put her off,' he says. More pressing was the fact that he had gigs to play the rest of the week.

'Everyone thought it was a prop, waiting for me to pull out a bunch of flowers. They spent the first five minutes just pointing and knocking each other and going, "Watch this!" and then I started to really struggle because they realised that it was broken and I wasn't going to do anything – nothing spectacular was going to come out of it.'

Peter Kay was lucky to be coming through when comedy in the north west was going through a renaissance. Spurred by the success of *The Fast Show*'s John Thomson, Steve Coogan and Caroline Aherne, Manchester felt it was at the centre of rock 'n' roll comedy. Yet, despite the power base shifting slightly from London towards the north of England, the venues in Manchester and Lancashire in 1996 were far from ritzy – performing in a smoke-filled L-shaped pub, the stage would invariably be a crate, there'd be no microphone and your choice of lighting would be on or off.

Speaking with the benefit of hindsight, Peter Kay claims that he misses 'the smoke, and the adrenalin and the sick and the closeness' and reveals that he told jokes faster because he was scared of being bottled off: 'You've got to keep moving, you've got to be a fast target, chucking it out at such a rate, otherwise they will kill you. I've seen comedians forcibly ejected out of clubs, I've seen people have their hair set on fire, I've seen people projectile vomited on, and it's all good stories, and it's all a strange way to earn your living, and it's very much like a zoo and a circus. I was very frightened of Manchester then,' he says. 'I was very frightened of the Manchester comedy scene; everything that it stood for put the fear of God into me.'

Times were changing, though, and while every pub in the city was attempting to catch the wave with its own comedy night, established clubs like the Frog and Bucket, once 'so rough you'd think bouncers chucked drunks in rather than out', were moving to bigger locations, while the Boardwalk and the Hacienda, previously known as rock venues, were hosting regular stand-up nights too. It was an anarchic period, but out of all the acts appearing regularly in the city Peter Kay was the one who was beginning to bring his own crowd with him. Even so, he still suffered from hecklers.

'Heckling's a very male thing,' says one of Britain's finest stand-ups, Adam Bloom. 'If you're playing to an audience of nearly all men, it's horrible because you're almost obliged to pick on someone and to beat them as an alpha male thing. It's really ugly.'

Peter's method was to invite hecklers onstage, all the time

hoping that they wouldn't accept his offer. 'But I've found it's best to humiliate them,' he says. 'Talk to them like a teacher: "Now, this is all just a bit of fun, why are you so upset?" They usually slink away.'

Not that he didn't appreciate a good heckle himself. Once when he was working as a compère of a talent contest in Liverpool featuring a very poor impressionist, in the middle of his Terry Wogan impression, Kay mockingly shouted out: 'Do Wogan.'

David Perkins, manager of the Frog and Bucket, remembering Peter Kay's early gigs, says: 'He was always so focused. You could tell he was special. When he was compère I got so many complaints – not from the audience but from the other comics. They said they couldn't follow him onstage – he was just too funny. One night he came onstage dressed as a lion – a really fed-up lion with a fag dangling in his hand …'

And it wasn't just any lion suit, either; it was the Cowardly Lion suit from his school *The Wizard of Oz* play. In the years to follow this suit would become something of a talisman for Peter, and it would make cameo appearances in nearly everything he'd do – from Bolton to Amarillo, it would never be far away. Some people carry a letter or a photograph to remind them of who they really are. Peter Kay dresses as a lion. In fact he only has to look at it and it'll make him laugh; transport him back to cocking his leg up a tree.

'The whole place fell about,' says Perkins. 'It's still one of the funniest things I've ever seen. As I run a comedy club, that's saying something.'

Perkins, whose Frog and Bucket is now one of the most successful independent comedy venues in Britain, says he knew immediately that Peter Kay was different from all the other comedians who had passed through his doors, that he was 'special' and 'focused' in a way he'd never seen before. 'I knew he'd be massive,' he says. 'Even back then, he said he wanted to be on telly – half seven on a Saturday night.'

According to one comedy agent of the period, who would prefer to remain anonymous, other comics at the time hated those evenings at the Frog and Bucket when the rising star was compère and she became accustomed to hearing her client's complaints. 'A compère has to take all the flak and heckles and ease the path for everyone else on the bill; they're not meant to be the star or hog the limelight,' she told me. 'The skill is to make everyone else look brilliant, but Peter Kay would want to be the star. He would do things like say, "Well, we've got another act coming on now, sorry about that, but I'll be back in a minute." '

Among his favourite playful tricks to sabotage his fellow comedians' routines was to take the microphone stand, lower it and tighten it to the point that when they came on they'd have to spend the first minutes, like a grandmother trying to open a jar of marmalade, trying to adjust it. 'First impressions are all important,' she says. 'And if you're wrestling with a microphone when you should be telling jokes it's likely that the audience will start thinking, "This is rubbish; we want Peter back." The first time I was told about it I thought that's a bit wanky; the second and third time I was like, "Oh my God, that's the most brilliant trick in the world." I'm laughing, but the comedians? Let's just say it pissed on their chips.'

According to seasoned compère John Marshall, the microphone trick is unpleasant and fairly standard in the profession and certainly not done exclusively by Peter Kay, but he says, 'He didn't make a great compère, he liked the limelight too much. You never felt as if you ever got to know Peter at all, that was my impression. He wasn't somebody I warmed to but he wasn't somebody I objected to either; you're not quite sure who the real person is. I was never sure whether he liked me or not.'

Peter's professional backstage oneupmanship went un-noticed by his audience, of course, who warmed immediately to his natural style, his tales from the mundane world of part-time work, memories of kids' TV shows and his gimmick of playing back songs he'd heard on the radio on his dicta-phone. He was engaging and charming, and while other comics seemed to be about confrontation, he just wanted audiences to have a good time. It was hardly a radical idea, but most people don't want conflict and aggression at a comedy gig – they just want to have a laugh.

In his early sets Peter did a great spot about misheard lyrics, playing David Bowie's 'Let's Dance' and asking the audience why Bowie was singing about 'Les Dennis', and do Sister Sledge really sing 'Just let me staple the vicar' rather than 'Just let me state for the record' during 'We are Family'. It wasn't the most original of ideas, but it didn't matter.

The bulk of the comedians on the north-west comedy circuit overlooked some of Peter Kay's trickery and put it down to youth and inexperience. Dave Spikey spread the word on Kay wherever he went, while Adam Bloom – a rising star of the era – told an interviewer, 'Peter Kay is the most natural performer I have ever seen.' There was also approval from the older northern comics still on the scene. After a gig in Rochdale, Kay was invited to the house of Irish jester and 1970s TV icon Jimmy Cricket, famed for his ' ... and there's more' catchphrase, and was delighted to find his red *This is Your Life* book suspended inside a glass coffee table in the living room.

Meanwhile, Oldham cabaret act Billie Bedlam, who was taking his routine of playing TV themes on a gigantic tuba and cracking gags around the northern circuit, saw some-thing he liked in the 23-year-old Boltonian: sartorial correctness. 'Most comedians at that time would be wearing a denim jacket and holding a beer bottle,' he says. 'Peter wore a velvet jacket. There was no effing and blinding. It was very much a throwback to people like Les Dawson; you felt he'd be around for a long time.'

But if stardom, sartorial correctness and Saturday nights on BBC1 seemed his birthright, Kay's first attempted step into TV in September 1996 was an utter disaster. Charged with booking comedy acts for ITV's Friday-night competitor to *TFI Friday*, the Anthony Wilson-fronted *Welcome to the Candid Café*, young researcher Dawn Panton toured Manchester's comedy venues looking for new talent. Johnny Vegas, Hovis Presley and Paul Edwards were all booked to appear in front of a panel at Granada's Manchester studios to decide who would appear as the resident stand-up on the show doing a five-minute routine every week. Peter Kay, who had been recommended to Panton by Lucy Porter, a budding comedienne and researcher on *The Mrs Merton Show*, joined the hopefuls.

'She told me he did this great routine on commercials and kids' TV, so I went to see him at the Jabez Clegg in Manchester,' remembers Panton. 'He was brilliant, but when he turned up at the audition he was dressed in a white shirt and a suit like it was a job interview. He looked really nervous. When he came out of the audition he was white as a sheet, sweating and shaking like a leaf. I asked the producers what they thought and they said, "He's rubbish." They said he kept fiddling with his hands all the way through. I got chastised for it and told to pull my socks up. But they didn't like Johnny Vegas either, they said he was crude.'

This shared failure was one of many times the paths of Peter Kay and Johnny Vegas would cross in the late 1990s. Invariably they would be mentioned together when anyone needed to make a point about the north being funnier than the south – a fallacy as sweeping as that claiming Northerners as friendlier. For a short period in 1997 the pair even planned doing a double act together with a view to taking it to the Edinburgh Festival. The sole performance of this momentous event was at a Midlands branch of the Round Table. Hours of Internet research result in one eyewitness report; it reads, 'They died on their arse.' Wisely, Vegas and Kay went their separate ways. For a while at least, however, they remained friends, and when they met in Nottingham in 1999 prior to a gig at the Old Vic, the *Independent* journalist Brian Viner described their hug as 'an impressive engagement of northern blubber'. In his book about the history of British comedy, though, author Ben Thompson claims that around this period Johnny was so enraged that Kay had been given a series by Channel 4 and he hadn't that he broke 'a room full of pots in an orgy of unhappiness'.

Rather than join forces (or stomachs) with Johnny Vegas, in early 1997 Peter Kay found a comic partner closer to home. The compère of the City Life Award show, Dave Spikey, had kept in touch since his victory and had employed him to write the links to a daytime quiz he had found himself presenting. In the emerging comedy world of Kay and Vegas, aged 46 and white-haired, Spikey was classed as a veteran. He'd certainly waited a long time for his break and even despite his TV presenting job had retained his job as chief medical scientist at the Bolton General Hospital – by day examining the 'genetic abnormalities of haemoglobin', by night telling corny jokes about coppers in kids' playgrounds: 'Two policemen sat by a seesaw. I said, "What happened to you?" "We've been tipped off." ' Spikey had been trying to make it as a comedian for years, but his handful of gigs in working men's clubs had been disasters and he'd had little luck sending scripts to the Two Ronnies', Russ Abbott and the Grumbleweeds. He'd even spent a summer opening for one-time Saturday-night institutions Cannon & Ball at the Blackpool Opera House. Sadly, he fell out with them in an argument about alternative comedy, which the born-again Christian double act deemed the devil's work. 'It's all eff, eff, eff. There's nothing funny about that,' were the words of the diminutive moustache-sporting legend that still is Bobby Ball. 'They say they're God's crusaders for comedy,' says Spikey. 'Then they'd go onstage and do homophobic gags – "He's a woolly woofter, he's a poofter." Double standards, or what?'

Thankfully, Spikey broke into the alternative scene when he met John 'Agraman' Marshall and played the Buzz – 'it was an epiphany'. Then, in 1991, at the insistence of the Chorlton promoter he entered the *City Life* Comedian of the Year competition and won, but until his compèring gig at the 1996 final and the offer from daytime TV that came off the back of his Jonathan Ross endorsement, things had been moving slowly.

Chain Letters was a daytime quiz show where the lyrics to the theme tune explained the simple concept of the show: 'Take a word … Change a letter … Do it again … And you've got a chain/Chain Letters!' Dave's job was to wear a shiny suit, flirt with the guests and encourage their chain-letter-making skills. With five shows filmed every day back to back in the Newcastle studios over a two-week period, Spikey needed as many jokes as possible to fill up his opening routine and between-round banter, so he decided to offer the job to Peter Kay. Tailoring his material to the daytime nature of the show, Peter penned family-friendly gags like: 'Bloke goes to a fancy dress party with his girlfriend on his back. His mate says: "What are you going as?" The bloke says: "A snail". His mate points at the girlfriend and says: "Who's that?" Bloke says: "That's Michelle." '

Sadly, no film exists of the most momentous moment in the series, one that is still remembered fondly by daytime quiz show lovers and fans of rude words alike: 'I remember a taxi driver from Manchester who was trying to beat the clock in the "Superchain" final,' says. 'He changed the "r" in "cart" to an "n" for "cant". Then said, "I'll change the "a" to a "u" to make ... er ... can I do that?" We stopped the recording and I just had this big C*** flashing behind me.'

After *Chain Letters* Spikey and Kay wrote a few rough scripts together (including a long-held idea of Dave's of a sit-com set in a local newspaper) and sketched out a few ideas for shows and took them up to Tyne-Tees Television in Newcastle. Nothing came of that meeting but on the journey back to Bolton they hit on an idea for a Lancashire version of *Coltrane in a Cadillac* – a 1993 series that had followed the extra-large actor Robbie Coltrane on a road trip across America in a car as enormously proportioned as he was.

For a short period in 1997 Granada TV, the north-west ITV region, which operated out of studios in Manchester, took Peter Kay under their wing with a view to developing some of his ideas. They enrolled him on a directors' course, where he was pleased to find another Salford graduate and Aspects Theatre player Sian Foulkes, with whom he'd appeared in *The Government Inspector* and *Electra*. Together the pair worked on a script, and then when he heard of a new Granada series called *Mad for It* – a series exposing people's mad obsessions like topiary or Wild West shoot-out re-enactments – he fleshed out his and Dave's road trip idea. Titled *Mad for the A6*, the final show saw the pair travel in a weather-worn VW dormo-bile from Buxton to the Lake District on their favourite stretch of tarmac – *en route* this somehow entailed attempting to dress a Jersey cow in a raincoat.

Despite playing to a small late-night audience, *Mad for the A6* convinced Granada to cast Peter Kay in *New Voices*, a series of one-off dramas intended to showcase emerging new talent. 'Two Minutes' was written by Johanne McAndrew, who would later create the private detective series *Nice Guy Eddie* for Ricky Tomlinson, and directed by

Jonathan Campbell, who would go on to direct *Shameless*, *Spooks* and the movie *Alien Autopsy* as well as the first series of *Phoenix Nights*. In 'Two Minutes' Peter Kay starred as a shortsighted getaway driver so incompetent he'd bought a decaying Vauxhall Viva rather than steal a decent car. His fellow armed burglars (played by Matthew Dunster and Pearce Quigley) were equally hopeless, choosing a bleak pub in the middle of an industrial wasteland to rob and then being outwitted by the ageing clientele. It was a neat, tightly scripted film that didn't allow much room for improvisation, but Kay impressed with a brilliant array of astonished stares as his accomplices revealed their flawed plan. 'Maybe we should rob a garage instead,' says Dunster when all three are still in the car. 'Or a chippy, I'm bloody starving,' pipes our man from Bolton.

'I don't have to do this for a living, I just do it for the luxuries like bread and shoes.'

Les Dawson

In less than a year Peter Kay had gone from a comic known only to an exclusive group of Boltonians to Manchester's best-kept secret, headlining sell-out nights at the Frog and Bucket and the Buzz. He'd travelled down to London to appear at the famous Comedy Store, but suffered at the hands of a few drunken members of the audience – he emptied a pint glass over one customer ('there were only a bit left in it')and threat-ened another with a fork ('I was going to throw it at him'). Fortunately Comedy Store managing director Don Ward found it hysterical. Even so Kay returned lambasting the London scene as McComedy, with comics simply doing their 20 minutes and then buggering offstage when their time was up, disappearing to another club to do exactly the same 20 minutes. 'If you go over in London, they bollock you,' he says. 'I remember doing the Comedy Store and I was supposed to be 20 minutes, and they come up to me and say, "Twenty-two, you did 22. We said 20, you did 22'. Up here, in most places, they'll take the batteries out of the clock, or they'll kind of put you in a position where you can't see the clock or stop it, because the more they go over, the more they're rubbing their hands together, because they're getting more for the money, so if you do 40 minutes, there's your 80 quid and thanks – but in London it's the other way round, and it's funny.'

London comedy, then, was deemed fast food; the northern circuit was a full meal. In fact, often, this was literally true as many clubs in the north offered pastie and pea suppers with the price of admission or, as the Frog and Bucket did, an evening called 'Curry and Quips': a chicken tikka with added jokes. What could be better than that? For Peter the other advantage of local dates was that he could drive home after a gig and get home in time for *Prisoner Cell Block H*. If he harboured ambitions, making it big in London, let alone Hollywood, was not among them.

'A lot of comedians sleep on people's floors,' he tells William Cook in his book *The Comedy Store*. 'I don't like doing that. If I wanted a life like that I'd go and work in an all-night garage like I used to.' Subsequently Peter would turn down many offers of gigs at the Comedy Store. London's streets may be paved with gold, but given the choice he'd rather be at home with his mum cooking him a cauliflower grill.

For someone to eschew the bright lights and big money pull of the capital at such an early stage in their career was seen as both incredible and arrogant by some of his fellow comedians, but despite his whirlwind year he still had little belief that he would make it as a comedian or as an actor, and so kept his jobs at the cinema and Manchester Arena, which included all five nights of Take That's final tour – 'they were fantastic'. In his words: 'One minute I'm making thousands of people laugh, the next minute I'm picking up Toffos.'

Among the regular places he played in his first year was the Levenshulme Palace, where he'd won the City Life Award. The venue held a special pull for him and he'd often used unbilled nights there to road-test new ideas. Among them, one night he pulled a TV set on casters on to the stage with him and played a tape of old TV adverts he'd collated at home to the audience, commenting on each one. At this point he was making all his own bookings himself, keeping the dates in a pocket *Angling Times* diary given to him by his old boss at Chris's News. He had an acting agent, but when he phoned them in the summer of 1997 to ask if they had any work for him, they offered him a two-week job filing at their offices. Then when they did find him some work in a Chekhov play in a small theatre in Middlesex he found himself feigning a sore throat to get out of it. At that point, he says, he was 'terrified of straight theatre'. Instead, he found himself taking on stranger gigs. In Birmingham he performed at a policeman's party. When they heckled him by chanting, 'Who ate all the pies?' he responded by asking them, 'Shouldn't you lot be out arresting wrong Irishmen?' He also played a Christmas party for Blackburn taxi drivers – organised for June because they were too busy over the festive period. 'They had a Christmas tree and decorations and a DJ with a party hat on playing Slade. But there were only 14 of them there. Typical bloody taxi drivers, most of 'em never turned up.'

Joining the trend of stand-up comedy shows that summer was a new Channel 4 series called *Gas*. Hosted by comedian Lee Mack, the idea was to feature British comedy acts deemed to be off the wall and with an edge. Producer Sandie Kirk and assistant producer Lisa White organised auditions at comedy venues around the country. From London Lennie

Beige and Martin Bigpig got their breaks, while at the Manchester showcase at the Frog and Bucket Kirk and White selected the surrealist Noel Fielding, future star of *The Office*, Mackenzie Crook in his guise as end-of-the-pier entertainer Charlie Cheese, and Peter Kay.

Among such madcap company Peter Kay must have seemed decidedly straight, but for Lisa White he shone out immediately. 'I was blown away,' she says. 'For somebody so young, who had been doing comedy for only a few months, he was amazing.'

Just before *Gas* was screened in July, Lisa White decided to supplement her TV work by becoming an agent for the Off the Kerb agency. The first person she called was Peter Kay.

With an agent on his side the money started improving and so did the offers. That year he appeared on every stand-up show going, including BBC1's *The Stand-Up Show* and ITV's *Live at the Jongleurs* and *Last Laugh Show*; suddenly 'women in leggings' who never gave him the time of day before started acknowledging him – 'Ooh, we've seen you on telly.' Meanwhile, Lisa White had entered him into Channel 4's 'So You Think You're Funny?' competition and the BBC New Comedy Award at the Edinburgh Festival in August, both events that would, she hoped, bring in more work.

A week before leaving for Edinburgh, Peter Kay did his first TV interview for a late-night ITV show called *Funny Business*, telling the show's host Iain Coyle, 'I've never been to Edinburgh before, except when we went to the Isle of Rhum with the school and that was just to buy a Twix from John Menzies.'

'We were based in London but it was a Granada show, so part of the deal was that we had to do some of the shows from the north. I didn't know anything about Peter Kay when I arrived in Bolton,' says Iain Coyle today, from the set of *Big Brother*, where he works as a producer. 'Originally we wanted to interview Johnny Vegas, who was causing quite a splash at the time, but he had this over-protective agent so in the end he wasn't allowed to do it.'

Unable to agree on a venue for the interview and what with the weather being unusually fine, Peter Kay suggested they film it in the back lane behind the house he still shared with his mother. The first half of the interview takes place with Peter Kay wearing some disturbing Bermuda shorts and sitting on a deckchair. Neighbourhood kids clamber on walls behind him, attempting to get into the shots – 'Watch yourself with that bike, you'll have your eye out,' he turns round and yells at one point. Then to a lad, all of seven years old, in shorts flexing his muscles behind him, he tells Coyle 'he used to be in Jo Boxers, him'. This was Peter Kay caught to a tee, funny without even trying and remembering reference points that everyone else had forgotten about years ago – who else remembered Jo Boxers and the perky hit 'Boxer Beat'? Coyle was immediately impressed and stunned by Kay's encyclo-pedic knowledge of popular culture.

A few minutes into the interview the location switches to Peter Kay's bedroom, but what we didn't see outside was that the small wild kids who had populated the background earlier had been replaced by what Iain Coyle remembers as 'two heroin addicts' wandering up the street towards them. 'I saw them and I was terrified. But he dealt with them in the same way he dealt with the seven-year-old kids: he started talking to them and sort of taking the piss out of them without them realising. It was so funny how he dealt with them. They were like "What you doing?" and Peter said, "We're on telly, do you want to be on telly? Have you been on *Crimewatch* before?" One of the blokes was incomprehensible he was so off his head. Ordinarily I'd have run a mile because I was petrified, but he sorted it. He disarms people with his humour.' Safely ensconced in Kay's bedroom and surrounded by his collection of hand-labelled *Mork and Mindy*, *Only Fools and Horses*, *Porridge* and Genesis video-tapes, Coyle was flabbergasted when he discovered that Kay still kept his Saturday and Sunday job at the ABC Cinema despite his run of TV appearances. But the comic told him it was good for material and started launching into his routine of the time.

'People phone up and say, "What's the queue for *Evita* like?" "A bunch of people waiting outside." These kids came in last weekend and looked at the kiosk and said, "Senior Citizens? What's that about?" I said, "It's like a Mexican version of *Cocoon*, now get out." People open the doors and lean in and go, "You haven't any idea what you're showing tonight, have you?" "No, no idea, mate, I haven't got a clue, I only work here." '

When conversation turned to famous Kays such as the Scottish comic Phil Kay ('like Billy Connolly with bulimia') and *'Allo 'Allo* star Gorden Kaye ('he used to work at the Bolton Octagon'), Peter remembered he had a *Tommy the Tuba* album by Danny Kaye and began rooting through his album collection to find it. 'There was just a wall of records and he had a stepladder to reach them all. He had an Evel Knievel album and really weird 1970s albums and all these reference points that were amazing.' Other records pulled out included German porn soundtracks by a chap called Otto Weiss (*Otto Weiss is Nice*), Tony Christie's *So Deep in the Night* and *The Collected Broadcasts of Idi Amin*.

Asked by Coyle whether his material was about Bolton, school, girls or sex, Kay replied: 'All of that – except the sex. I'm not a prude, but people say I'm very mainstream. I don't think I am but I like stuff that's funny and old. I don't think there's mainstream or alternative; if something's funny it's funny.'

He went on to say that not much made him laugh other than Ronnie Barker – an idol he would later exchange fan mail with (Barker sending Peter letters on HMP Slade notepaper). 'I'm more of a laughter giver than a laughter taker,' he remarked, stifling a giggle.

'I don't think he ever believed he was as good as he was,' says Ian Coyle now. 'But when I was interviewing him, he was almost like a Victoria Wood character. All the references and what he was saying, you could just tell he was going to do something great.'

As fate would have it Iain Coyle was about to play his own small part in Peter Kay's next brush with greatness when he managed to sell a programme idea about the Edinburgh Fringe Festival to ITV and accidentally became a comedy award judge.

Chapter Four
None of That Effing and Blinding

'I not only use all the brains that I have, but all that I can borrow.'

Woodrow T. Wilson

'Adrian!'
'Rocky!'
'Adrian!'
'Rocky!'
'Adrian.'
'Rocky.'

Talia Shire and Sylvester Stallone, Rocky

The Edinburgh International Festival began in 1947 and in the wake of the Second World War was given a perky remit to 'provide a platform for the flowering of the human spirit'. For most of the visitors this entailed watching a fireworks show and a spot of military bombastics, but seeking to take advantage of the crowds a group of eight uninvited theatre companies took over a disused pub on the Royal Mile and started staging daily productions – the Edinburgh Fringe Festival had begun. Decades later the Fringe – a mecca for experimental dance troupes and one-armed jugglers alike – had expanded to include a Comedy Festival which quickly became the stand-up comedian's equivalent of the World Cup. In the late 1980s, when alternative comedy was in bloom, comedians would centre their entire year on hour-long shows. By the 1990s TV producers were using the festival as a place to spot upcoming talent and do deals. It is also one of the few occasions all year when a rising star can find himself reviewed in a national newspaper.

As each year has passed the Comedy Festival has become less adventurous and less fun. Comedy is big business, but once you realise this it's harder to enjoy it. Countless careers have been launched off the back of successful Edinburgh runs: Stephen Fry, Frank Skinner, Eddie Izzard, Steve Coogan and Lee Evans all gained TV contracts after being nominated for the coveted Perrier Award. As well as these big names, hundreds of lesser-known acts pour into the Scottish capital like so much seaweed washed up on the shore, desperately hoping that some passing comedy bigwig or at least a couple of tourists from Canada will notice them. In 1988, as a way of encouraging this fresh talent, the founder of the Gilded Balloon venue, Karen Koren, started the 'So You Think You're Funny?' competition aimed at amateur stand-ups who couldn't afford to hire a theatre for their own showcases. The initial prize in its first year was £250 from Koren's back pocket, but as the years progressed and Channel 4 climbed on board the prize fund swelled to £1,500 and the biggest carrot of all was that commissioning editors from the TV company as well as journalists and radio producers would be watching. Despite Channel 4's involvement it still had an edge that the Perrier Award didn't; if the big-name comics were the major-league movers then the entrants of 'So You Think You're Funny?' were the far cooler, eager comedy underdogs.

Iain Coyle, from ITV's late-night comedy programme *Funny Business*, was overjoyed to find himself in Edinburgh interviewing various comedians in the Pleasance Theatre Courtyard – the main congregation point for ligging and revelry – one night. After being approached by one of the

Gilded Balloon employees he found himself roped in to judge one of the four 'So You Think You're Funny?' heats. He was delighted.

'When I saw the name Peter Kay on the running order I thought there's no point watching any of the others,' he laughs. 'Paul Foot was on as well and he was really good, but then Peter came on and just blew the whole place away. Afterwards you have to go into this little room in the Gilded Balloon and discuss what you thought, and me and Fred McAuley just went, "What are we bothering even talking about this for?" The people from the Gilded Balloon were going, "Paul Foot was very good." And Fred, who was on the panel with me, said, "Look, are you mad? If he doesn't win this, there will be a riot." '

At the final a few days later comedian Adam Bloom, who'd been a 'So You Think You're Funny?' entrant three years previously and was beginning to make a name for himself on the various stand-up TV shows, went along to the Gilded Balloon to check out this 'fat Northern bloke' everyone was raving about. One of Bloom's favourite acts, Paul Foot, had made it to the final as a runner-up but the other comedian Bloom remembers from the night was a Liverpudlian called Anton who was like a 'cross between Alexei Sayle and Steven Wright with some of the funniest one-liners ever'. The host was Julian Clary who, as usual, was adorned in glittering purple camp finery with vast shoulder pads and protruding peacock feathers. Clary's put-downs were as subtle as his outfits and, on withering form, every time he mentioned the title of the show he would make his thoughts clear on the proceedings by emphasising the word 'think' in 'So You Think You're Funny?'. Sadly, it didn't go well for Anton, who was overcome with nerves. To make matters worse he left his carrier bag of props on the stage and had to shuffle back on to collect them while Clary was in the middle of his between-act banter. 'Anton came walking back on to collect his carrier bag just like a passerby would in a street,' remembers Adam Bloom. 'There was no respect whatsoever for Julian Clary in all his glamour onstage; it was as if he'd left his carrier bag in a café and was just going back to pick it up. Hilarious.'

After such a pitiful opening the stage was set for Peter Kay, who was on second. He didn't disappoint. Instantly Adam Bloom realised that the majority of the audience were here to see the Boltonian. 'He walked on storming,' he says. 'It was incredible; before he'd even got to the microphone the crowd were roaring. He'd won the audience over before he'd even spoken; I'd never seen anything like it. The other thing I remember was that he was wearing bright white, brand-new trainers, and I thought, "You should have scuffed them up a bit, mate." '

Peter Kay's set included a routine where he pretended to be a dad miming to the keyboard part in Soft Cell's 'Tainted Love', which is ridiculously basic and simple to begin with before it goes off on a spectral synth journey. When he told the audience where he was from, he remarked, 'Bolton, the only place in Britain where people still point at the sky when they see an aeroplane.'

'The room was in stitches. We all knew he'd won it when he came off; everyone thought no one's going to top that,' says Adam Bloom. 'But the real moment I knew he was going to be a star was when he came on to collect his prize. The stage had all the contestants on it, the people from the Gilded Balloon, Channel 4 people, the stage was crammed, and he was among them all with his award and he said, "It's like *Rocky* this," and he went "Adriiaannn". We've all seen *Rocky*, the ending when he's in the ring covered in blood; we're all emotional and he can't find his wife and he doesn't care about all the press and all the boxing industry, he just wants his wife. And I just thought to myself there couldn't be a more appropriate line for that moment and I roared. It was cocky because at the moment of humility – he'd just won an award – rather than say "I can't believe this" he carried on being funny. You could say that's slightly obnoxious because there's a time to just take it and be humble, but it was brilliant. The audience adored him. They're loving him already, he's won, then he hits them in the stomach with the *Rocky* line. And I just thought, "Do you know what? You're just too, too good." '

As if witnessing the 'So You Think You're Funny?' victory wasn't enough confirmation, Adam Bloom became certain Peter Kay was going to become a megastar when, a few weeks later, he found himself on tour with him. Comedy promoters Avalon had arranged a short stint at northern universities for Bloom and called him to say, 'There's this new bloke we think is really great. We want him to support you, he's called Peter Kay.' Their first gig together was at John Moores University in Liverpool, where only three years previously Kay had limped through a year as a student before moving to Salford.

'He turned up to the gig; it was the first night of the five we did and he was in the dressing room and he was sat there in the chair,' says Bloom. An expert in the slight nuances of human behaviour, the southern comedian detected something out of the ordinary in his fast-rising support act. 'There's a difference in status; whether you acknowledge kudos and hierarchy or not, it clearly exists. New acts don't make jokes at the expense of established acts in dressing rooms because there's a subconscious feeling that they might get their gigs pulled or miss out on a TV show. There's a pecking order, dos and don'ts, just like there is in any industry. Although he didn't say anything out of line, the way he was sitting in this chair looked like *he* was the star. He was just a man sitting in a chair, he wasn't lording it, he wasn't strutting, he wasn't smoking a cigar, he wasn't wearing anything special, he just looked like he had the presence about him, that he was a man who was about to go onstage to thousands of people, not 128. And I remember thinking, "There's something different about this bloke"; it wasn't arrogance, although there must have been a bit to make me think, "F***, I'm your support act!"

'If you just imagine being ushered in to meet God by a load of angels,' laughs Bloom. 'When you got there there'd be something in his posture that would be different to a normal person, yes? Now, I'm not saying the guy's a god, I'm just saying that the guy acted like it was his show. I slightly resented it,' Bloom adds. 'I'd appreciate that if you put the God reference in, you also put the resentment bit in.'

Like a confessional, Kay used the Liverpool show to own up to his sin of lying to get into the university. The students in the hall found it hysterical. But then he could have read out the Funeral Directors section of the *Thomson Local Directory* and people would have been in creases.

After each gig Peter would drive home, back to his mother's house in Bolton, while Bloom stayed in a local hotel. Just before their final date together at St Martin's Teacher Training College in Lancaster, Peter had to visit the hospital, and turned up at the gig with his arm in a sling. As ever, he turned what had happened into a part of his routine that night, but it wasn't so much the joke that impressed Adam Bloom as how easily he won over the audience. 'The poster for the gig that went out over the campus had me on it and no mention of a support,' he says. 'So he was unadvertised, there was no MC to introduce him and the audience had no idea who he was. He walked onstage, grabbed the microphone and told a story about the tube that had been put into his arm when he'd had this operation. He didn't look up at the audience, which is an extraordinary sign of confidence, and he trusted that his charisma was enough to make them want to listen and he told a story about the nurse putting a tube in his arm and she slipped and went, "Oh shit." His point was you don't really want someone talking like that just before they're about to operate on you. But the thing that blew me away and made me realise that he was going to be a star was that he hadn't even established himself with a hello, he hadn't made some funny generic comment about the room or himself, he'd just walked on unannounced, unadvertised. It was the Adam Bloom show, he was just there to warm up the crowd, and he walked on and within one or two seconds the whole room was his friend. They cared about his arm and wanted to know the story. I'd never seen that before in my life.'

After the gig Bloom regrets not approaching Peter Kay and telling him 'I bet my life you are going to be a big star and please give me 1 per cent of your future revenue in return for my confidence in you.' But he didn't. Instead, he went back to his hotel and tried to figure out how Kay had managed to charm the audience so easily and how, after three years in the game, with nothing but good reviews, he was being overtaken by a kid from Bolton.

The truth was Peter Kay wasn't like any other comedian on the circuit. The normal rules did not apply. 'He acted like a star who they loved and they just went, "Yeah, he's a star who we love." For me that's a mind-blowing level of confidence and belief in your likeability. I remember racking my brain to try and understand how it was possible. He had no fear.'

Adam Bloom ended the short tour with Peter Kay with mixed feelings. He was awestruck by Kay's confidence with the audience and was confident he had witnessed somebody with huge potential, but equally he felt aggravated by some of the tricks Peter Kay had pulled to undermine him. Kay was booked to perform 25 minutes each night, but at Lancaster after 15 minutes he told the audience, 'I'm sorry, I've got to go now', and waited for them to respond with an 'ahhhh'. Before the gig Adam Bloom had told him he could do 35 minutes if he liked, but getting the audience's sympathy, getting them subliminally to demand more was part of the stagecraft he'd picked up from Salford.

For Bloom it got worse. 'He said "I've got to go now" and the crowd groaned so he said, "Unless Adam Bloom will let me do some more." He left me in an extremely unfair position. Now I'm the Elephant Man's evil owner whipping him in the cage. I've already become an oppressor before I've even gone onstage – what chance do I stand now? Peter Kay is a very, very clever manipulator of situations and there's no way on this earth that he didn't know what he was achieving. That's my only beef with him. But I don't actually think it was anything more than another driver throwing tacks on to the racetrack behind him. I just ran over some of his tacks.'

Despite possessing superhuman evil comedy powers, back home Peter Kay behaved as if nothing extraordinary was happening in his life. If anything, away from the comedy clubs, he became even more normal. Conscious of his weight, which had climbed in direct correlation with his success, he joined Slimmers' World and attended meetings with his mother, Deirdre, every Tuesday evening. Those who recognised him there suspected they were being filmed as some elaborate candid-camera joke for a future TV show, but he weighed in with everyone each week and stayed for the motivational chats by the club organiser. Now, no longer working in factories and warehouses, it also gave him a chance to check in on regular conversations and keep his comedy hearing alert to some unintended comedy pearl. The low-calorie chocolate bars were also pretty good.

With the money he earned in Edinburgh from 'So You Think You're Funny?' and the BBC New Comedy Award he bought a second-hand Ford Fiesta and went back to his job at the cinema. Even when his manager Lisa White landed him a regular slot on BBC2's *The Sunday Show* he would rush from the studios on Oxford Road in Manchester to rip tickets and show people to their seats at the ABC in the afternoon. 'People would give me a double take and say, "Weren't you on telly just now? What are you doing here?" But I just liked it. Plus I got to see all films for free.'

'I don't sell the ice-cream,' he would add. 'People throw things at you and it's a girl's job – the union would be on to me.'

The BBC's Head of Entertainment Features, John Whiston, had been keeping tabs on Peter Kay for the past year and had even caught him at an end-of-term revue by Salford graduates the previous summer. With Channel 4 chasing Kay too, Whiston was keen to give him work, and as well as *The Sunday Show* he was hoping to develop a sit-com idea of Kay's called *Seaside Stories* which was to be set and filmed on location in Blackpool, Southport and Morecambe, following the adventures of coach parties of pensioners.

Quizzed by the *Bolton Evening News* on the eve of his debut on *The Sunday Show*, the local lad who 'still lives with his mum' appeared to be taking it all in his stride and told the paper: 'It's a thrill unlike any other to be presenter of *The Sunday Show*, an excitement that few people on this earth get to experience. Who would have thought that those bright lights existed somewhere over the rainbow.' Sarky bugger.

The Sunday Show was into its third series when Peter

Kay joined presenters Paul Tonkinson and Donna McPhail as part of the regular cast of a show designed to help viewers recover from the night before. He was joined by Jenny Ross – whom he'd competed against in the City Life Award Final the previous summer – offering a comic slant on showbiz news; and by Bez, the dancer from the Happy Mondays and Black Grape, whose enthusiasm for class-A drugs had once led him to be described as 'a walking medi-cine cabinet'. Here though, Bez was trying something different ... DIY. Each week, after he'd hammered together a shed or dispensed technical advice, he'd end on his catch-phrase – 'Job's a good 'un.' Kay was there to take the place of Dennis Pennis, Paul Kaye's brash American interviewer who had hung around film openings and asked celebrities like Demi Moore 'Would you ever consider doing a movie where you kept your clothes on?'

Although initially the production team at BBC Manchester wanted Peter to do short two-minute stand-up slots, he came up with 'Peter Kay's World of Entertainment' instead, where he would play dodgy old vinyl records or reminisce about old children's TV shows with the help of grown adults dressed as schoolkids. In one episode Billy Bedlam appeared – playing the theme from 1980s afternoon programme *Jonny Briggs* on his tuba as Peter goofed in the background.

'He were a bit raw,' remembers Billy Bedlam – a man who, among his many accolades, can rightly claim to be the world's fastest trombone player. 'But he was great at ad-libbing. He had to read everything off an autocue and I remember he really struggled with that. At one point he got it all wrong and just went up to the camera and started dusting the screen.'

With Dennis Pennis, who had been handed his own BBC2 series off the back of *The Sunday Show*, gone, *The Sunday*

Show was deemed low-budget trash by the critics and roundly ignored. For those lucky enough to see it, Kay shone. It had a huge and immediate effect on his popularity. A couple of weeks after his *Sunday Show* debut he performed at the Frog and Bucket in Manchester and the tickets sold out in a day, the manager telling the *Guardian* on 21 October 1997, 'We had to turn down 500 bookings.' The *Guardian* was the first national newspaper to pick up on the phenomenon of Peter Kay and, travelling to Bolton, discovered a comedian slightly disbelieving of his newfound celebrity, joking that the people who did make it into the Frog and Bucket gig 'even waited until the interval to go to the toilet'.

'Kay's style of comedy demands your attention,' wrote the reporter Collette Walsh. 'A bit like Dave Allen on speed, he reels out stories and observations about life and people: his family, old schoolteachers and staff at the cinema where he works are the main targets.' Despite being wide of the mark with the Dave Allen comparison, the *Guardian* got it right when they noted that Peter's audience was a lot more main-stream and not strictly limited to twentysomethings, like most acts on the comedy circuit. Peter Kay told them: 'It's just a matter of taking out the swear words I suppose. You have to read the audience to know what you'll get away with. I really don't see the point in offensive comedy. With *The Sunday Show*, I've got to watch my language; it's daytime telly and although it's assumed that hungover students are watching, there are probably kids and parents too. Anyway, people don't want to hear heavy Ben Elton stuff these days. I'm not into comics who go on about politics and sex, or who slag off their audience.'

To help him remember not to swear he jokingly asked *The Sunday Show* if they could put a cardboard cut-out of his mother in the row. Maybe they should have: his first words on air were 'I am the bastard son of Alf Roberts'.

Mrs Kay attended many of Peter's biggest shows and whenever he found himself swearing he'd always put his hand over his mouth and apologise. Indeed, in the early days, Peter indicated that his mother played a far bigger influence in his act than those impressions of her dancing to Sister Sledge. 'She's pretty cool, my mother,' he told the *Manchester Evening News*; 'in fact she writes half of my material.'

'When we were kids Deirdre had a good sense of humour,' says Peter's old schoolfriend Michael Atherton. 'She seemed to act as a kind of yardstick for things that might cross the line for being too sick or facetious. Peter's "impression" of her in his act, by the way, is fairly accurate.'

Deirdre Kay acted as a filter, attempting to remove the bad language from his act, but most people simply did not even hear it. 'That was one of the nice things about Peter,' says Billy Bedlam. 'He made it with none of that effing and blinding.' 'What I'm doing is really old school,' admitted Peter Kay at the time. 'I think if I'd come along and done this five years ago it wouldn't have worked.'

In an early profile in the *Independent*, comedy writer Simon Fanshawe said that the clubs of Manchester were 'not the natural habitat for this oversized, six-year-old-looking man-child of a comic whose face is too young to talk about sex, that kind of crowd's standard fare, or to swear, their staple vocabulary'. He wasn't that innocent, but there was something decidedly old-fashioned and uncomplicated about him. In response to the publicity about this 'new Alan Bennett' who looked like a young Alf Roberts with a clean-cut non-sweary act (ignoring the occasional slip-up), Kay noticed his audiences getting older. At one point a whole coachload of pensioners appeared at a Blackpool gig. 'It's like we raided Age Concern,' he joked.

This pan-generational appeal was something that Lloyd

Peters, the stand-up comedy teacher at Salford University, had noted in his protégé early on. 'Peter's gift was that he had lived a bit, so he had a store of material you wouldn't see in a normal young comedian,' he says. 'He worked as an usher, with the bingo crowd, he's worked and lived with old people and therefore has a whole range of old connections and observations about old people and how they live and work. The secret of his success is he connects with the old, middle and young age groups unlike any other contemporary comic, and that's his great gift, so when he got up and told jokes about old people's homes and how old people can't work answering machines it was from his experience.'

Graham Linehan, the Irish writer of the sit-com *Father Ted*, agrees. 'When you see his live show he will do impressions of old women at a wedding, for instance, and it'll be spot on, and then he'll do an impression of the six-year-old kid at the wedding and that'll be spot on as well. He's not isolating his targets to one particular age group. There are some comedians and they are just aimed at 16- to 35-year-olds, so it's acid and satirical and very ironic or clever; Peter Kay's clever but he's not trying to be clever; it's really, really intelligent, brilliantly observed, very sweet and very funny.'

'Peter Kay's genius is recalling a more innocent past,' says writer and broadcaster Andrew Collins, whose book *Where Did It All Go Right?* is chiselled from the same mound of childhood happiness as Kay's. 'I don't know how calculated it is, but he appeals to the part of us that finds the modern world confusing and depressing. Weren't things easier in the old days? His persona belies his actual age. He comes across as a middle-aged man, and always has done, and that endears him to older audiences. I have no idea why anyone under 30 would find him funny. But I have sat at suburban dinner parties and listened as people in their forties who don't even watch that much telly swap Peter Kay quotes, just as undergraduates used to with Monty Python. He really tapped into an older market.'

As Collins points out, Peter Kay was 'predestined to appear in *Coronation Street.*' The warm, gentle humour of the programme and Kay's reputation as a working-class comic with old-fashioned values meant he was a perfect fit for the show with its cobbled streets, corner shop and neighbourhood pub, something most towns and cities in Britain had lost decades ago. But his first appearance on the soap opera was a blink-and-you-missed-it cameo broadcast on 17 November 1997, in which he played a shop fitter helping Fred Elliot expand his emporium with a new shop sign and a few new cabinets – Fred's rival Maude sneaking a raw kipper inside one of them. 'Do you like blue?' asks Peter Kay in the background as Maude goes about her evil work. Peter Kay was only on screen for four minutes, but found himself being recognised and stopped in the street because of it and, as ever, started weaving his Weatherfield experience into his comedy set. 'They all talk posh,' he told his stand-up audiences. 'But they're putting it on, they are. Gail Tilsley's on the phone [puts on posh voice] – "Yes, well it will have to be two o'clock," and I'm like, "Stop it and talk proper." '

We hate it when our friends become successful
And if they're Northern, that makes it even worse
Morrissey, 'We Hate It When Our Friends Become Successful'

As much as the public adores Peter Kay, his fellow comedians, who will groan and grumble at the merest mention of his name, loathe him. The root of their beef is that he uses other people's jokes without giving them credit. But when it comes to going on record with these accusations they clam up.

'I've got major problems with Peter Kay,' says one Manchester comic.

What are they?

'Do you think I'm mad? I do want to work again, you know!'

'He stole a joke off me once,' says one, reciting a popular Kay pun before backtracking: 'Please don't print that, he's richer than me.'

'Other comedians live in fear of him coming to their gigs,' says one Blackpool-born stand-up. 'Because you know he's watching for what bits of your act he can subtly change and make his own.'

Other current comedians cite a long forgotten act called Woody Bop Muddy, whose performances consisted of him playing a cheesy single on an old record player then ripping it off the turntable and destroying it in a series of inventive and violent ways. Peter did a similar thing on *The Sunday Show* – not every week, just once, but it is highly unlikely that he was aware of the obscure Muddy. Besides, Peter's taste for cheesy vinyl was established when he was twelve. The accusations demonstrate how far back some people in the comedy business are prepared to go to prove their point.

One London agent told me that she didn't feel Peter Kay used remarkably similar material to some of her clients maliciously. He just had a different 'old school' mentality to everyone else. 'In the 1970s you'd hear Bruce Forsyth tell a joke on the Saturday, then hear Tommy Cooper tell it again on a different programme the next week. It never used to be an issue. Jokes were seen as fair game; they didn't belong to anybody. Now, though, there's an emphasis on writing your own material.

'Mention Peter's name on the comedy circuit I'm on and people spit blood,' says the wickedly funny Glaswegian comedienne Janey Godley.

'There is a sense of resentment towards him, certainly within the London comedy world,' says comedy writer Andrew Collins. 'Having said that, there are few professions as insecure or paranoid, so perhaps it's nothing to do with what he does, merely that he did it outside the traditional radar. Perhaps because he arrived fully formed.'

Today, animosity directed at Peter Kay is expressed cagily in dressing rooms or behind the disguise of a nickname on an Internet message board, but when Kay was starting out in 1996 and 1997 they almost put a halt to his career. At the 'So You Think You're Funny?' heat in Edinburgh, Iain Coyle remembers that several of the judges were adamant that he shouldn't win because they'd heard several of his jokes before. 'The thing is, jokes aren't what makes Peter Kay funny,' he says. 'I remember talking to Paul Zenon, who was very big at that time, and he said that he'd take it as a compliment.'

Perhaps one of the reasons other comedians dislike Peter Kay so much is not that he tells similar gags to them but because he tells them better? When he was on tour at the tail end of 1997, another comedian at a Manchester date told him about the rumours. Discussing it two years later, Kay told Chris Oliver Wilson of *The Times*: 'When I started doing stand-up, a lot of comedians accused me of stealing their material. It really upset me. I was naïve. I didn't know there were a thousand other comedians talking about Jerry Springer and *Teletubbies*. So I thought, "Sod you. I'm going to talk about my family." Then comedians can't come to me and say I've lifted it, because they are my own stories and real things that happened. But there's still a lot of jealousy. They accuse me of lifting material. Some people are bitter because they had a career plan and it just hasn't happened for them. They begrudge other people having success.'

Janey Godley agrees: 'I like him, but other comics they'll say they like him then say that they want to kill him behind his back. It's the same with Jimmy Carr. For what? For being successful?'

Then as now there is a feeling that Peter Kay had it easy – that all the doors magically sprang open for him and slammed shut for them. Adam Bloom can understand the feeling towards Kay in the industry because, he says, 'For most comics overnight success takes ten years. The only other person I can think of who was as successful as quickly as Peter Kay is Jack Dee.'

Google a few of the corny gags Peter Kay tells at the start of any of his live DVDs and you will discover that many of them are also credited to one-line expert Tim Vine, some to Tommy Cooper and a couple to high-voiced American eccentric Emo Phillips. But discovering the origins of jokes, unlike song lyrics, is impossible – nobody copyrights gags. Muddying the water further is the fact that in the era of email forwarding, two lists – one entitled 'The Genius of Peter Kay', the other 'Peter Kay's Universal Truths' – have been circulating for several years. Despite being very funny and containing the kind of thing you can imagine Peter saying – triangular sandwiches taste better than square ones; you never know where to look when you're eating a banana – he wasn't the original author of either list; somewhere along the back lanes of what Clive James used to mockingly call 'the information super highway' his name got attached. The truisms originate from two ex-students from York, Tom Sharp and Andy Milson, who published them in a book called *100% True* in 2001.

Perhaps Peter Kay's attitude towards the end of his 'Mum Wants a Bungalow' tour in 2003 was the right one: to let the audience tell the punchlines to his oldest gags, like a joke version of karaoke. Jokes in themselves are not what makes Peter Kay funny; he is a brilliant storyteller, actor and observer of human quirks. Terrible cliché it may be, but never has the phrase 'it's the way he tells them' been more accurate.

'It's his ability to be loved onstage that makes him a genius, not his ability to write jokes,' says Adam Bloom. 'Woody Allen said a comedian's a funny person doing material and not a person doing funny material, and I think that's hit the nail on the head with what Peter is. He can say anything and be funny. Who needs clever twisty turny jokes when you can just be funny without doing anything? What an amazing way of being.'

Writing on the <chortle.co.uk> message board recently, Toby Foster – who had starred in *Phoenix Nights* as a member of the the Phoenix Club's backing band, Les Alanos – defended his friend from a fresh wave of allegations: 'PK is great at what he does, and a lovely bloke. Stupid personal attacks like this just make you sound like a c***. People seem to imagine that Peter was just hewn from some rock and bunged onstage at the Albert Halls to sell out crowds, forgetting the years he put into stand-up ... I can honestly say that I never saw him do anything other than storm in every club gig he did. A chancer? He worked his bollocks off, and became successful, that's the fact.'

Just as at the Edinburgh Festival, where Peter had made the audience laugh long after his act was finished by quoting *Rocky*, often the thing that people laugh most at is the bit after the punchline has been delivered – 'You can have that. You can keep that one.' It is both a Kay family trait he'd caught off his father and an excellent tool for leading into the next joke or section of his routine. Technically it's brilliant, and in a business that feeds off laughter, where an ordinary comic would get one laugh Peter Kay manages to get two, or three.

Peter Kay doesn't claim his work is 100 per cent original – on the DVD commentary of *Phoenix Nights* he admits borrowing some gags that he'd seen in other sit-coms, although he couldn't remember their titles. In fact, the one time Peter Kay has fully owned up to using someone else's material it was with a joke that got him the sack: 'I was on Preston train station and this announcement came on. Ladies and gentlemen, the next train is an express to Carlisle. We advise passengers to move away from the yellow line at the edge of the platform as they may get sucked off … bit of blue for the dads there, bit of blue.'

He told this joke during his spell as warm-up man on *Parkinson*, where he worked in January 1998. According to the *Daily Mail* it was allegedly Mary Parkinson, Michael's wife, who objected to the 'blue' nature of the gag (ironic though it was). Either way, he admits that being sucked off at Preston station was the reason he got the boot eight weeks into the job.

The person who got Kay that job was his Mancunian friend Danny Dignan, who was also Parkinson's producer. Being a warm-up man is a difficult task. You need to welcome the audience and get them to comply with the house rules – no going to the lavatory during recording, no leaving before the end, no heckling – and you have to keep them happy between the endless breaks for adverts, make-up and reshoots. Then, in the middle of one of your jokes, the floor manager will shout, 'Going to taping. Quiet please.' Not easy. These were all qualities that jarred some-what with Peter, and typically he saw the challenge slightly differently. As well as the guests on the show he wanted the audience to go home each evening remembering him, too. Not everyone on Parkinson's team found Peter perfect warm-up material. Michael Parkinson thought he was fantastic.

Peter described the job to the *Bolton Evening News* on Friday, 23 January as 'scary' and told them it meant that finally he would be giving up his usher job at the ABC Cinema in Bolton – finally, 18 months after winning the City Life Award, he had accepted he was a full-time comic.

'I have to follow people like Billy Connolly – it's very difficult,' he said. 'During every interval between guests I come on and talk to the audience. They usually use a comedian who has been in the business for about 30 years. To choose someone like me is amazing. But they wanted something a bit different.'

A perk was that he got to take his parents to the shows. His mother and nan travelled down to London for the Billy Connolly appearance and, as a 50th-birthday treat, he took his father along to a show where Phil Collins and John Prescott were guests. Backstage, before recording, Peter told them it was his father's birthday and Michael Kay was treated to a surreal celebrity moment as the former Genesis man, the Deputy Prime Minister and his son sang 'Happy Birthday' to him. It was a peculiar show that was filmed on Thursday, 5 February 1998 – Prescott breaking free of the normal expectations of a politician by going into the orchestra and playing the drums. Peter Kay's memory of the night, though, was the way in which his father spoke to the Hull MP. 'I remember seeing him and saying, "Hello John", whereas my dad said, "Hello, Mr Prescott." It's funny how different generations behave.'

Whereas other people in Peter Kay's position might have been star-struck by Parkinson's guests he treated them like regular mortals: 'I'd just say something like: "The kettle's over there." Seeing all these famous people was a bit strange. It was a bit like being in Madame Tussaud's, yet everyone was real.'

The day after the Prescott show, Peter was booked to play at the Comedy Store in the West End and took his father along with him, the pair having their photograph taken next to the sign outside the famous venue with Peter billed as the headliner. Kay's second performance there was a bigger success than his first – despite struggling against a noisy bar, he took it all in his stride. 'What's going on back there?' he asked. 'Someone got a car boot sale on or something?'

When his invitation to clap along to the *Jim'll Fix It* theme tune at the end of his set was met with a muted response, he asked the audience, 'What do you need? A metronome?' In William Cook's *The Comedy Store*, Peter says, 'I had fears that I wouldn't translate outside the north west.' But he had no need to feel afraid. 'It's the rhythm, isn't it? Sometimes you can tell a joke and if it's said a certain way they'll laugh even though they don't know what they're bloody laughing at. When I first started, I tried losing my accent,' says Peter, revealing that at his first show south of Birmingham, in Bristol, he'd tried to 'take the Northern out of my voice. It didn't work. I was self-conscious about it, but it turned out that it was one of my strongest things.'

This was more than apparent later in the year when Peter was approached by an American woman on the Royal Mile in Edinburgh who told the comedian: 'I thought you were really funny. I've no idea what you were talking about, but you made me laugh.'

Back at the Comedy Store there was another difference Peter noticed between himself and his counterparts on the southern circuit. In London there are so many clubs that acts can polish the same 20-minute set over and over again and never perform to the same audience. Up north, because there are considerably fewer comedy venues, Peter felt he had to change the act every night. He'd always take his tape recorder to gigs with him and record his shows – not only to see what bits got the biggest laughs, but also to ensure he didn't do the same act when he returned a fortnight later. His method wasn't to write his act but to have themes which he'd expand upon. In the first two years of his stand-up act part of the reason his regular followers loved him so much was that, unlike with so many comics, you never saw the same show twice. Despite the loose nature of his sets there was a structure. As he says: 'I always try and go full circle on a story. Then it becomes more like a piece of theatre to me.'

'That's the trouble with stand-up comedy: people want to hear jokes.'

Peter Kay, Live at the Comedy Store

Losing the Parkinson job was a minor setback to be filed away alongside all the other temporary jobs he'd lost. In fact it led to another warm-up-man job, this time on a couple of episodes in the first series of *Rolf's Amazing World of Animals* on BBC1. It was, says Peter, 'the easiest job I've ever had. I was supposed to fill in between all the technical breaks but Rolf would always appear to entertain the audience and I'd be sat there getting paid £200 to watch Rolf Harris play his didgeridoo.'

Rolf and Parky notwithstanding, 1998 was the year when things really began to step up a gear for Peter Kay – not that they hadn't moved quickly enough already. On Saturday, 23 May Channel 4 was due to air the terrestrial première of Robert Redford's movie *Quiz Show*. Building a whole themed evening around the event, the film was sandwiched between Bob Monkhouse with a personal history of his years as a game show host and, at 11.30 p.m., *Let's Get Quizzical*, in which Peter studied bizarre moments in quiz show history. It was a great programme, with Peter's links done from a mocked-up living room featuring him in a stuffed armchair as he played clips, such as the man who answered 'Turkey' to every question in *Family Fortunes*. Peter also astutely noted that Steve Coogan's Alan Partridge character was surely based on Fred Dineage, host of *Gambit* – a corny TV version of blackjack but with the added appeal of Fred and his glamorous assistant Michelle Lambourne (job description: hold giant playing cards and smile) flirting. In the clip Peter played, Dineage was revealed as a man who made it obvious that he assumed all TV hostesses were thick when he remarked, 'Michelle is the thinking man's Muppet.' Kay, an expert on UK game shows, having spent the bulk of his childhood weekends watching *3-2-1* and *Bullseye* as well as writing the jokes for Dave Spikey's *Chain Letters*, made the point that in order to appear on TV ordinary people had to be willing to have the piss taken out of them. To demonstrate the point he showed a scene of Bill Grundy hosting *In My Opinion*, a game in which three middle-class panellists had to guess a working-class person's political opinions.

'What is comedy? Comedy is the art of making people laugh without making them puke.'

Steve Martin

Having just gone to the Edinburgh Fringe Festival for three days to compete in the competitions the previous year, Peter Kay found himself having to find a temporary apartment in the city when he returned in 1998, as Lisa White had arranged for a full three-week run at Pleasance over the Road – one of the many outbuildings of the Pleasance

Theatre, the hub of the Comedy Festival. It was the longest he had ever been apart from his mother and away from Bolton in his life. The digs he hired weren't up to much; despite paying out a fortune (many Edinburgh residents hire out their homes during the festival at extortionate rates) he was appalled to discover that his landlord had left piles of dirty laundry everywhere. 'I mean my house is not much more tidy,' he said. 'But when it is someone else's it's different, isn't it?'

Edinburgh 1998 was regarded as a vintage year for emerging talent by many observers, including Nica Burn, the producer of the Perrier Pick of the Fringe, who compared it with the year when Emma Thompson, Stephen Fry and Hugh Laurie shared the bill of the Cambridge Footlights show. Among the buzz shows were several with surreal leanings that some journalists saw as a signal of the end of stand-up comedy. Among them were two comedians called Julian Barrett and Noel Fielding, who had created an off-kilter parallel universe called the Mighty Boosh in which they performed as two disillusioned zookeepers attempting to unravel the mysteries of the space–time continuum. Invited to join the debate about standard comedy's demise, however, Barrett and Fielding declined. 'It's ridiculous the way we keep on being asked on radio shows to slag off stand-up,' Barrett told *The Sunday Times* in an article headlined 'The Surreally Useful'. 'Why would we want to do that? We're not anti-stand-up; it's what we do for a living most of the time. You can't have a wild man dressed in strange fur with Polos instead of eyes running on to the stage in a stand-up routine, whereas we can in the Mighty Boosh.'

If anything, Edinburgh 1998 proved that regular mainstream stand-up, rather than weird comedy psychedelia, remained the dominant force. The angle was debunked even further by anyone who got the chance to see Peter Kay that year. Reviewing his show in the *Independent* on 27 August, James Rampton wrote: 'The Edinburgh Comedy Festival this year has been full of pontificators predicting the death of straight stand-up. But in Peter Kay's case, it is very much alive and kicking; in fact, it's in the rudest of health.' Rampton noted that Peter Kay's subject material of taxi drivers, bad DJs, *Bullseye* and the embarrassing way your mum dances at wedding receptions was hardly breaking any new ground but 'Kay gets away with his hackneyed choice of material by the sheer verve with which he performs it'.

Hackneyed or not, the audience lapped it up, and despite the slightly negative reviews, he was very much the people's choice when he was announced among the five nominees for the much-coveted Perrier Award alongside Canadian Sean Cullen, pub landlord Al Murray and two Irishmen, Tommy Tiernan and Ed Byrne. 'I am really, really chuffed to be nom-inated,' Peter told the *Bolton Evening News*. 'I'm confident – confident that I won't win it, and I know they all say that, but I do really mean it.'

Peter's hunch was correct. Among the Perrier voting panel there was a perception that Peter Kay didn't need it. 'There was a feeling that the Perrier was already too small for him,' one of the panellists later revealed. Possibly an additional factor was the fact that he disappeared for a week of his run to a former lock keeper's cottage in Bow, East London, and the set of Channel 4's morning show *The Big Breakfast*. With regular presenters Johnny Vaughn and Denise Van Outen on holiday, Kay (who'd impressed as a sharp-witted guest a couple of months previously) was invited to be a host for a week alongside Melanie Sykes, the actress and model who had shot to stardom on the back of her adverts for Boddington's beer ('by 'eck it's gorgeous').

Kay was worried that they were a beauty-and-the-beast combination. 'Have you seen the state of me?' he asked. 'Most of the viewers will be a sight better-looking than me.' But the pair quickly settled into their place as the north's answer to Johnny and Denise, Peter even developing a bit of a catchphrase – 'yes indeed, ladies and gentlemen'. It was a chaotic week, full of blunders – Peter stepped on Sykes's toe and left her gasping and he struggled with his autocue – but it all added to the anarchic fun of the show. One morning, hosting a game show within the programme on which three women appeared, he very obviously let one of them win – but then she was his girlfriend Susan! When the wind blew open the living-room curtains when he was mid-link he rushed to close them and in disgust at the weather shouted 'August!' at the camera as if he was a dinner lady worried about the weather at break time. At Channel 4 and among TV critics the verdict on Peter's *Big Breakfast* week was positive. On the Tuesday after the first show, Kathleen Morgan in the *Daily Record* wrote, 'While Vaughn is off, he should sharpen up his repertoire. He has some tough competition back home.'

It's tempting to assume that Peter's career took off on the back of Edinburgh 1998 (Channel 4's comedy commissioning editor, Katie Taylor, was among the judges on the Perrier panel) and his successful five days on *Big Breakfast*, but the wheels were already in motion long before. Sandie Kirk, who had produced the *Gas* TV series where Peter met his manager Lisa White, had been commissioned earlier in the year to develop a new strand for the channel called *The Comedy Lab* to encourage new names. The idea was that these new comedians and writers would put together half-hour shows – screened in the post-pub 11.30 p.m. slot – and hopefully one or two series would come out of them. The first person she approached was Peter Kay.

Chapter Five
It Smells Like a Rotten Alsatian

'Still to come, the man with the enduring twinkle. And that's
David Essex. Plus, the five-year-old boy who knows the name
of every motorway junction from Land's End to John o'Groats.
The amazing walking, talking map-boy.'

Judy Finegan, Richard and Judy

'There used to be a real me, but I had it surgically removed.'

Peter Sellers

Peter Kay's contribution to Channel 4's *The Comedy Lab*,
'The Services', was written mainly while he was in
Edinburgh in 1998 and while he was presenting *The Big
Breakfast* for a week in London. Earlier in the year, when the
offer had first been made, he'd surprised producer Sandie
Kirk, as well as Jack Dee's production company Open Mic
who were behind the series, by telling them he didn't want
to do a stand-up special ('mainly because I'd use up most of
my act', he told them). Instead, he saw it as a chance to do
some acting – and not the highbrow stuff his acting agent in
Manchester was still phoning him up about: 'Now I could do
comedy acting.' Kirk – who knew him only as a stand-up act
– was surprised, but gave him his head. After all, the idea of
The Comedy Lab was to give emerging talent the opportunity to express themselves, and the other episodes in the
series were no less adventurous – Dom Joly's *Trigger Happy*
pilot, which followed a week after 'The Services', with its

actors in giant squirrel costumes fighting in a shopping precinct springs to mind.

Peter began by developing further a rough script he had started with Sian Foulkes on the Granada TV directors' course and came up with the idea of spoofing the docu-soap genre that was overrunning the terrestrial TV schedules like a plague of ordinariness at the end of the 1990s – everyone from clampers to bin men were being filmed for the nation's fix of funny realism.

'I always used to love Victoria Wood when she did documentary spoofs on *As Seen on TV*, like "A Fairly Ordinary Man", "Winnie's Lucky Day" and "Swim the Channel". I thought that's what I'd really like to do,' he says. 'At the time there were programmes like *The Cruise* and *Lakesiders* and *Hotel* and I thought I really wanted to do something like that so I came up with the idea of a service station because I thought it was a really classless place – upper class, working class, they've all got to stop at the services. It seemed like the perfect place with so many people passing through from bin men to rock stars, from school trips to pensioners on mystery tours, it had it all – not to mention the staff.'

Originally Channel 4 wanted to film the show close to London. The budget for each episode of *The Comedy Lab* was around £40,000 and this had to pay for everything: cast, the crew (who were all based in the capital), catering, transport as well as the standard rate for first-time scripts (approximately £4,000 according to former Channel 4 employees). But first Heston services on the M4 wouldn't give Channel 4 permission, then every other service station followed suit. 'Because of all these documentary programmes dishing the dirt they all said no,' says Peter Kay.

At first Peter and Sian were faced with the unwelcome prospect of having to rewrite the script and set it in a supermarket instead. But then Channel 4 came back and told them that there were two independent service stations in the British Isles – one in Swansea and the other in Bolton, four miles from Peter's home – and they'd agreed to let them film there. Kay was chuffed; not only would he be filming locally, where his characters were based, but also First Services Bolton West was perfect because nobody ever stopped there, it was run-down and quiet. In other words 'a bit of a shithole'.

His *Comedy Lab* show was given the title 'The Services'. It came together with suggestions from Dave Spikey (who came up with the outline for manageress Pearl and the storyline about the missing French tourists – 'blooming French, they don't know a word of English') and Neil Anthony (who would later change his surname to Fitzmaurice), a Liverpudlian comedian Peter had become friendly with after they'd competed in the same BBC New Comedy final at Edinburgh in 1997. Neil had told him about a screenplay he was working on about a Liverpudlian gangster and told him, if it ever got made, there'd be a part for him in it. Although both Dave and Neil were uncredited when the show was aired, Peter made sure to mention them in interviews surrounding the screening. Ideas for what the characters should wear were fleshed out on the way to live dates in early summer – invariably with Paddy McGuinness who'd drive with Peter to some of his further-flung shows.

'I remember working it out with an A4 pad sat on a bed in a cheap £10-a-night B&B in Bristol,' says Peter. 'We were watching *My Cousin Vinny* with the sound turned down and I was sketching out a mullet hairdo.'

Three weeks before filming was set to begin the bulk of the script was yet to be written. In fact, Peter penned most of it during the holiday to Las Vegas he took with Susan after the Edinburgh Festival. Instead of gambling away his life savings or going to watch Siegfried and Roy getting mauled by white tigers, Peter spent the majority of the seven-day break writing in his hotel room, then wandering the Vegas strip attempting to find somewhere he could fax his final drafts to Sandie Kirk in London. 'It cost me £50 and I never got it back on expenses!'

Mind you, Peter and Susan did take some time out and lots of it wound up entering the stand-up shows he'd perform through 1998 and 1999. 'If you think I'm fat, you want to go to America; it's like *It's a Knockout* out there,' he tells audiences, miming some ten-chinned beast wobbling around a shopping mall.

In Las Vegas Peter also had his first taste of alcohol for years. He and Susan had gone along to a *Stars in Their Eyes*-style tribute show and, not wanting to waste the free drink voucher that came with the ticket, Peter ordered a Baileys because he likes Baileys-flavoured Häagen-Dazs. The result? Susan having to pull Peter away from the dancefloor as he danced like his dad to a Four Tops tribute band.

Most of the parts in the 25 minutes of 'The Services' were to be played by Peter Kay himself – partly because, as a fan of the Peter Sellers movies *Dr Strangelove* and *The Party*, he saw this as a comedy tradition, but also because he didn't trust another actor to pull off exactly what he wanted – and certainly not without being paid. Apart from Peter Kay and Sian Foulkes (who would progress to roles in *The League of Gentlemen* and *Emmerdale*), the only other actor in the show was Paddy McGuinness. McGuinness, Peter's schoolfriend who would give Foulkes the nickname 'Does she?' on account of how her name sounds with a Bolton accent, had two lines. 'Are we getting time and a half for this lot being here?' he asks, gesturing towards the unseen camera crew during a staff meeting. 'Standard rate, Equity, surely.'

'One word, Terry: Job Club,' replies the service station manageress.

The real staff of Bolton West Services and the customers became unpaid extras. Not that Paddy was really an actor either. Just as Peter had done, he was stumbling through a succession of low-skilled jobs, and after a spell as a building-site labourer was working as a fitness instructor and lifeguard at Horwich Leisure Centre. When he heard how much Peter was earning from his stand-up act he thought, 'I'll have some of that' and began hatching plans for his own comedy career.

'The Services' was put together extremely quickly, filmed over three days in October then screened on Channel 4 as the first show in the *Comedy Lab* series less than three weeks later, on Wednesday, 11 November at 11.30 p.m. There was just one review in the national press, by Brian Viner in the *Mail on Sunday*, but it was brimming with enthusiasm. 'The Services' was screened in the same week as Victoria Wood's long-overdue debut sit-com, *Dinnerladies*. Viner noted that *Dinnerladies* was all but welcomed to BBC1 by a team of buglers in gold smocks, which makes it a little unjust that "The Services" barely snuck on to Channel 4 before midnight, for *Dinnerladies* was nowhere near as funny.'

Brian Viner had been tipped off about Peter Kay during an interview with Caroline Aherne and Craig Cash, who were promoting their sit-com *The Royle Family*. In his review of 'The Services' he was quick to point out their shared 'acute ears for the absurd banalities, not to mention the banal absurdities, of everyday conversation' and also mentioned Steve Coogan, writing that Kay was 'blessed with a comparable genius. However, there is more warmth in Kay's characterisations than in Coogan's, and more humanity.'

In true docu-soap style 'The Services' centred on a typical day in an everyday workplace and featured a voice-over, by Peter, midway between bored and patronising, that was typical of the shows of that era. The spoof was completed by a generic saxophone instrumental even Kenny G would have found repellent. The characters Peter appeared as would all reappear later in his TV career, with the exception of Pearl Harmon, the bolshie service station manageress who believes the appearance of the TV cameras will be the start of her life as a celebrity.

In one of the early scenes we spy Pearl on the phone to her friend Carol, through the half-shut door of her life-sappingly dull office, boasting about being on TV. 'Look at the Mo, she only passed her driving test, she had a record in the Top 40 and they did her bloody life, did you see that?'

'I loved that line,' says Peter. 'People always say stuff like, "Did you see that Claire Sweeney on *This Is Your Life*? She hasn't had a life. She's only 12." '

As well as Pearl, Kay played Mathew Kelly – a customer care assistant in the final year of a drama degree who would rather be onstage than cleaning toilets: 'It smells like a rotten Alsatian. Why can't they flush, the filthy bastards'; Alan McLarty – a disgraced ex-employee of the RAC ('She was fifteen and a half, what's six months?') who has set up his own motor recovery service called the ARC and holds strong views on corporal punishment, believing that they should 'hang joy riders on the National Lottery. And when the body drops the foot sets the balls rolling'; Utah – a coach driver whose real name is Craig: 'Utah's my wild west name,' he explains; and Paul LeRoy – the mullet-haired 1980s-obsessed DJ staging a roadshow at the service station to drum up interest in his radio station Chorley FM. 'We've got a foot spa, health spa and a £20 voucher for your local Spar, so near so,' says LeRoy to an empty car park. 'Three fantastic prizes and all available today from Chorley FM, your favourite waste of time.' Cue – 'You're My Favourite Waste of Time' by Paul Owen.

Of the five, he admits that Mathew Kelly is basically Peter

Kay playing Peter Kay, albeit slightly camper and with an Irish accent – his thespian pretensions picked up by studying the mannerisms of the drama students at Salford University. In an out-take Kelly tells the cameras he's from the small Irish town of Coalisland – the birthplace of Peter Kay's mother, Deirdre. All five characters have classic scenes: Utah shakes the interviewer's hand and asks him to 'watch my trigger finger'; Paul LeRoy's impassioned paean to the 1980s – 'Every year something different happened' – as he played 'I Think We're Alone Now' by Tiffany to an audience of exactly zero; and best of all angry self-employed Scot Alan McLarty suffering a mental breakdown and last seen wandering down the hard shoulder of the M61, with his trousers around his ankles, singing 'We Will Rock You' by Queen. 'The police had truckers ringing up saying there's a madman loose on the motorway,' laughs Peter. 'But we had permission.'

After filming Peter revealed that LeRoy was based on a local radio DJ a friend had seen doing a roadshow at the far end of a Tesco car park once, while the inspiration for Utah was a coach driver he'd personally experienced while on a family holiday to Barmouth in Wales in 1991. This man spat a bottle of orange squash over his windscreen when he realised it was undiluted cordial and attempted to impress the teenage Peter Kay by referring to his coach as 'a big girl'.

'The Services' began two recurring motifs that would run throughout Peter's TV career. One was Chorley FM – Paul LeRoy's radio station with its unintentionally (by the fictional radio station) cheeky slogans 'Coming in your ears' and 'Where the listener comes first'. The other, rather bizarrely, was Bob Carolgees, who with his puppet Spit the Dog used to terrorise guests on the riotous Saturday-morning kids show *Tiswas* by gobbing on them. Such discourteous behaviour then was inspired by punk rock, but today, in an era where children are practically doused in tinned tomatoes the second they enter a TV studio, Carolgees's phlegm-based capers seem a little tame. In 'The Services' 'TV's own Bob Carolgees', as Pearl calls him, is an unseen presence but he still sends the staff into a tailspin when the manageress gets wind of his imminent arrival – the cynical Mathew Kelly even rolling out a red carpet and removing all the adult magazines from the shop.

'I don't know why we were obsessed with him,' says Peter. 'When we met him he asked about it, but I couldn't really explain it.'

The biggest surprise for Peter's friends watching 'The Services' and for those who had witnessed him performing in smoky northern clubs was seeing him convincingly pull off the role of Pearl. It was even more bizarre for Peter, because the make-up and Dorothy Perkins blouse turned him into the spitting image of his mother's sister, Auntie Bernie.

In the DVD commentary of 'The Services' Paddy McGuinness says that he finds it weird seeing his mate dressed as a woman, but Kay enjoyed the experience. So did his mother, who 'bagsied' the clothes after the shoot, although wearing a skirt previously worn by your son is not something every mother can claim to have experienced.

'I loved playing a woman actually,' Kay tells McGuinness on the DVD. 'And I didn't play it in a woman's voice … Andrew Gillman the director told me not to, and it works.' In pre-publicity for the show Peter told the *Independent* on 10 November 1998: 'I've always been able to write female characters – I find women funnier than men, and I love the rhythm of women's speech. I go to Slimmers' World, where it's mostly women, and I get so much material – they have no taboos about what they'll discuss.' Coming from a matriarchal Irish Catholic family, Peter Kay found adopting a female voice far easier than that of a man's.

Father Ted, *Coogan's Run* and *The IT Group* writer and

admirer of Peter Kay, Graham Linehan, agrees and likens some of his stand-up to an Irish comedian he once saw – 'the name escapes me I'm afraid' – who would perform all his gigs with his mother and all her friends on the front row and 'would more or less play to them. The rest of the audience were just along for the ride. I think Peter Kay is very feminine as well,' he added. 'If you notice, a lot of his reference points are from not the usual male references of *Star Wars* and things. His references will be *Dirty Dancing* and, for want of a better word, chick flicks. I think that comes from being close to women and understanding women a bit more. It also tends to take some of the nasty edge off your comedy when you show the female side of yourself. I think that's a real secret to him. If he was from a household full of boys his humour would have been more edgy and defensive, because he'd be coming from a more combative direction, but he's warm and welcoming and that appeals to a lot more people. I'm so sorry for sounding so pretentious!'

Indeed, Peter's acceptance of his X chromosomes stretches to his music taste, which incorporates a love of musicals like *The Kids from Fame* and housewives' pin-up Michael Bublé. 'He's got a special kind of magic, that guy,' he told Radio One's Edith Bowman recently.

Even before 'The Services' aired, Channel 4 had decided to give Peter Kay his own series. Comedian Billy Bedlam remembers appearing on the bill at the Frog and Bucket with him shortly after *The Sunday Show* in 1997, and Peter telling him about a TV series he had planned that was inspired by the 1995 series Graham Linehan had helped write, *Coogan's Run*. 'We chatted backstage and I remember him telling me all about this idea,' says Billy. 'As he was explaining it to me he kept on saying it was like the Steve Coogan series where he played Paul Calf and lots of different characters.'

In early November Peter and his manager Lisa White travelled down to London to meet Channel 4 chief executive Kevin Lygo. The recently appointed Lygo and comedy commissioning editor Katie Taylor had some ideas on how they would like him to develop, but Peter shocked them by outlining in great detail six episodes of a series that continued with the format of 'The Services' with all of the shows set in his native Bolton. They were stunned. He worried that the London-centric TV company might find the last part of his idea hard to swallow, but fortunately it worked in his favour and became one of the deciding factors in the commission. Then governed by guidelines to provide set amounts of hours of different types of shows for as broad a range of viewers as possible, Peter's idea fell into their remit for 'regional programming'. Hurrah! Job's a good 'un, as Bez used to say.

When he spoke to Simon Fanshawe of *The Sunday Times* shortly after the meeting with Lygo he told him he had the green light for the series but 'now it just needs the green, green light ... apparently ... whatever that is'. 'There was some opposition,' Katie Taylor admits. 'We had to fight to get it through.' A couple of weeks after the meeting with Kevin Lygo the 'green, green light' flickered and Peter Kay was signed up to write and perform in six episodes of an as yet untitled series, again to be produced by Sandie Kirk with filming dates scheduled for spring 1999.

'You ... you what? Lancashire against Yorkshire? Bloody hell, Jerry, you don't mix the counties ... Ike and Tina, Chalk and Cheese. They don't go. You're asking for trouble.'

Brian Potter, Phoenix Nights

In the winter of 1998 Peter Kay was to perform to the biggest audiences of his career to date, but first there were smaller, less glamorous local gigs to attend to. One of them was co-compèring an event at the Frog and Bucket club during the Manchester Comedy Festival entitled Raw of the Roses – owner Dave Perkin having come up with an idea to stage a Lancashire versus Yorkshire open-mic comedy duel. It was an evening ripe for disagreement. As Charles Nevin describes the difference between the counties in *Lancashire, Where Women Die of Love*: 'The Pennines are a boundary far more significant than the Trent. On the one side lives a warm and whimsical race, ever ready to chuckle, even laugh, in the face of the sheer ridiculousness of life; on the other, a sad and surly people, unable to understand why they haven't been let in on the joke.'

'My dad used to say people from Lancashire wake up funny,' says Eric Morecambe's son Gary. 'They have the ability to see the world slightly askew, they don't actually see it the same way we do. He wasn't thinking what he was going to have for breakfast, he was just thinking funny, what funny things were going to come his way today. It's completely unique to the north west. And I can definitely see that in Peter Kay, that Lancashire way of looking at things. They look at life differently to everyone else.'

On the Yorkshire team for the Raw of the Roses battle, compèred by Roger Monkhouse, was one man who would later become friends with Peter, Toby Foster from Barnsley. Foster's best material was when he was being heckled by the partisan crowd. When a wag shouted 'Hey fatty', he replied: 'Why do they always pick on comedians? No one ever shouted that at Elvis, did they?' And then he asked, 'Any other Yorkshiremen in?' When a handful responded he told them, 'Great! Enough for a strike. I'll keep them looking this way while you go through the till.'

'I'd never seen Peter before, and he was absolutely fantastic,' says Toby Foster today. 'He blew the room away.' A month later Toby booked him for the comedy night he compèred in the function room above the Fleece and Firkin pub in Barnsley (it's not there any more, sadly). It wasn't very well attended, but Peter Kay fan Steve Alcock, who is now the editor of the blog <stevestate.blogspot.com>, has fond memories of the evening. There were only about 17 people in the room, all on chairs round tables, and Steve and the only friend he'd managed to persuade to shell out the £7 entrance, Neeki, blagged a table down the front. Not letting the small throng bother him, Peter launched into his normal routine – his mum dancing at weddings, people's conversations on buses – when midway through his act Neeki's mobile phone rang. 'She went bright red but didn't switch it off,' says Steve Alcock. 'She answered it and started to whisper into it that she was at a comedy gig. I was so embarrassed, especially when Peter Kay snatched the phone from her and started talking to Neeki's boyfriend, who was calling her. "Could you call back later," he said. "Only we're a bit busy. Ta ra." '

Still, it was better than the previous time he'd played in the Yorkshire citadel. 'Some of the places I've played,' he said. 'In Barnsley once there was a f***in' horse in the room – he got stuck in the doorway.'

After Edinburgh and 'The Services', playing in Barnsley was something of a comedown, but since his Perrier nomination he had appeared at Her Majesty's Theatre in London and the High Hall at Birmingham University. Then came the call that every alternative comedian dreads and every mainstream comedian dreams of, an invitation to appear in the Royal Variety Performance. It used to be called the Royal Variety Command Performance but, as befitted a family lurching from one embarrassment to the next, they no longer had the right to command anyone, let alone the showbiz elite of Great Britain.

'I got a letter asking me if I wanted to do it. I knew it were real because it said I weren't getting paid!' laughs Peter, who nevertheless accepted the call.

Before Peter got himself togged up in a dinner jacket and bow tie for his appointment with royalty he was booked to entertain an entirely different set of queens. On Sunday, 28 October Peter was among the acts booked to perform at the Royal Albert Hall as part of the annual Equality Show, which raised funds for Stonewall, the pressure group lobbying for gay and lesbian equal rights. The show was directed by famous Bolton old boy Sir Ian McKellen and presented by Rhona Cameron and Graham Norton.

Peter had run into Graham Norton a year previously when they shared the bill in Manchester. Norton was headlining, and in the dressing room before the show he asked Peter: 'What's the name of the gay area in Manchester?' Rather than tell Norton it was the area around Canal Street, he replied, straight-faced, 'The gay area of Manchester is Bury.' At the end of his set Graham Norton told his audience, 'I've got to go now, ladies and gentlemen.' And seeking to seal his approval with the gay members of the crowd, he added: 'I've got to get down to Bury.' Silence.

With no concessions to the audience, Peter held the Royal Albert Hall crowd in the palm of his hand. For a comic performing for the first time at such a large venue it was little short of miraculous. 'Before he went on I gave him one piece of advice,' says his manager, Lisa White. 'The Royal Albert Hall is massive and the acoustics for a comedian are not great, so I told him to wait for the laugh. It takes a while for the laugh to get to the back. And he did. And he absolutely stormed it.'

Just as at small comedy clubs, his forensic observations of life, TV and childhood reminded the audience of things they'd forgotten they knew. Like the fact that 'there's always a full gateau left at the end of weddings', or when you need to use up a roll of film from your holiday you take a picture of the dog in front of the fire or your mum on the patio. If you were looking for proof that Peter Kay could appeal to everyone, this was the night. Peter didn't get the biggest laugh of the evening, though. That came when *EastEnders* 'songbird' Martine McCutcheon attempted to reach out to her gay audience by murdering Diana Ross's 'I'm Coming Out'. 'I'm coming out, I want the world to know ...' sang the actress formerly known as Tiffany. 'Yeah, you wish,' came the heckle back. McCutcheon was booked to play the 77th Royal Variety Performance too, at the Lyceum Ballroom a month later, but instead of bawling out a camp anthem she joined Barry Manilow, Boyzone's Ronan Keating and Stephen Gately to croon Frank Sinatra's 'They Can't Take That Away from Me'. It was not the finest of cover versions although Manilow and McCutcheon made an amusingly mismatched couple – like a Concorde parked next to Budgie the Little Helicopter.

Peter Kay toned down his act too, but suffered one of the most embarrassing moments of his career during rehearsals: 'You do a quick run-through of your act and there were people hammering nails in behind me and Barry Manilow stood in front of me,' he says. 'I had a small tape player which I played songs through as part of my act, but the radio mic I was using caused the tape to speed up so everyone sounded like Pinky and Perky. But everyone in the audience was roaring with laughter, including Barry Manilow. I was saying: "This isn't my act!" They were saying: "But it's funny. Can't you make do?" I said: "I can't make do, the Queen's coming!" So they sent out for another dictaphone and I got five back in the end. That really frightened me. But in the end it was fine.'

In fact Peter needn't have worried about the Queen catching him off guard. She'd decided to stay at home and watch *The Vicar of Dibley* with a few cans of Stella and a thin-crust pepperoni instead (well, possibly), leaving the duty of mixing it with showbiz hoi polloi to the Prince of Wales. As Paul O'Grady in his Lily Savage guise remarked in the direction of the royal box during the show, 'I bet when that envelope comes through the front door you all draw straws for who comes to this.'

Peter's mother, Deirdre, and nan, Edith, were in the audience though for his big occasion. The £100 tickets were a gift in return for constantly answering the phone from people offering him work. Eventually Peter would buy an answering machine for his business calls, the contraption telling callers, 'Hello, you've reached Peter. If it's about showbiz call my agent. Ta ra.' Sadly the Royal Variety Performance wasn't Peter's finest 10 minutes on a London stage. As Charlie Catchpole wrote in the *Mirror*: 'Typically, the most original act on the bill – the brilliant comic from Bolton, Peter Kay – died a death. His revelations that "Turn, Turn, Turn" by the Byrds is really the theme from *Crossroads* and that Celine Dion actually sings "I believe that the hot dogs go on" went over the audience's head like a Cruise missile.' Instead it was cruise ship entertainer Jane McDonald and rubber-faced impressionist Phil Cool who pleased the attending Prime Minister Tony Blair and Prince Charles the most. Maybe Peter should have stuck with Pinky and Perky after all.

This year, 1998, was the one when the Spice Girls grabbed all the headlines at the event. Not because of their singing, but because in the traditional meet and greet after the show the Prince broke with centuries of royal protocol and lightly touched the pregnant Victoria Beckham's bump. This invasion was possibly in return for having his arse pinched by the Girls when they last met. Two places along, as Charlie boy was getting all zig-a-zig-ah with Posh Spice, Paul O'Grady and Peter gurned mock 'Carry On' looks of surprise.

The next day Peter was due to attend a gala luncheon – ham and egg pie, Quavers, all good stuff – with some of the cast, but didn't make it because he was due back in Manchester at the Levenshulme Palace to play a benefit gig for victims of the Omagh bombing. 'He has not let the fame and fortunes of his two-year meteoric rise to fame go to his head,' Palace owner Lawrence Hennigan told the *Bolton Evening News*, as if he were reading from an autocue. 'All he wanted was a plateful of scampi and chips and a pint of Pepsi Cola.'

A few days after this slight return to his 'will perform for food' early years he was back in London at LWT's South Bank studios for the 1998 British Comedy Awards. The comedy elite were all there – Steve Coogan, whose *I'm Alan Partridge* was the comedy hit of the year, Harry Enfield, Dawn French and Paul Merton. The organisers had hit upon the idea of it being a fancy-dress event and for everyone to turn up in a Latin theme. But being a cynical bunch, every single one of the comedians attending the event dressed in their normal suits and ties – apart from *Jonathan Creek* actor and stand-up comic Alan Davies, who sheepishly sat at a table dressed as a matador. As the evening progressed and the guests got increasingly drunk a new game began called 'Throw Things at Alan Davies' and bread rolls hurtled through the air as Jonathan Ross attempted to keep order. Not that Peter joined in. He was too busy feeling awestruck by being in the same room as Victoria Wood.

Peter had been nominated in several categories, both as Top Television Newcomer and Top Stand-Up Comedian, but in the event lost out to Irishmen Dylan Moran and his Perrier Award conqueror in Edinburgh, Tommy Tiernan, respectively. He didn't win, but in the eye of the discerning comedy connoisseurs the nominations still ranked as another promotion.

Peter found himself in demand with the media and in one extraordinary interview with the *Scotsman* he took the journalist on a tour of Bolton's finest shopping precincts (principally because he had to visit Susan in Boots and take a couple of videos back to the library and didn't see any reason to change his plans for the visiting gentleman of the press). Such a matter-of-fact approach to publicity took the visiting journalist by surprise. 'Peter Kay doesn't want to meet you in London, at the Groucho Club or some such see-and-be-seen watering-hole just so you can appreciate what an accomplished air-kisser he is,' wrote Aidan Smith. 'You have to go to Bolton.' Bolton? he must have wondered. Don't people become famous so they can leave places like Bolton? Peter continued to give the journalist a tour of the sights pointing out the market and the town's Christmas lights: 'A pig switched them on last week, Bolton's very own Babe. It's got foot-and-mouth apparently.'

Ah, Bolton, land of dreams, a town of dreaming spires and campaniles, college squares and willow trees. No, hang on, that's Oxford. Bolton's a bit more down-to-earth than all that, a town built on hard graft and fed on pies and gravy with a proper Victorian town hall looming over the lot of it and casting the bulk of the town centre in perpetual shadow. It's a glorious sight. Beyond the town centre Bolton today is made up of half a dozen other towns – Kearsley, Farnworth, Horwich, Blackrod, Little Lever and Westhoughton – and when you add it all up it makes Bolton the second biggest town in England (Northampton claims first prize) – although Wigan also boasts of the same thing, which feeds the healthy rivalry between the two neighbours. In fact the bulk of Dave Spikey's live set centres around Wigan jokes. Bolton's people were voted the friendliest in Britain, according to a survey carried out by the British Society for the Advancement of Science. It is home to the world's largest manufacturer of disposable bedpans, a national school for training the blind, the most zealous traffic wardens in the world (just try spending 30 seconds longer than it says on your parking ticket!) and thanks to good town planning, no tower blocks and a far lower mugger-to-pensioner ratio than most places in England. Cunningly, it is surrounded by a complex ring of motorways and one-way A roads, making it rather like Las Vegas casinos in that it's easy to go into but virtually impossible to leave. In common with the rest of the country, most Mancunians have never set foot in Peter Kay's home town and regard Boltonians as a different species who talk oddly, like the old joke: 'A bald cat gets on a bus in Bolton without paying and the driver asks, "Where's your fur?" ' Southerners may like to imagine that avocados and lapsang souchong have yet to make it this far north, but Bolton's booming. There are hundreds of wealthy Asian entrepreneurs, hotels spring up everywhere and a gleaming new football stadium. Oddly, however, it seems to have retained a 1950s identity that other towns and cities have long since lost.

Of course Peter Kay's a Boltonian, he couldn't come from anywhere else – his humour suits his accent (or is it the other way round?), he's canny, daft and no-nonsense. He's fortunate enough to come from a town where people still talk to each other in shops, but unfortunate to live in a place where pastry is included on the list of a day's crucial vitamins and minerals.

Bolton was once famous for its football team, Bolton Wanderers, and their valiant captain Nat Lofthouse, who scored a goal in the 1958 FA Cup Final by pushing Manchester United's goalkeeper Harry Gregg and the ball he was holding into the back of the net, and also for the soot and grime produced by the town's multitude of mill chimneys. Then it became even more famous for the man who helped pull them all down, steeplejack Fred Dibnah, who enjoyed celebrity after nearly being crushed by a falling stack during a BBC news report. As much as his hair-raising demolition jobs, it was Dibnah's rough-hewn manner, permanent flat cap and pearls of Lancastrian wisdom that made him a star. 'A man who says he feels no fear,' he said, 'is either a fool or a liar.'

As well as Dibnah (RIP), Bolton is the birthplace of no fewer than three former Radio One DJs: Sara Cox, Vernon Kay and Mark Radcliffe; Badly Drawn Boy man Damon Gough; children's TV presenter Johnny Ball, pop art painter Patrick Caulfield; *Crackerjack*'s Stu 'I could crush a grape' Francis; actor Frank Findlay; film critic Leslie Halliwell; and teenage female arm-wrestling champion Dawn Higson (arm currently insured for £40,000). Despite such stiff competition even before Peter Kay had turned it into a TV location, he was Bolton's favourite son. Such was the local newspaper's obsession with him that in December 1998 they even ran photos of a Peter Kay look-alike who couldn't have looked less like Peter Kay if he'd been wearing a balaclava – unless the look-alike bit was confined to his waist measurement. Even so, Bolton loved Peter Kay and Peter Kay loved Bolton right back. It wasn't just the fact that he felt at home there, that he could 'go to the chippy in my slippers (you can't do that down London, you'd get arrested!)', it was special.

'I love Bolton. I really, really love it,' he has said. 'You could do a Woody Allen in Bolton, do 40 films and still find something new because there's something new in every house.' Over the forthcoming three years he'd be doing just that.

For Peter, Bolton was home, inspiration and shortly location for his new series. Unlike the other acts who had recently emerged from the north-west area – Steve Coogan, *The Royle Family* cast of Caroline Aherne, Craig Cash and Ralf Little, *The Fast Show*'s John Thomson, Paul 'Lily

Savage' O'Grady – he saw no reason to leave his birthplace and relocate to London.

'Bolton is home, and it's normal,' he says. 'People never treat me any different and I like that. I'm not anti-London, but I just think, "Why do we have to go to London?" I love being at home. Life is all about your family and friends. I'd rather pack it all in than go and live there. I can go down to London and perform at some flash corporate do, and the next day I'm in my tracksuit bottoms eating me mam's cooking. And it seems to me like the only real bit was Bolton – the rest of it never happened.'

Fortune if not fame seemed to hold little appeal for Peter Kay in 1998 and, when pressed on where his ambitions lay, he replied frankly that all he wanted was to 'get married and buy a house and settle down. And they would be, like, the most important things in my life. So it wouldn't matter what other people thought, as long as I could find some way to keep on writing, or whatever, even if it was some chat show on cable.'

Ending his article for the *Scotsman*, Aidan Smith concluded, 'Make no mistake, Peter Kay is going places. Today Bolton, tomorrow Bolton, too.'

The words Peter gave to Pearl in 'The Services' as she drives in for another day's work seemed to apply to him and his feelings for his home town. 'I must have driven down here a million times,' she says, glancing flirtatiously into camera. 'Still brings the hairs up on the back of me neck, though. You know, they say home is where the heart is. Well, my heart definitely belongs here, in First Services Bolton. She's my first, my last, my everything.'

The way that Peter Kay has rooted his entire career in his home town is incredible. He has said, 'You write about what you know, and what I know is Bolton.' But there must be more to it than this. In trying to quantify what it is that makes him funny, the answer is always 'Bolton' – the people, his memories, his family (his father's side go back centuries in the town). It is almost as if he feels that if he leaves the place of his birth some magic and luck will disappear.

The other thing that roots him to the town is his mother. He was always a mother's boy, but the bond grew when his father left home. Leaving Bolton would feel like desertion, so when he is in the business of househunting for himself and for her his major criterion is that they shouldn't be more than two songs away from each other on the car radio.

Like all sons who are particularly close to their mothers, the need for approval is never far away, and it's not just laughs Peter is looking for when he passes his scripts on to his mum, it's endorsement.

Carry on caravanning: A teenage Peter with teacher John Clough and friend Michael Atherton in Bouth, Cumbria.

It's spitting: Peter aged 17, in the Lake District, with school friend Michael Atherton.

Roar potential: Peter the Cowardly Lion relaxes backstage during the school's performance of *The Wizard of Oz*.

Bowled over: At home the day after winning the *City Life* 'North West Comedian of the Year' competition in 1996.

Playing his joker: Showing off his prize after *That Peter Kay Thing* wins 'Best New Comedy' at the British Comedy Awards in December 2000.

In the club: As nightclub owner Don Tonay, with Steve Coogan as Tony Wilson, in Manchester music movie *24 Hour Party People*.

Her indoors: Peter and his wife Susan arrive at the London Palladium for the 2003 BAFTA Television Awards.

Friends United: At Manchester United's annual UNICEF charity dinner with Susan, *Coronation Street*'s Sally Lindsay and Justin 'Young Kenny' Moorhouse.

Put big light on: Switching on the Christmas lights in Bolton, 2003.

The dynamic duo: Filming *Phoenix Nights* spin-off *Max And Paddy's Road To Nowhere* in Bolton, June 2004, with Paddy McGuiness.

Teenage kicks: Peter as *Phoenix Nights'* Brian Potter at the Teenage Cancer Trust Comedy Night at the Royal Albert Hall, London, in April 2005.

Boltonian rhapsody: Peter sends Hyde Park radio ga-ga as warm-up to Queen in July 2005.

Little and large: *Little Britain*'s David Walliams and Peter backstage at Live8, London, in July 2005.

Salutes you, Sir: Peter hails the crowd after mass 'Amarillo' sing-a-long at Live8.

Meat and potato pie piper: Peter mimes playing the panpipes at the Live8 concert in Edinburgh.

Channel fir: Appearing on the *The Paul O'Grady Show Christmas Special* with Barbara Windsor in 2005.

With the band: Peter Kay joins the Kaiser Chiefs at the 2006 Brit Awards.

Chapter Six

Give Me Three Rings When You Get In

'Money can't buy you love, but it can get you some really good chocolate ginger biscuits.'

Dylan Moran

'All you have in comedy, in general, is just going with your instincts. You can only hope that other people think that what you think is funny is funny.'

Will Ferrell

In December 1998 Peter Kay began writing his as yet untitled debut series for Channel 4. He had a rough outline for all six shows and knew that all the episodes would stand alone but that some of the characters would interconnect. As with 'The Services', all would be fly-on-the-wall documentaries shot with a hand-held camera to capture that authentic docu-soap feel. And, importantly, all six would be set in and around Bolton.

It was an ambitious project that would need six separate locations, six huge casts and six unique scripts, but Peter Kay's attitude was to see it as a challenge. 'I want to stretch myself,' he said at the time. 'My logic is, I might only get one crack at this TV lark so I'm climbing on big time.'

The process was an arduous one, not because Peter struggled for material but because he had too much of it. Lots of scenes had to be completely cut from the script. Among them was a brilliant interview with Peter's psychotic ice-cream man Mr Softy which reveals that he'd enjoyed more of a romance with his vans than with any women. 'I had my fair share as the years passed on,' says Mr Softy in Peter's script. 'They got bigger and harder to handle. I had a crack at Pamela and then Madam Georgia, then I fell for Christabel, she was the big love of my life, she was everything to me, we were inseparable, we were together for seven years, I was in bits when she died, it was on the A6 outside House of Rajas.'

Characters who have enjoyed little luck with the opposite sex were to become a recurring trait over the years for Peter Kay, from Brian Potter to Max to Keith Lard – women are a foreign country yet to be explored for every one of them. As borne out by his sentimental gifts for his first girlfriend Catherine Hurst, Peter himself is an old-fashioned romantic. The pair were engaged a year into their relationship and did not live together until they were married.

Having agreed the storylines for the new series, Peter would write ideas then send them on computer disks to his co-writers, Dave Spikey and Neil Anthony, who would then post them back with their suggestions, changes and ideas along with some ideas of their own. Additionally, he'd try out some of the gags in his live shows and, judging on the audience response, would weave them into the plots or spike them – hapless pop duo Park Avenue were born from a routine about the kind of trashy acts you see in Blackpool cabaret clubs. Next, Peter would edit the whole lot down and bash out final scripts on his PC in his bedroom. This was before any of them had access to the Internet, which would have speeded up the process somewhat. Incredibly, throughout the six-month period of writing Peter, Dave and Neil met up together only once – in a pub near the hospital where Dave worked.

'It were a bit like Bernie Taupin and Elton John,' joked Peter, who also says that he did everything he could to avoid

actually sitting down to write the shows – not just alpha-
betising his CD collection but also splitting it into genres
and subgenres.

A pleasurable part of the development was what Peter
called 'field trips'. Peter and Dave would visit a variety of
businesses as background research for the series. At one
working men's club in Daubhill, they stifled laughter as they
watched a committee being briefed on the latest advance-
ments in urinal block technology and immediately wrote
what they witnessed into the script.

Meanwhile producer Sandie Kirk hit on the idea of Peter
taking a video camera to Southport Film Fair to try and find
some characters who would inspire him. A year later, in the
run-up to the show being screened, Peter explained Kirk's
technique: 'Normally people would get suspicious, but at a
film fair they were more easy-going, as they were used to
people pointing cameras. Afterwards I would point out
people we saw and say, "I want that moustache, I want that
hairstyle." The actual characters are from people I know, or
I'd steal voices from people we interviewed when we did
research for the series.'

One of the first episodes to be written was the final show
of the series, 'Lonely at the Top', which cleverly rounded off
the characters we'd meet in the very first episode. '"Lonely at
the Top" was Neil's idea,' Peter reveals. 'He wanted to take a
look at what the recent trend of TV documentaries had done
to the members of the public who had become the stars. The
media had made them into celebrities for the simple reason
that they had appeared on TV – Mo from *Driving School*,
Jeremy from *Airport* and, most successfully of all, Jane
McDonald. We decided to use Park Avenue from the first
episode of the series, "In the Club", and look at what would
happen to them as a result of that first episode being broadcast. It was a clever idea, turning the whole thing on its head

and highlighting what we and the media do to these so-called celebrities.'

In late December 1998, Peter found himself doing a series of 'Turkey and Tinsel' Christmas-meal shows every evening for a week at the Porthouse Hotel in Birmingham and staying at the hotel every night. It wasn't the most glamorous of engagements, but it paid well. 'I had borrowed a laptop and gave myself a challenge, that for the duration of the week I had to write the episode. I managed to do it.'

He also completely rewrote one episode at the eleventh hour. Utah, the coach driver, and Mathew, the drama student from 'The Services', were set to reappear in an episode called 'The Trip', which concentrated on the adventures of an A-level school drama field trip to the theatre where they were due to take part in a drama workshop. On the way Utah's coach breaks down and after a lot of wasted time he decides that it's too late to go to join the other group at the theatre, so they end up going to Knowsley Safari Park instead. Ever the perfectionist, Peter decided that the episode wasn't strong enough and transformed the coach party into the story of two girls from Birmingham travelling to a show in Manchester (keeping Utah as the driver), while Mathew was transferred from a budding actor in a drama workshop to a budding actor working as a steward in the MEN Arena.

The series had lots of working titles – *Six of One and Half a Dozen of the Other*, *Peter Kay's Friends in the North*, *Peter Kay's Midget Gems*, *Pack of Six*. Desperate to name the series, Peter was at the house of his close friend Danny Dignan (the producer who had landed him the *Parkinson* warm-up-man job) discussing possible titles into the early hours of the morning. Then, in a moment of revelation, Dignan said, 'Whatever you call it, people will still go into work the next day and say, "Did you see that Peter Kay thing last night?" ' So, *That Peter Kay Thing* it was.

'Tragically,' says Peter, 'we had a lot of media arsehole types getting the complete wrong end of the stick and assuming it was "That Peter Kay THANG". We had to put them right on that, of course.'

The scripts were finished in March 1999, but still had to be trimmed down and rewritten ready for filming. Travelling down to a meeting at Channel 4 in London, Peter later claimed he was physically sick on the train because he knew he'd be spending the entire day 'arguing and defending the scripts' with Sandie Kirk, executive producer Ivan Douglass and director Andrew Gillman. Peter won the arguments and ended up with the scripts he wanted. He knew he was right; indeed, as an actor on the set of 'The Ice Cream Man Cometh' episode would later tell him, 'It's you that's f***in' the goose, they're just holding its neck.' Worryingly, this pearl of wisdom came from an extra dressed as a policeman! There were, though, some regrets about changes he felt forced into, and one in particular that would rankle for years to come. About the multiple parts he was due to appear in, Peter wrote on his official website that he had reservations about being labelled 'the new Steve Coogan': 'But after much deliberation I thought f*** 'em, there's enough room for everybody, and if it wasn't going to be him then it would be Dick Emery or Peter Sellers. Journalists will always pigeon-hole you somewhere, as sadly some of them are lazy bastards after free meals and weekends in Jersey.'

With the scripts rewritten and the series given a title, *That Peter Kay Thing* began filming in May 1999.

As with 'The Services', the production team working on the 'Eyes Down' episode had tremendous difficulties finding a bingo hall willing to let them film inside because of the tremendous trend of prime-time docu-dramas dishing the dirt on ordinary professions and basically revealing what we all knew already: nobody knows what they're doing, least of all the people in charge. Eventually they managed to persuade the Apollo Bingo Hall in Blackpool to let the cameras in, Peter even charming the manager and staff into appearing in the show. Unpaid extras were essential to Peter's idea, and gave it an air of authenticity he felt he couldn't achieve with actors. When they were shooting 'Eyes Down' they even provided some of the funniest lines – not that they realised it. Ivan Douglass hit on the idea of asking the old ladies what they thought of Tom Jones and George Clooney and filmed their responses, but for the show it was as if they were swooning over Peter's misogynistic bingo caller – 'Wigan's famous for two things, rugby players and beautiful women. What position do you play, Sheila?'

The MEN opened its doors, too. It had been less than a year since he'd stopped working for them and, proud of an ex-steward made good, they were more than happy to give Peter access all areas, even though they knew he would more than likely be making a mockery of the place in an episode that would follow the life in a day of the venue. The managers of the bingo hall and the arena, believed producer Sandie Kirk, gave their trust because of what she described as 'Kay's gift' – that although his comedy is hysterical and subversive, as with Victoria Wood before him, it is done with respect. 'We all recognise those people,' she says of his characters. 'His comedy is gentle, but gentle with bite.'

Nowhere is this better demonstrated than in the opening episode of *That Peter Kay Thing*, 'In the Club', which was shot at the Farnworth and District Veterans Club, a local social club heavily populated by the over-sixties. Like all the subject matter of *That Peter Kay Thing*, Peter is drawn to working men's clubs because they connect to his personal past (he attended countless parties and wedding receptions in them) and because he is fascinated and amused by disappearing institutions.

'It's nostalgia,' Kay has admitted. 'I used to go as a kid. I loved the names of the acts and the pictures of them pinned up outside. I used to ask if I could have them to put on my wall. I love the fact that outside it's car alarms going off and razor wire, and inside it's like Vegas. The nightlife always fascinated me. The acts, butcher by day – Elvis by night. The escapism of it all, of these people trapped by a mortgage and family by day, living out their fantasies by night.'

In 1999 he told a reporter visiting the set of 'In the Club': 'I'm interested in the sort of jobs that won't make it to the next millennium – ice-cream men, paper boys – and following people as they try to hang on to the past. Look at ice-cream men. No one wants to stand queuing for a cornet in the rain when you can go down the shop and get a Ben and Jerry's. And ice-cream men don't make any money so they resort to anything to get by.'

At the Farnworth Veterans Club the visit of the film crew was the biggest event to happen in the area since the opening of the Lidl superstore – although some of the older members could recall James Mason recording a scene from the movie *Spring and Port Wine* on the canal at Nob End. As well as requiring the members of the club to appear as themselves in the episode, Kay also booked several real cabaret acts to appear in the Talent Trek competition, including a limbo dancer from Southampton, local singer Marie Perrigo and Oldham's very own one-man band, Billy Bedlam.

'It was great fun,' says Billy, who appeared on the show in his clown suit and blowing a tune through a shower tube. 'Everyone treated it like a real talent show and we all had four minutes each to do our act. There were lots of bits that they cut out. In my scene Dave Spikey grabbed my bass drum and started marching around the hall with it. Peter was a bit less friendly than he'd been in the past,' claims Billy Bedlam. 'But that was understandable; he had a lot on his plate. You could tell it was very much his show, that he was in charge.'

In fact Peter's desperation to get everything just right in the series drove many of the crew potty. His obsession was such that when he was filming 'The Arena' episode he spent 40 minutes arguing with the stylist over whether or not his character's hair had sufficient curls on top. The art of delegation was not a strong point, courtesy of his years of stand-up, where there was no one to tell him what to do, but it was a trait that went much further back than that. At school, his friend Michael Atherton remembers that 'he wanted to hold the camera and be in front of it as well'. Peter, though, held the vision of the series in his head, and having studied films and TV for years he had an in-built sense of how things should be done. For example, he knew how to capture the absurd in the ordinary without veering too far into the unbelievable.

'I often have to pull back because the screen enlarges everything anyway,' he said during filming. 'Some people say that Mike Leigh's characters are not believable, but I know those people. It's just that he will put six great characters in a room and it becomes a caricature – it's too much on screen at the same time.'

He also saw *That Peter Kay Thing* as maybe his sole chance on TV, and he wasn't prepared to let go – even if that meant arguing with people about hair. In a typical illustration of his latent Catholic guilt, imagining the world is going to come crashing down around you the moment something good happens to you, he was fatalistic about his chances of success and shrugged, 'If I fail, I'll go and work on the bins; at least I've given it a go.'

Despite his controlling nature and worries about a project that was very much his 'baby', the team of Gillman, Kirk and Kay worked well, with director Andrew Gillman even having a part in an additional scene in 'The Ice Cream Man Cometh' which replicated – albeit above a takeaway called Kebabylon – a famous scene from Martin Scorsese's *Taxi Driver*.

After each show was completed Peter would go down to London for the post-production editing, where he would stop overnight at the house of his friend from *The Royle Family* Craig Cash. Cash's keen ear for comedy and knowledge of the machinations of television production were crucial to this final stage of the series. Each night the pair would review unedited tapes and Cash would offer suggestions. One of them was that in order to retain the dry docu-soap feel of the shows some of the more obvious jokes should be taken out. As much as Peter appreciated his input, crucially it was the fact that he found the shows funny that Peter enjoyed the most. The pair were good mates and for some while there was talk of them writing together on various projects such as a *Royle Family* movie and a spin-off series (later to become the brilliant *Early Doors*), but neither came to fruition.

Despite the exhaustion and the fears of compromise, Peter described the experience of filming *That Peter Kay Thing* as 'overwhelming'. One of the most difficult and eye-opening scenes he filmed was as Leonard the elderly god botherer, who wheels a giant cross into Bolton's Victoria Square and begins preaching and reading from the Bible to passers-by. The film crew were a hundred yards away, above Clinton Cards, so Peter with just a small radio mic was effectively alone as he stood clutching the 10-foot cross as nonchalant shoppers passed by assuming he was another of the town's resident eccentrics.

'Leonard really opened up my eyes to some things that I never knew existed,' he said. 'I spent over an hour wandering around unrecognisable to anybody and it really affected me. I was treated so differently by the public. The majority of people treated me with contempt and looked through me rather than at me. I do realise that probably had a lot to do with me carrying a 10-foot crucifix. Or did it? I also had a few people coming up to me when I was praying and chatting to me about the word of the Lord and spreading God's good news. I never knew that so many people were actually interested or believed in anything else or needed some kind of guidance in their lives. They stood and prayed with me and sang with me. That really freaked me out, but in a good and surprising way.'

Among the life-enhancing experiences of filming there was also a near-death incident. His role as Marc Park – the Talent Trek winner who suddenly shoots to fame – entailed Peter shooting a cliché-laden seasonal pop video for Park's pretentious stab at a seasonal number one, 'Christmas 2000', with fake snow falling as he mimed the lyrics. Mucking around between shots, one of the dancers threw a snowball at Peter and a piece became lodged in his throat. Unlike real snow, it didn't melt. 'Next thing I knew, it had mixed with saliva and expanded like a tampon. I was choking and apparently turning a funny colour. There was all of a fuss and confusion, and I was outside with my head between my legs and being given oxygen. I felt like a right idiot, and what was even funnier was, my face went white and my false nose stayed tanned.'

With the series done and dusted, it was originally due to première in early November, but in a very late change of heart Channel 4 decided to move the series back to January 2000. The wait was terrible, but after all the trauma of putting *That Peter Kay Thing* together, returning to his stand-up was a welcome relief, even though he found himself beginning to stretch his itinerary beyond the limitations of a drive back to Croston Street. However, it was on home ground, at the Frog and Bucket in Manchester, where Peter made the first ill-advised decision of his career – that's if you don't count those Bermuda shorts he wore in *The Wizard of*

Oz – when, shortly before he was about to appear onstage, another one of the comics told him a sick joke he'd heard and Peter decided to incorporate it into his act.

It was DJ Mark Radcliffe's 41st birthday that evening and to celebrate he and a dozen members of staff from the BBC Manchester studios, where he recorded his Radio One show, had decided to visit the Frog and Bucket to see Peter Kay, who was headlining. Peter began in his normal fashion with a series of one-liners, but 10 minutes in discussed people making sick jokes, such as the one about Rod Hull, the puppeteer famous for his narky bird alter-ego Emu, who had died after falling from his roof trying to adjust his TV aerial: 'The funeral was great but the reception was crap.' Asking the audience, 'What's black and white and eats like a horse? A zebra', he followed it with, 'What's black and white and wants feeding?' The answer? 'Jill Dando's cat.'

It was a mistake. A big one. Jill Dando, who presented the BBC's *Crimewatch*, was a popular personality who had a few weeks earlier been murdered on the steps of her home in west London. Among the BBC party was someone who had worked with Dando, who although saying nothing at the time, was upset enough to report it to a journalist friend. The following day, back home in Bolton, someone phoned Peter to ask if he had 'any more Dando jokes'. It was a reporter from the *Sun*. Later, two more *Sun* reporters called round to his house. The next day, the story loomed large on the front page. 'Sick comic makes disgraceful joke' they bellowed, labelling him 'Podgy Pete'. It was a story nobody would ever have expected to be associated with a comedian who had such an avowed aversion to unpleasantness as Peter Kay.

'I just thought, "That's me finished now, that's it," ' he said later. 'It was ironic, really. I'd never done anything about sex or anything like that. I just didn't think.'

Although padded out with a few half-truths in the press, the story caused a nationwide backlash and Peter went into hiding. The BBC issued a statement that read: 'Clearly this was unacceptable and we apologise for the offence that has been caused and are speaking to Peter Kay about this ill-judged attempt at comedy.' A few days later, Peter spoke of his regrets to the *Bolton Evening News*, telling them it was all 'a big mistake' and 'God knows, I feel bad about it. If I could rewind it and unsay it, I would ... I apologise. I did tell the joke. I would be a liar if I said that I didn't,' he told them. 'I have never done it before. When I said it I just looked at the audience and said: "Oh, I really shouldn't have said that." '

Illustrating that comics find it harder to accept a joke that bombs than a joke you regret, he went on to claim that although the *Sun* had said the audience was shocked and fell into a stunned silence, the crowd actually laughed. 'I'm not making excuses – I just didn't come on and tell the joke straight off. It was all part of a routine I have been doing for a year about people who tell sick jokes.'

Even if the rest of Britain hated him for laughing at the untimely death of TV's golden girl, the people of Bolton supported him. Long after the national press had let go of the story, the controversy rumbled on in the *Bolton Evening News*, following a letter from an outraged reader who wrote: 'He insulted the memory of Jill Dando, with his sickening joke about her cat.' The letter writer went on to promise that she would no longer watch TV or read the *Bolton Evening News* if either featured the evil Kay. Rather than prompt more demands for the head of Peter Kay, the newspaper received a flurry of correspondence defending him, one replying: 'Try being proud of what Peter is doing (putting Bolton on the map).'

The strength of the response affected Peter deeply and only strengthened his loyalty to Bolton. Immediately after-wards, when the story first broke Peter said he felt 'ashamed, but me mum especially were great about it'. Typically, his dad said that he didn't get the joke. 'He said: "Tell me again. Wants seeding?" I said, "No, feeding!"

'When I rang up me nan to warn her, she went, "Oh my God. Oh Peter, Peter, Peter, Peter … why don't you think before you open your mouth?" And then she thought for a bit and went, "Anyway … I don't think Jill had a cat." I thought, "Well, I'll ring them up and tell them to take it off front page … Hullo, it's Podgy Pete here, take it off, she hadn't got a cat." '

The whole event does illustrate a darker side to Peter Kay. Although he is portrayed as a family-friendly comic he is not without an edge that often frays the boundaries of political correctness, and for some often cuts too close.

'It was the best of times, it was the worst of times.'
Charles Dickens, A Tale of Two Cities

Having fallen foul of the redtops with his ill-judged gags about Jill Dando and her non-existent cat, his image as an entertainer with a populist worldview was repaired when he contributed to TV's *100 Most Memorable Moments*, broadcast on Channel 4 on 11 September. Peter's appearance came at no. 97 and centred on public information films, for which Peter wrote a hilarious commentary claiming 'they were like mini-Ken Loach films when I was young. There was one that sticks in my mind,' he said. 'It's the one with a child running down a beach, a little boy, and there's a piece of broken glass, a lemonade bottle. That still upsets me now and I still can't rundown a beach. I'm 26 and I still can't run down a beach with nothing on my feet.'

He went on to remind viewers that after Dave Prowse had stopped doing the Green Cross Code adverts, saying things like 'Make sure you find a safe gap between cars' in a broad Cornish accent, he was replaced by Dr Who, Jon Pertwee, and a new acronym for children to remember as they crossed roads: SPLINK. 'SPLINK!' laughed Peter. 'Find a safe place ... Pavement ... by the time I'd got to P I'd been hit by a bus.'

Then, on 18 November he began his first proper headline tour, ten dates starting at the Derby Assembly Rooms and ending at the Barracuda Club, Lincoln, on 6 December. The biggest date of the tour was at the 1,600-capacity Bridgewater Hall in Manchester – an event which Peter saw as a massive leap forward from the usual venues he'd played in the city over the years.

'It obviously meant a lot to him,' says his former lecturer at Salford University, Lloyd Peters, who was in the audience that night. 'I remember him taking photos of the audience.' Nervous, and somewhat incredulous that he should be playing such a premium venue, Peter asked the audience, 'What the f*** are we doing here, eh?' before launching into a 90-minute set that featured his tried and trusted reminiscences of school trips and the pop aisle at Asda on top of new material about people nagging him to book a holiday on Ceefax – 'Booked it, packed it, f***ed off' – and people who blow their lifelines on easy questions in 'Who Wants to be a Millionaire?' – 'How many legs has a dog got? Can I phone a friend?' At Sheffield City Hall he slid, as usual, energetically across the stage on his knees in his imitation of children's giddy abandon at weddings and ended up covered in hairs shed the evening before by Elkie Brooks's golden retriever. While at the Nottingham Old Vic, *Independent* writer Brian Viner reported sitting next to two student teachers, Heidi and Mel, rolling with laughter 'as Kay starts to evoke, with devastating accuracy, the last day of school term, when you were allowed to take in Etch-a-Sketch and Kerplunk, and Mastermind with that Vietnamese lady on the front. His next routine, about school dinner ladies, is the point at which Heidi rushes to the loo,' wrote Viner. 'Later, Mel forces her to admit that she had actually wet herself laughing. "Yeah," she protests, "but only a tiny bit." '

Meanwhile, on Peter's website message board, a fan who attended the same show wrote: 'As an asthmatic, I found the performance drained me and had to catch a taxi home at the end of it all as I couldn't bloody walk!'

With people wetting themselves and wheezing home from his gigs and *That Peter Kay Thing* just weeks away from being aired on national TV, Peter's career was hitting a new peak. Then, the day after the final date of the tour at the Barracuda Club in Lincoln, he received a call from Margaret Faulkner, his father's partner since he had left his mum nearly 10 years previously. His father was dead. The cause of death was liver failure. He was a few weeks away from his 52nd birthday.

Michael Kay had played a huge part in his son's future profession – not just through the corny jokes he told, but also via his taste in comedy (he had adored Morecambe and Wise and *Only Fools and Horses*). Humour was the thing that united them, and after his dad left his mother Peter would visit him at the one-bedroom flat he shared with Margaret, where they'd stay up late into the night laughing. Later in life Peter had found the things that had irritated him as a child about his dad now amused him, and were a rich source of material. For his part, Michael was proud of his son and would boast of his achievements in the pub – sadly, he didn't get to see *That Peter Kay Thing*. Peter was due to pop round later in the week he died to show him the tapes. According to Margaret, the 50th birthday he spent with Peter in London – at the *Parkinson* show and the Comedy Store – was one of the best weekends of his life.

At the time, Peter coped as best he could, taking a few of his father's records and helping Margaret donate his clothes to a charity shop. Organising the funeral kept him occupied and helped keep his mind off his bereavement. 'Dad always said I was not funny enough to be a comedian,' he told the *Stage* a couple of weeks later. 'But he ended up the biggest fan of my work. I always asked him if he wanted to come to my gigs. I think I made him feel it would make me feel uncomfortable, but I told him I'd always love him to come. I don't know why he said no.'

Even in tragedy Peter was able to find things to amuse him, and at his father's funeral he found it hysterical when one of the mourners told him: 'I've just come out of hospital. Rectal abscess.' But then Peter Kay's comedy recorder is seldom switched off, and throughout his career he has kept a finely tuned ear out for the normal everyday things people say, which when you step back from them are actually quite strange: 'You've brought the weather with you'; 'Is it hot in here or is it me?'. Or the time when Peter's mother visited her local library and the librarian said, 'Your Peter's doing very well. Mind you, he's very quiet when he comes in here.'

Peter also really loved a friend of his who would talk about himself in the third person. 'He'll say, "Baz went out last night. Baz had a great time." And we're like, "Well hang on, you are Baz, you idiot." I find things like that very funny.'

As with everything, Baz was locked away in the Kay comedy cupboard, to be brought out many years later when he came to write *Max and Paddy's Road to Nowhere*, re-created in Max's pa's groan of 'Paddy has needs'.

Although in his grief Peter didn't realise it, on Christmas Eve he was the main attraction of Channel Five's schedule when they broadcast a show he'd recorded a few months earlier at the Comedy Store in London. It was one of a series of half-hour-long stand-up sets that Five broadcast, but this was the only one that found itself on at such an attractive prime-time spot. For many viewers it was the first time they'd experienced Peter in full flow. The show was just wonderful and an excellent demonstration of how far his act had advanced in the two-and-a-half hectic years since that gig at the Pint Pot in Salford. Of course to those who had seen his act in Nottingham or Derby or at the Birmingham Glee Club there was also the realisation that Peter's act wasn't quite as wildly improvisational as they had imagined. Over the year he'd develop the incredible feat of making people believe he was almost making it up as he was going along, that he was confiding in his audience for the first time. Then there were the brilliant sideways glances and eye-rolling looks that you'd never notice in venues the size of Bridgewater Hall, such as when he recounts the story of telling his nan that Elsie Haslam ('Do you know her?') has died.

'She said, "When?" I said, "Wednesday." ' He mimics his nan sucking her teeth. ' "I only saw her in supermarket on Tuesday." ' Pause. 'I said, "And? What does she expect? Grim Reaper pushing a trolley behind her? Come on love, get in, come on, you don't need bleach where you're going, come on. Soap-filled pads? KP choc dip? Come on, time's time." '

Most brilliantly of all, when a woman gets up on the front row to visit the toilet, he waves after her, as if she were a relative leaving after a visit: 'See ya love. Take care. All the best,' he calls. 'Give me three rings when you get in, let me know you've got home safely.'

Give me three rings when you get to t'next chapter, three rings ...

Chapter Seven
Garlic Bread?

'The British working men's club. Yesterday's dream factory. But now with each passing year there are fewer and fewer people to peddle those dreams to. The Neptune is one such club. With attendance figures dwindling and a permanent lack of funds, it continues to struggle in an effort to appeal to a younger generation with more modern tastes.'

Andrew Sachs, narration on 'In the Club',
That Peter Kay Thing

'You'll have to forgive him. He's from Barcelona.'
Basil Fawlty, Fawlty Towers

Of all the shows in *That Peter Kay Thing* it was 'In the Club' that would have the most lasting significance for his future TV career and, crucially, the decision to cast comedians instead of actors – among them Toby Foster, whom he'd met at the Raw of the Roses show; Archie Kelly, who had a brilliant act where he performed as old-time crooner Jackie 'Mr Goodtime' Valencio; and of course Peter's writing partner Dave Spikey, who auditioned for the role of club compère Jerry St Clair, even though he'd played a major part in creating him. It gave the episode a naturalness that really worked. The comics were joined by the Talent Trek competitors, most of whom were real acts on the club circuit in the Manchester area, and the real audience of the Farnworth Veterans Club who, plied with cheap drinks, treated the event like a real variety show.

'When Michelle Coffee sang "Don't Go Breaking My Heart" you can see some of them feeling sorry for her,' says Peter. 'They were amazing.'

There was some opposition from Channel 4, who were worried about the comedians' acting inexperience – something that was exacerbated by the fact that Peter also wanted to cast his schoolfriend Paddy McGuinness as the Neptune's bouncer. There were also arguments at Channel 4 over the Neptune's social secretary, Brian Potter. Did he have to be in a wheelchair?

'I remember at Salford, Peter showed me a few script ideas for TV shows,' says his former lecturer Lloyd Peters. 'And I remember one featuring a love affair between an able-bodied man and a disabled woman. I told him to be careful, but I think it spurred him on. In my opinion some of his best stuff is when he's ruffling feathers.' Feathers were ruffled but, yet again, Peter's argument – 'Why shouldn't he be disabled, there's no other disabled people on TV' – won through.

Peter also liked the idea of planting a doubt in the viewer's mind that Brian Potter was so low, such a skinflint, that he might actually be feigning his disability in order to claim benefit. Indeed, his story as to how he became para-lysed didn't exactly ring true: 'I was managing the Aquarius Club,' Potter tells the documentary cameras. 'We had a big Christmas bash, 15 quid a ticket, sell-out, everyone were there, but then tragedy. The pipes burst, water everywhere, utter chaos. People running round getting electrocuted. It was like something out of *The Poseidon Adventure*. I were terrified, me. I had to swim for the safe for the night's takings and that's when I saw it coming towards me, fruit machine pinned me to the serving hatch. I blacked out; all I can remember is this warm, bright, pulsating glow ...' As Brian delivers his speech one of the Talent Trek singers, Marie Perrigo, can be heard singing in the background: 'Walking back to happiness, whoop a oh yeah yeah.'

Peter would have preferred to leave viewers' suspicions there, but unfortunately, having won so many conflicts with Channel 4, he agreed to a closing scene, with the Neptune Club burning down. In his horror at seeing his 'dream factory' in flames, Brian Potter stands up out of his chair to bully the firefighters. 'The idea was that we gave the viewers little clues, made them wonder,' Peter Kay told me a couple of years later. 'I'm still a bit annoyed by it, to tell you the truth; it were never supposed to have gone in. I buckled to pressure.'

The opening scene of 'In the Club' sees the committee debating the entertainment for the forthcoming Christmas party, with Brian campaigning for an entertainer called Nobby Alcock. 'Now hear me out, I know he's blue but he does a smashing sideline in Punch and Judy.' When Toby Foster's character, Les, swears in response, Brian responds by saying, 'There's no need for that foul language please, I've got a photograph of my wife in the pocket.'

'It was brilliant, absolutely spot on,' says Billy Bedlam of the re-creation of a working men's club committee meeting. 'They'd be run by men who worked on the buses or in factories during the week but then when they'd get to committee meetings they'd turn into little Hitlers, arguing about whether or not they should have a cigarette machine in the corridor.'

The show was broadcast at 10.30 p.m. on Wednesday, 12 January 2000. Directly after it, Peter took part in a live web chat on <Channel4.com> and had to respond to a series of bizarre rapid-fire questions from people hiding behind pseudonyms such as Applejack, ERV200 and Banzai Barber III. 'Have you ever ridden a camel?' ('No.') 'Do your family own Kay's catalogue?' ('Yes.') 'Is playing characters just dressing up for adults?' ('That's a bit deep! Go out. Kiss a girl.') Among them, though, one barbed comment from a viewer called 'Pople' stood out. 'Why were you so crap in *The Sunday Show* and suddenly come up with something as subtle and clever as this?' ('Erm, because I was getting more money?')

It was a question the critics – who had written *The Sunday Show* off as dead the moment Dennis Pennis left anyhow – were asking too. The *Herald* reported: '*That Peter Kay Thing* went about its creator's task with seamless subtlety' and that 'Kay delivered a ton of slow-burning corkers'. Not that all the reviews were undiluted praise. In the *Observer*, TV columnist Kathryn Flett compared the programme unfavourably with *The Royle Family* and wrote, 'what you get with Kay is a near forensic obsession with the source material which unfortunately has the effect of negating most of the comedy'. Which missed the point of what Peter had achieved. However, she did compliment the use of narrator Andrew Sachs, as did Charlie Catchpole in the *Mirror*, who described his commentary as containing just enough 'authentic, energy-sapping dullness'.

Getting Sachs, the actor best known for his role as Manuel in *Fawlty Towers*, on board was a huge coup, especially as he was fresh from narrating *Parking Wars*, one of the terminally eventless docu-dramas *That Peter Kay Thing* was sending up. 'Andrew Sachs was brilliant,' says Peter, revealing that the actor had even lowered his fee to take part, having been impressed with 'The Services'. 'Although I never got to meet him. We'd just send him the scripts and he'd do them in London, then they'd send the finished tapes up to us in Bolton.'

As well as Brian Potter, for 'In the Club' Peter played three more characters: Max the doorman, Marc Park – one half of Park Avenue, a double act in the Talent Trek Final ('If you can't be the song then let the song be,' he pompously tells his singing partner) – and a reprise of Chorley FM DJ Paul LeRoy from 'The Services' as the judge of the Grand Final of

Talent Trek 99. LeRoy had no lines, except mumbling 'I'm not' when his girlfriend catches him staring at Cheryl Avenue and tells him to 'stop looking at her tits'.

As with his stand-up set, many of the storylines mirrored things that had happened to Peter in his real life, such as being disciplined at the bingo hall for time-wasting and Mathew Kelly in 'The Arena' being given the wrong name tag on his first day at work. While the speech Marc Park pretentiously gives about yoga – 'yoga: I find it stimulates my mind and my body' – is taken almost verbatim from a *South Bank Show* special on the singer Sting, Park's brother's speech about him showing off in a school play was very reminiscent of Peter's own life. 'He ruined the nativity. He was the innkeeper, he only had one line, "There's no room at the inn." He offered them en suite with full English. You can't ad-lib the Bible.'

It could have been Sister Barbara talking!

In the remaining five shows following 'In the Club' Peter would appear as a dozen other characters, many of them inspired by his part-time jobs over the years and others by the strangers he'd interviewed at Southport Film Fair. The line-up of larger-than-life personalities includes: Leonard de Thomkinson, the world's longest-serving paper boy, who was closely based on the real elderly eccentric whom Peter had befriended during his time at the Esso petrol station; Robert Edge, aka Mr Softy, inspired partially by a kid from Mount St Joseph's who'd tried to sue the school in an incident involving a Bunsen burner; Rose, a middle-aged bingo player who says, 'We never had time for sex, we were too busy having babies'; Mathew Kelly and Utah from 'The Services'; and Tom Dale the bingo caller, who charms the old women with the dabbers with lines like 'Thanks for coming tonight, was the cemetery shut?'

At first Peter was open about his inspiration, admitting

that Brian Potter was based on an amalgamation of his ex-bosses. But first Tom Henderson from the bingo hall where Peter had worked said, during an Internet interview, 'I want royalties because he used me in a piece in one of his sketches, I know he did.' And then a fire safety officer from Bolton Council, called Keith Laird, appeared in the *Bolton Evening News* claiming that Peter's character in the bingo hall episode, also a fire safety officer, and with the incredibly similar name of Keith Lard, was based on him. 'I've never met Peter Kay,' Laird told the local paper. 'But he must have seen me somewhere because there's no doubt it's me. He's got everything down to a T. The facial expressions were spot on. He kept saying it's not fire that kills, it's ignorance – I say that all the time.' He went on to claim that he had 1,300 witnesses at the council. Indeed Laird was something of a legend in Bolton, alleged to be so obsessed with fire safety that he would pack a pair of smoke alarms in his suitcase whenever he went on holiday. No doubt the similarity would have been easier for Mr Laird to take if it hadn't been for the fact that in *That Peter Kay Thing* his almost-namesake was rumoured to enjoy illicit romantic liaisons with canines. As Laird revealed to the *Bolton Evening News*: 'My new nick-name is Woof-Woof. It's a good job I can see the funny side.'

As for Peter Kay, he claimed innocence: 'Honestly, the character was just made up. I never met him, even when I worked at Top Rank bingo. I can't believe it's almost the same name but then again, a Brian Potter came forward after I featured a Brian Potter character in the first show. I suppose this kind of thing is bound to happen, but I've never met him in my life. There are bound to be similarities,' he said. 'There are nine Peter Kays in the Bolton phone book.'

Once the show had been screened and his colleagues tired of barking at him, Laird went quiet. For now ...

For the people of Bolton there were also other references

in the show that only they would get. The *Bolton Evening News*, for example, is known locally as BEN; for *That Peter Kay Thing* the invented local paper is called the *Bolton Independent Leader*, BIL for short. While in the Leonard episode, the main character is fleetingly caught in conversation with a local elderly gentleman who was something of a legendary eccentric in the area because in the summer he enjoys frequenting pubs dressed in tennis whites and carrying a racquet.

Before *That Peter Kay Thing* was broadcast, Peter already had the idea of expanding the first episode and in January 2000 began mapping out a whole series following Brian Potter's new venture. The moment of realisation that this was the episode to follow up came at the mecca of old-fashioned, outdated northern clubland: Bernard Manning's World Famous Embassy Club.

Manning, in the enlightened era of the 1980s and 1990s, had found himself marginalised by the comedy establishment because of some of his racist and sexist jokes, but still managed to fill his own club three times a week. As Jonathan Margolis claims in his biography of the overweight millionaire, 'Manning was a potential working-class hero, a master of the comedy of vulgarity and insult whom Chaucer would have admired, but who ruined it all by being racist.' However, even in his own heartland he was beginning to appear past his sell-by date. Nowhere is the old-school comedian's struggle to keep up with changing trends better illustrated than in John Thomson's ironic pastiche of a fat northern comic in *The Fast Show*, Bernard Righton, whose jokes began worryingly un-PC before redeeming themselves: 'There was a Jew, a Paki and an Irishman in the pub. What a fine example of racial integration!' In 1999, more than aware that times had changed and that his father was well behind them, 39-year-old Bernard Manning Jnr (who once got sent off for Stockport County reserves when the referee asked him his name) took over the venue, renamed it the New Embassy Club and started booking acts from the new breed of Manchester comics. Headlining the opening night was Peter Kay.

'It's been turned into an alternative comedy venue,' he said. 'But it's kept the same audience Bernard would play to. I find that hilarious. That's when I realised the "In the Club" episode from the last series had potential for a series of its own.'

Once *That Peter Kay Thing* finally made it on to our screens, Peter himself loved watching them screened live – somehow it all didn't seem real unless there were adverts and other programmes around it. The series and all the accompanying publicity had helped take his mind off his father's death, but once the run was complete he felt a strange purposelessness. '*That Peter Kay Thing* has shuffled off into the distance and that's a shame,' he wrote on his website in a March 2000 message to fans. 'It all seemed to go so fast, the six episodes flew by.'

His feelings of emptiness weren't helped by some senior people at Channel 4's lukewarm reaction to the series and their reluctance to schedule a repeat run. As had been proved in recent years with *The Fast Show*, *Father Ted* and *The Royle Family*, repeats were crucial to a series' lasting success with the word of mouth from the original showing pushing up ratings when it was moved to a new slot. The show had been well received by the public and most of the press, but the peak viewing figures of just 1.6 million were relatively low. Frustration led Peter to start an Internet campaign urging fans of the show to bombard Channel 4 with requests for another chance to watch it. Upset by the lack of plans, he wrote, 'Why? It was critically acclaimed, it got viewers, it wasn't the best programme in the world, but it was a lot more charming than some of the shite that's on. Anyway, if you would like to see it repeated then write to either Katie Taylor or Kevin Lygo in the Entertainment Department at Channel 4, 124 Horseferry Road, London, SW1P 2TX. Good luck!'

Elsewhere on the site, in a question-and-answer session Peter says: 'I went to see Channel 4 the other day and surprisingly they said that they don't think the series would be repeated unless it was to promote a second series. Now whether this was an attempt at convincing me to do another series or sheer blind f***ing stupidity remains to be seen.'

Peter's official website <www.peterkay.co.uk> had been started by a pair of Peter's friends, Glenn Jones and Chris Greeney, in June 1997 as a bit of fun but as Peter's fame grew the site got more serious and in July 1998 it became a fully formed beast rather than an amateurish affair hosted on AOL's free webspace. The site had a major part in spreading the good word of Peter Kay by publishing tour dates and booking information and long before any other comedian had noticed how important this new technology could become Peter Kay was taking an active role in it with monthly messages to fans and answering reader's messages. As well as all the normal website fare, the site also included reviews of his shows, fans' jokes and some original material penned by Peter. Some of this, like his rant against public transport, veered more into the territory of irate commuter rather than quick-witted comic: 'Why are two hundred people packed into economy while there are two "business" men in first class?' he grumbled.

The website also included a couple of rough ideas for what might have been developed into future characters, such as Roy, the manager of the Majestic Cinema: 'Unfortunately, due to neglect and abuse the old girl's gradually wearing away, so much so that she's now turning into a stale decrepit hell hole. In fact only this morning my u-bend in the Gents went all to cock, but never mind.'

One development in Peter's career went unreported online, though it would be another turning point in his career. In the spring of 2000, after being recommended to him by his friends Craig Cash and Caroline Aherne, Peter left Lisa White, his manager and agent for the past two years, and appointed Phil McIntyre as his new representative. McIntyre was a huge player in the theatre industry and in addition to Cash and Aherne handled some of the biggest names in British comedy (Victoria Wood, *The Fast Show*). His involvement instantly gave Peter Kay some weight (no pun intended) at Channel 4.

Robert Popper, who was a commissioning editor at the channel at the turn of the century, says that 'If you heard Phil McIntyre's name associated with someone you would certainly take it more seriously. He's a big, big name in the industry, someone who knows what they're doing, so whatever he brings to you, you're going to listen.'

With a background in live rock concerts, McIntyre also brought experience in areas Peter Kay hadn't begun to think about, and one of the first decisions was to get a video done of Peter's live performances.

'The idea is to get paid for something you really want to do!'
Michael Palin

In February 2000, on the front page of the site, Peter Kay alerted his fans to the fact that this April he would be recording his first live video in Blackpool. Originally the two gigs were booked for the theatre on the North Pier, but then when all 1,000 tickets for the first show sold out in a couple of days and the video crew suggested it might be a bit dicey taking all the filming equipment down a pier, it was moved to the theatre at the foot of Blackpool Tower, usually the home of the resident circus.

'I wanted to do it somewhere special, rather than some faceless theatre somewhere,' he says. Early in the year he had cancelled a few dates in Liverpool, Birmingham and Preston because so much of his act was about his dad that he felt it would be uncomfortable. But when he went on holiday with Susan to Egypt in March he found himself writing more and more material about him. 'Maybe that was my way of grieving and coping with losing him,' he tells people before the Blackpool gig. 'Don't get me wrong, the material's not sad or nothing and I'm sure he'll be pretty chuffed with it.'

The new material about his father found him recalling his dad holding him in a headlock when he was a kid and yelling out to passing police cars, 'It's OK, I've got him', and witnessing cheesy cabaret shows like the singer with an American accent called Tony Colorado, about whom his dad said, 'I know him, he's from Burnley.' On top of this, because it was Blackpool there was a whole new section about foreign holidays – how you hate it when you get home without a suntan, how terrible it is having to check out of a hotel at 10 a.m. when your plane doesn't leave till midnight, not to mention how dads on holiday abroad always manage to find a place where they can eat English food and none of that foreign muck. 'Garlic bread?' he says, mimicking his dad. 'Garlic? And bread? Am I hearing you right?'

With the audience in on the joke, he calls the video *Live at the Top of the Tower* – 'How'd you all get up here in the lift?' He also films a series of small sketches and in one of them he takes a sideways pop at his comedy enemies when future *Phoenix Nights* regular Archie Kelly, dressed in his Jackie

Valencio wig, says to camera: 'He steals all my stuff, you
know. "Smack Me Bitch Up", I've been doing that for years.
And he swears. It's rude, it's crude and its f***ing offensive.'

The music for the *Live at the Top of the Tower* was recorded
by Toni Baker, a musician from Bury (not the gay area of
Manchester, by the way). Toni had been in a few bands in the
1970s and 1980s (Shabby Tiger, very big in Belgium, apparently), and following a divorce was making some extra money
by giving piano lessons, advertising his services in the north-
west edition of *Loot*.

'I got a call from this guy saying he'd like to play piano,'
says Toni. 'So we talked for a little while about what he
wanted to do and we found out we both liked the same kind
of music – Billy Joel. When he told me who he was it were
incredible cos I'd just watched *That Peter Kay Thing* so I
said, "What? That Peter Kay that did *That Peter Kay
Thing*?", which were absolutely brilliant. He came round, we
had a couple of brews and had a couple of lessons, then later
he came back with a keyboard and he told me what he was
learning for. He said he didn't want his fiancée to know
because he wanted it to be a surprise. He wanted to play
"Dancing Queen" at the wedding.'

Peter and Susan had got engaged a few months earlier,
Peter proposing outside Andy's Records in the town centre
because it was where they'd had their first kiss. After a few
weeks, and having found out about Toni's background, Peter
asked Toni if he'd like to perform the music for his *Live at the
Top of the Tower* video. 'He said what he'd like was three or
four pieces for the opening titles in the style of [organist]
Reginald Dixon but songs that you would never expect him
to play. So he said he wanted "Shaft", "Sussudio", "Deeply
Dippy" and "Bat Out of Hell".'

Over the course of the next couple of months Peter visited
Toni every Tuesday and Wednesday afternoon but when

Susan began to suspect he was having an affair, Peter had to tell her he was having lessons. Then Peter told Toni, 'I'm going to have to knock this on the head. I'm doing a new TV series. Do you want to do the music?'

'I thought about it for about a second,' says Baker.

Despite their initial reluctance to schedule a repeat of *That Peter Kay Thing*, when Peter and his new manager Phil McIntyre visited Channel 4 to discuss Peter's idea for a new series they were instantly sold on the idea when he described it as 'Ken Loach does *Cheers*'. The docu-spoof style was binned and instead it would be a sit-com picking up from where the *That Peter Kay Thing* club episode left off, with Brian Potter trying to start again after the demise of yet another club. There would be no laughter track and the whole thing would be filmed on location in Bolton. How could they say no?

As with *That Peter Kay Thing*, the new series remained untitled deep into the writing process. To help name the series Peter turned to the regular visitors of his website, who sent in suggestions – a bit like the Peter Kay version of naming a new *Blue Peter* pet. *Out of Order, On Its Arse, The Club, Phoenix Rising, Potter Files* and *Brian Potter and the Ring of Fire* were among the suggestions, but knowing a good thing when he saw it, Peter plumped for *Phoenix Nights*. Later Channel 4 would twist it slightly to become *Peter Kay's Phoenix Nights* in order to give some continuity between *That Peter Kay Thing* and the new spin-off series from it.

Phoenix Nights was co-written by Peter Kay, Dave Spikey and Neil Fitzmaurice, with occasional remarks by Patrick McGuinness ('He's the George Harrison of the group,' said Peter). This time, as a measure of their newfound professional status, the series wasn't to be written via a complex game of Royal Mail tag but in an office where they would spend each day from nine to five together from June to August.

'You never really clock off, not when you're writing. It does take over your life and your thoughts. I would lie awake for hours thinking of lines and structure. Worrying that we'd got everything in.'

Writing together was good fun, although sometimes they'd waste an entire day giggling over an idea like Keith Lard setting fire to a bonsai tree with his lighter or a scene where Brian Potter would go to Jerry Dignan for sexual advice and all his answer would be masked by a hand dryer in the toilets except the last line 'covered in piss'.

'At the end of the day,' says Peter in the *Phoenix Nights* DVD commentary, 'you can write the best jokes in the world but nothing beats a good fart gag when it's done properly.'

Before they started writing those fart gags, though, there was serious work to be done. 'The first thing we did was research,' says Peter. 'We went out and chatted to local club owners. But I only spoke to about three because they all seemed to have the same stories. They were like, "We had Matt Monro and then we had this woman who swallowed birds." ' As with 'In the Club', Peter noted how the clubs he'd visit had a strange sadness to them and that they were becoming more rundown and derelict. 'Yet to the people running them there is no slump,' he says. 'They don't see it, just like they don't see the bit of tinsel left on the ceiling after Christmas that's still there in July.'

Getting this right was the key for Peter, who says, 'To me, it has to be rooted in some kind of reality or it isn't funny.'

With *Phoenix Nights* Peter, Dave and Neil developed a new skill. Annoyed that so many of their gags had been lost in the editing process of *That Peter Kay Thing*, they decided to layer every single scene in the new series, taking every chance for a funny line even if it was hidden as a sign on the wall or a song on the radio.

The next task was to cast the show which, apart from one

or two actors including Sian Foulkes as Paddy's love interest Mary (she's Holy Mary's daughter, whose brother is called Joseph) and Alex Lowe as the slightly unhinged mind reader Clinton Baptiste – a brilliant invention of Neil Fitzmaurice's – was to be completely made up of stand-ups. It was an incredible masterstroke and one that would be replicated in the following years in the casting of the movie *24 Hour Party People* and in the West End production of *One Flew Over the Cuckoo's Nest*.

'Stand-up comedy is acting,' Kay said. 'It is going onstage every night and making it sound real and making it sound like it's the first time you've ever done it. They make you believe they've just remembered it or it's just happened, and it's the skill of making it sound fresh. Going on and knowing verbatim every little intonation, every little "oh" and "ah" and making it sound like it is, and getting people's eyes to widen and taking a full room with you. You see a spark and you go "They're good", or "She's not", and I got all these ones over the last three or four years that I'd seen. We had about 20 or 30 or 40. Some were really good at stand-up but no good at acting – some were better actors than stand-ups!'

Among the cast who hadn't been seen in the pilot (as everyone was now referring to the *That Peter Kay Thing* episode as) were Janice Connolly, who was making a name for herself with her housewifey alter ego Barbara Nice – perfect for the saintly Holy Mary, who'd be wearing a Princess Diana sweatshirt in most of her scenes; Steve Edge, who became the new keyboardist in the house band Les Alanos; and brilliant Scouse legend Ted Robbins, transforming himself from the most charming man on Merseyside into the dastardly Den Perry. In all, 22 stand-up comedians appeared in the series, which was filmed on location at St Gregory's Club in Farnworth, Bolton, during September and October 2000.

It was around this time that the BBC began screening their *I Love the 1970s* series. It was a bit like Paul LeRoy's speech in 'The Services'. Someone at the corporation had noticed that 'every year something different happened' and came up with the idea of combining old clips with the comments of a few comedians and social experts. Each episode was presented by somebody significant to the year in question, be it David Cassidy in 1972 or Carrie 'Princess Leila' Fisher in 1977. Despite barely being out of their prams in the years being discussed, it was Peter Kay and Johnny Vegas who lit up the show.

Because it was the first year of a new century there was a huge wave of nostalgia going into the new millennium. Suddenly it didn't seem sad to wallow in the past a bit, in fact it seemed quite vital and fun. Like Friends Reunited and the relaunched Mini, the *I Love ...* series surfed this wave of re-examining our recent history.

'*I Love ...* was the child of *TV Heaven and TV Hell*, the first BBC clip show,' says author and *I Love ...* contributor Andrew Collins. 'One of the achievements was that it completely redefined the seventies as a decade of fun and innocence and plurality, of sweeping cultural change and speeded-up shifts in attitude. For most of the eighties, the seventies was "the decade that style forgot".'

It was also – when Vegas or Kay were on screen, at least – fantastically funny. Kay's finest moment was during the 1977 episode (remember, he was four years old at this point in his life). In all the rest of the shows, the talking heads said something quickfire – 'it were all crackly in my mouth' or something when talking about space dust – then we would hear from the next one 'you'd put a load in your gob at once'. There was no room for pontificating, but it was a bit annoying. However, just once in the entire series, they let one person speak uninterrupted for about four hysterical minutes. The occasion? Peter Kay's incensed rant against *Take Hart* and in particular Tony Hart's plasticine pal, Morph. 'It was a show where Tony Hart got to do all the things you weren't allowed to do in art at school,' he began. 'A lovely man, though, but I think he were off his head cos he talked to Morph. You know, a bit of plasticine ...'

He went on to recount in incredible detail a whole episode of *Take Hart* – 'Sophie sent this picture in and as you can see she's created a beach effect ... by using sand.' The piece featured an interview with Morph's animator David Sproxton, a man who to this day still lives under the misconception that people actually watched the show to catch the annoying adventures of his creation. Thankfully, Peter Kay delivered the thoughts of a nation ...

'I wish you could just get a mallet and squash him ... bye, bye Morph, eh! Mind, he'd be gone to the other side of the studio before you could get to him.'

As the series progressed into the 1980s Peter got the chance to reveal his views on Samantha Fox's ample bosoms – 'She could breastfeed a crèche, but that were it' – and recite the lyrics to Nik Kershaw's 'The Riddle' – 'There's a tree by the river ... who gives a shit?' While both Peter and Johnny Vegas confessed an infatuation with *No Limits* presenter Jenny Powell, especially her rather appalling taste in American soft rock bands like REO Speedwagon and Journey – 'That's how I got into that music,' croaks Vegas. 'If that's what Jennie's listening to that's what I'm listening to.'

The *I Love ...* programmes were the harbinger of hundreds of similar clip shows – some of which would feature Peter Kay discussing adverts or pop music. What docu-soaps were to the end of the 1990s, talking-head list shows were to the start of the 2000s – they were on all the time. *I Love ...* was the format at its peak.

If his 'Smack My Bitch Up' gag on the Blackpool video

indicated that the accusations that he borrowed material still rankled with Peter Kay, he received validation that he was pleasing some of his peers at the 2000 British Comedy Awards in December 2000, where *That Peter Kay Thing* scooped the prize for Best New TV Comedy, beating *Alistair McGowan's Big Impression* and another show that had originated from *The Comedy Lab, Trigger Happy TV*. *Trigger Happy*'s Dom Joly was regarded as the strong favourite, and when *That Peter Kay Thing* was announced as the winner by Richard E. Grant and Cerys Matthews from the Welsh rock band Catatonia, Peter Kay, Dave Spikey and Neil Fitzmaurice were shocked, none more so than Peter.

'I know people always say they are shocked when they win, but I genuinely could not believe it when they announced my name,' he says. 'I made a joke just before the announcement saying that if we won we should stand up and pretend to throw our chairs in disgust. In the end I was gobsmacked.'

Perhaps swayed by the fact that, along with Sandy Gall, Geoffrey Palmer, Ken Dodd and Miss Coal Board 1981, a photograph of himself had adorned the bedroom of Peter Kay's loveable eccentric Leonard, veteran broadcaster Dennis Norden – who was on the voting panel – had swayed the other judges with an impassioned plea.

'I didn't have a speech prepared,' says Peter. 'But I was keen to make sure I thanked the people of Bolton.' As for Dave Spikey, he said of the evening, 'It was like a dream.' Although he wasn't talking about winning an award so much as Carol Vorderman asking to have her picture taken with him.

There was no chance for Peter to get too many fancy showbiz ideas. 'No, because a week later I were doing Eccles Masonic Hall,' he says. 'The British Comedy Awards were on the Saturday, and this were Friday after. I were on after a Cher look-alike, although she looked more like Shania Twain.

The DJ said to me, "How do you want your lights?" I said, "What are me options?" He said, "On or off." I did raffle and all. It were for my fiancée Susan's Auntie Anne, to raise money for motor neurone. You can't say no to family, can you, especially your fiancée's family.'

The 2000 Comedy Awards were viewed as a triumph for the north. As well as Peter Kay, other winners that night included Victoria Wood's Lancashire *Dinnerladies*, the Manchester-based *Cold Feet*, *The Royle Family*, Salford-set movie *East is East* and Yorkshire legend Alan Bennett. *Liver Birds* and *Bread* writer Carla Lane made a speech saying that the televised awards were the 'north's finest comedy hour' and that 'with the exception of the fantastic *Only Fools and Horses*, northern comedy has always been the funniest because of the very real, everyday situations it has dealt with'. The press agreed, and in the eyes of the redtops it was no longer a case of it being grim but grin up north.

Seeking to capitalise on Peter's triumph at the Comedy Awards and the prevailing mood of north is best, anti-Margot and Jerry sentiment, Channel 4 decided to bring *Phoenix Nights* forward in their schedule to the second Sunday of the new year. Not only that but the show would have a prime-time slot, 9.30 p.m., and be repeated on Thursday evenings. It was a bold move, a sign of Channel 4's increased confidence in their rising star, and perhaps Phil McIntyre's negotiating skills. But there was a slight problem. They hadn't finished making it yet.

Each episode of the first series of *Phoenix Nights* was finally edited only one day before transmission, a ridiculously tight deadline for such a major programme. Among the last things to be added was the music, Toni Baker adding new background pieces when required, right up to the last minute. Indeed such was the rush to get the show ready that the first episode didn't have a theme tune. After watching it on the Sunday evening Peter decided that he'd like one after all and visited Baker in his Bury home.

'I wasn't going to have a theme tune to *Phoenix Nights*,' he says. 'I'll tell you the full story. I have always loved the James Bond teaser at the start of Bond films when they have a little thing beforehand then you get a bit settled and you think, "Oooh, James Bond", and I wanted that. Channel 4 weren't really keen on me doing it before each episode comes on, but I like it; I like having a little two-minute thing before it comes on. Then a friend said to me you should have a theme cos it's like that thing where you're in the kitchen making a cup of tea and someone shouts out "It's on ... it's started." '

Peter likes the fact that the first show has no theme tune; it makes it special – and he would later repeat the trick in subsequent shows. But for now they needed a theme and they needed it quick. 'His brief was that he wanted something jolly but with a slight hint of menace,' says Toni, on the phone from a music shop in Manchester. 'He wanted it on a solo instrument. The parallel that he drew was with *Some Mothers Do 'Ave 'Em*, which is done on a piccolo flute. So we tried it on various instruments – guitar, piano, cello, trombone like *Hancock's Half Hour* – but it sounded too obviously comic. So, in the end, we settled for the glockenspiel – it gives you that feeling like when you're watching a horror film and it's in a child's bedroom and there's a creepy jack in the box moving in the corner.'

There was also late trouble clearing some of the music for the cover versions used in the show. 'One of the reasons music is always last-minute is that you're always waiting for tracks to be cleared,' says Toni. 'Sometimes Peter would get clearance on what he wanted, sometimes it's got to be the fourth choice. I know that he really wanted to use something by the Smiths and by Prince, but it's hard with artists like that.'

Despite the stress of the deadline, Toni Baker hails Peter as 'the easiest person I've ever worked with'. The pair would collaborate on all the music for the series, Baker coming up with ideas and Peter adding to them. 'He was looking for comedy all the way through,' he says. 'So no matter how good it is musically, it's got to suit the scene perfectly. Previously I'd worked with other musicians, and there's always someone who wants to stamp his feet. It ends up great, but the process is painful. I never have that with Peter. At the end of the day it's his gig so I'll bow down to him anyway. There's only been a couple of times when I've said "No, you can't do it like that" and he's said "Give it a go". And when I see it on the TV he's always been right. He's got the vision of what the cameras see. It's like having another ear. He knows what he wants and 99 per cent of the time I know how to achieve it.'

Over time it would transpire that not everyone was as happy to work alongside the Bolton boy made good. For now, though, it was more a case of 'top of the world, Ma, top of the world'.

Chapter Eight
Can You Hear Me Now?

'In the rich chocolate box of life, the top layer's gone and some-body's nicked the orange cream from the bottom.'

Bob (Rodney Bewes), The Likely Lads

'Sometimes you want to go where everybody knows your name.'

Theme tune to Cheers

It wasn't only Dennis Norden whom Peter Kay could count among his growing flock of celebrity worshippers – darts player Jocky Wilson, snooker legend Tony Knowles and DJ Chris Moyles were all confirmed fans of the Bolton funny man. With *Live at the Top of the Tower* out on video, Peter also saw himself become a tour-bus favourite of dozens of rock acts, whose arduous trips around the world sampling free lager were enlightened by watching TV on the road. Peter's musical followers included Texas, Eric Clapton, Doves, Fatboy Slim and Starsailor. There was, though, one exception to this expanding list of musical Kay disciples: Liam Gallagher of Oasis.

Talking to the *Observer Music Monthly* in June 2005, his brother, Noel, explained why. 'Liam hasn't got a sense of humour, f***ing full stop,' he says. 'Like with Peter Kay. If you're a northern guy about our age, all the reference points are spot on – you can't not like him. We were on the tour bus one night and somebody put a Peter Kay DVD on and I thought: "This is going to be a disaster." There's a few Mancs in our crew and everyone was laughing their heads off. And Liam's just sat there going: "He's a f***ing shit, f***ing fat idiot." So he gets up to go to the bog and someone goes: "Why doesn't he like Peter Kay?" Because he'd been to the NME Awards when Liam won a trophy for being hero of the year – and Liam wouldn't go up and collect it ...'

The night was 6 February 2001. Not wishing to see the reluctant Liam go without his prize, Peter clambered down from the stage and waded through the tables of rock stars until he got to Liam Gallagher who, despite the fact that he wouldn't feel the benefit when he went outside, was wearing a vast white fur coat. Peter brought his trophy over to him and went, "Ere you are, lad.' And then, as he walked off, he said: 'Me mam's been looking for that coat.' 'F***ing uproar!' says Noel. 'I was laughing like f***.'

The first episode of *Phoenix Nights* was broadcast on Sunday, 14 January 2001. Within the first five minutes it was obvious to everyone watching that the show was destined to rank alongside the likes of *Rising Damp*, *Porridge* and *Father Ted* as a comedy classic on UK TV. And the main reason is Brian Potter – played by Peter Kay in grey wig and a disturbing assortment of brown and beige cardigans – the disabled club secretary. Our first glimpse of Potter comes as he trundles over the brow of a hill on his shopmobile, Bolton glimmering in the sunlight beyond him, to a soundtrack of 'The Only Way is Up' by Yazz. To anyone over 30 it's a shot reminiscent of an old Hovis ad of a boy pushing his bike up a cobbled northern lane. Within those opening minutes Potter produces more cantankerous outbursts than Victor Meldrew has managed in the past ten years of *One Foot in the Grave*. The string of bulbs on the club roof isn't impressive enough ('Think Las Vegas'); the builders have gone on their dinner break at half ten in the morning ('It's a bloody disgrace'); he has to settle for a *Das*

Boot fruit machine instead of the *Matrix* one he ordered ('It's the last one on the van,' says the delivery driver. 'I don't care if it's the Last of the Mohicans'); one of his staff is filling religiously sloganed balloons with helium ('Pop 'em. It's a club not a mosque'); and social secretary Jerry 'the Saint' Dignan is sat on the loo reading a pamphlet about colon care when he should be rehearsing ('Stop crappin' and get cracking. Avanti!'). The laughs come so thick you feel as if you're in fear of missing half of them. The next 20 minutes don't disappoint either, as we are introduced to the regular cast of loafers – Ray Von (an electrician who becomes the Phoenix's resident DJ), Kenny Snr (a compulsive liar who claims to have played on Centre Court at Wimbledon despite being unseeded), Potter's gormless Manchester City shirt-wearing slave Young Kenny, and the doormen Max and Paddy, whose thrill at wearing radio microphones extends to Paddy going on a bus ride while still wearing them.

Max: 'Can you hear me now?'

Paddy: 'I can see ya, you dick.'

The next day in the *Daily Express* critic Ben Walters wrote that *Phoenix Nights* 'was as perfectly pitched – and as bitterly funny – a parody of working-class lassitude as *The Royle Family*. Think of Jim Royle on wheels and armed with a random – yet weirdly resonant – list of pop culture references.' While Charlie Catchpole in the *Mirror* wrote that *Phoenix Nights* was so good he was going to tape them all so he could watch them again – quite an accolade for someone who watches TV for a living. 'Each time I spot some new, tiny detail that delights me – like Kay's wheelchair-bound club owner Brian Potter drinking whisky from a vase because he can't reach the optics behind the bar with a glass.'

Bloody Rafferty!

Picking up where 'In the Club' had left off, we discover that Brian's last club, the Neptune, had been burnt to a crisp and this was his new chance to run the best club in Bolton. Like the American sit-com *Cheers*, which had an often unseen rival bar, the Olde Towne Tavern, the Phoenix too had an adversary – the flashy Banana Grove, whose malevo-lent owner Den Perry (brilliantly portrayed by Ted Robbins) is like some dark northern gothic cut and shunt of Les Dawson and Dr No reincarnated in a double-breasted suit. Perry's Banana Grove was about profit; Potter and his crumbling Phoenix Club was about survival and not ruining the cork flooring. As Paul Sandland, the chairman of St Gregory's Social Club, where the majority of *Phoenix Nights* was filmed, explains: 'Social clubs, Catholic clubs, working men's club, everything you make on the door and at the bar goes back into running the place. You're always scraping by and improvising and worried about how much things cost.'

Indeed a lot of southern viewers, not immersed in working men's club culture (not to be confused with Culture Club) and how they operate, might have imagined Brian Potter as a tight arse, looking after his own back and giving the change in the disabled boy statue in the entrance hall a shake to see if there's enough money in it for a holiday ('Corfu for Christmas'). Potter, it seemed, was a million miles (well, at least as far away as Stranraer) from the personality of his creator we knew through his stand-up – open, warm, friendly. Kay's Potter seemed to be culled from all the unpop-ular bosses Peter had ever had. But there were family traits, too, like Brian's constant consumption of Teacher's whisky, which he imbibed as if it were Sprite, and his creative collec-tion of alternatives to swearing and coyness regarding 'filth', mirroring his mother, Deirdre, and her calling of saints' names and shock at the relationship between the priest and Rachel Ward in *The Thorn Birds*.

Brian is a conservative curmudgeon, as he tells the stand-up comics getting ready to take part in the Phoenix's alternative comedy night, Funny Farm: 'There's a picture of Her Majesty the Queen out there and as far as you lot are concerned she may as well be sat on the front row.' But he is also strangely loveable.

As each episode went by, Brian Potter became less and less of a grotesque, so by the time of the singles night in episode four, where he meets Beverly Hillscopto and is hopeful of a sexual liaison with her, you are rooting for him to succeed – especially after his own admission that he hasn't seen much action in that department for years. As he tells Jerry, 'It's been twelve years. He thinks he's in for life, you know.'

'Who?' asks Jerry.

'Him!' Brian says, pointing to his crotch. 'He's up for parole soon. If he gets out I want him coming home in style.'

'TV's own' Roy Walker cut the ribbon of the Phoenix Club in the first episode and after that each week revolved around a theme night. Originally they were going to ask Bob Carolgees to do the honour, but Peter was worried about overdoing the joke. So instead they featured him as the celebrity endorser of Jerry's colon care leaflet.

In episode two, Brian takes delivery of a bucking bronco in exchange for a wonky snooker table, but improvises to create a Wild West theme night. 'Give it a couple of days and it'll be shitting money,' says Potter's provider of dodgy entertainment gear, Eric (brilliantly played by Bolton comedy and folk music legend, Bernard 'the Bolton Frog' Wrigley). 'If not it better learn how to shit snooker tables,' says Potter.

Just like classic sit-com *The Fall and Rise of Reginald Perrin*, which was awash with regular jokes ('I didn't get where I am today without ...', '17 minutes late ...', 'Take a letter Miss Jones ...'), Peter, Dave and Neil gave the *Phoenix Nights* characters a bevy of recurring gags. Among them were Brian's malapropisms, where he'd get words just slightly wrong – acapulco instead of a cappella, 'a Catch-21 situation' instead of Catch-22. Dave Spikey's Jerry St Clair and Neil Fitzmaurice's Ray Von had their motifs too – Jerry and his string of appalling cover versions, Ray asking as if he was still at a funfair rather than calling the bingo for six old-age pensioners. There were other running gags too: the auditions at the end, such as the escapologist who couldn't escape, a clumsy fire juggler and a pair of geriatric gymnasts. These were dubbed by Peter, Dave and Neil as 'the Last Supper shots'. As Charlie Catchpole had suggested, there were things you missed out on first time around, like various signs dotted around the Phoenix Club, song lyrics dropped into conversation (such as when Brian is jilted by Beverly: 'I've bigger fish to fry. No woman, no cry'), and Jerry's obsession with bowel movements.

Jerry: 'Are you regular?'

Brian: 'As a Kennedy funeral. You could set your watch by my arse.'

'Oh, *Phoenix Nights*,' sighs Scottish comedian Janey Godley. 'I really love *Phoenix Nights*. It was just so clever and real, they captured that world so accurately. I used to run a pub just like that called the Riverside in Glasgow. I'd have bingo and bands that were as bad as Les Alanos, climbing out of the window after gigs cos they had punters chasing after them.'

'Up until that point,' says Toni Baker, who appeared in the first episode as the guitarist in the racist folk band Half a Shilling, 'I think all most people, especially down south, knew of working men's clubs was *The Wheeltappers and Shunters Club*, which was this old flat-capped variety show that was on in the seventies. *Phoenix Nights* really caught it how it really is, with all the acts and stuff. If you played at a club like that and you didn't go down well or get paid, what they'd always do was find the bingo machine, which was usually at the back of the stage, and take out this clip on top so that the next time they used it all the balls would go whizzing up in the air.' Which is exactly what happens in *Phoenix Nights*, of course, Jerry having to improvise with bucket bingo instead – pulling the numbered balls from a white pail straight out of Bolton Market.

'I love that show because I've lived with that; it's like watching my life,' says Brian Lloyd, a comedy act from the 1960s who supported the likes of Tommy Cooper and Frank Carson on the northern club circuit. 'The doormen are just right. It's absolute perfection.' Brian says he saw plenty of incidents that were straight out of *Phoenix Nights*. 'We once had a singer who had got one of the first radio mikes and he thought he was the bee's knees,' he said. 'I introduced him and he came on looking very suave. However, halfway through we heard "243 come in" on the mike. He'd managed to pick up the local taxi firm!'

Not everyone, though, was impressed by the show's absurd twist on realism. Keith Laird, the fire safety officer who claimed Kay's dog-bothering fire safety officer from the 'Eyes Down' episode of *That Peter Kay Thing* was based on him, was upset to discover, when he picked up *TV Quick* that week, that Peter had reprised the role for *Phoenix Nights*. Especially as his colleagues at Bolton Council had only recently tired of barking whenever he walked past. Fire was an essential linking factor between the Neptune Club and the Phoenix, but Peter could have changed the character, given him a different name and facial features. He couldn't resist bringing back the much-loved Lard, however: he liked the continuity and the idea of people from the mythical Bolton of *That Peter Kay Thing* continuing to exist in his new vision. The scenes with Lard – giving a fire safety speech at Den Perry's Banana Grove club – are some of the funniest moments in the first series. Attempting to get the audience of club bosses' attention he reads a letter he has received from America about a burning tower block that seems to bear an uncanny resemblance to the lyrics of 'Disco Inferno' by The Trammps. 'Burn, baby, burn, burn that mother down,' he reads. 'Another child orphaned.'

For Laird it was too much and in the week after the first episode aired it was reported across the press that Channel 4 had apologised to Mr Laird and agreed to pay him £10,000 in compensation. A spokesman from the broadcaster said, 'Channel 4 and Peter Kay would like to state that the character of Keith Lard may have led some persons to wrongly believe that the character was based on Mr Keith Laird. We wish to make it clear that this was not the case and would like to apologise to Mr Laird and his family for the distress caused.' In February, at Manchester United's Old Trafford stadium, Laird handed over cheques worth £5,000 to two charities – the National Fire Safety Charity for Children and the Fire Service Benevolent Fund – while on Channel 4's part, whenever Keith Lard appears in a *Phoenix Nights* or a *That Peter Kay Thing* repeat it is accompanied after the closing credits with a disclaimer page and information on fire safety.

For his part Peter continued to protest his innocence. On an interview on his official website, he draws a line under the matter when he is asked, 'Are any of the characters based on real people?' Answering, he says: 'No. And I can't stress that enough. No! All the characters are fictitious and any similarity whatsoever is purely coincidental. One of the most frequently asked questions is did I know Keith Laird. The answer is NO.'

Mr & Mrs
Be nice to each other
Mr & Mrs
You've got to love one another

Mr & Mrs *theme tune*

On 27 April 2001, Peter Kay realised his lifetime ambition when he spent £187,000 on a detached home in a middle-class suburb of Bolton. On the Bolton pages of the knowhere guide (<knowhere.co.uk>) some wag wrote on the message board that you can tell which house is his because 'it's always got big light on'. Possibly in preparation for this, Peter and Susan didn't get to move in till long after their wedding day because they 'had the electricians in'.

Peter and Susan Gargan were married on Friday, 7 September 2001 at St Osmund's Roman Catholic Church in the pretty Bolton town of Breightmet. If he'd had his way *Mr & Mrs* host Derek Batey would have married them, but in the event, being a sentimentalist, it was Father Flatley, Peter's priest when he was an altar boy at St Ethelbert's, who conducted the ceremony.

Despite good intentions, Peter didn't finish learning how to play 'Dancing Queen' as a wedding surprise for Susan; that duty fell to *Phoenix Nights* theme tune composer (and Half a Shilling member) Toni Baker, who performed the Abba hit on the church organ after Peter and Susan had finished signing the register and were leaving the church. Most of the cast of *Phoenix Nights* were there to see Peter and Susan on their happy day, but guitarist Eric Clapton, who was a fan of the show and was invited to the wedding, was unable to attend. At the reception, which was held at Mytton Fold Farm in Blackburn, actor Paddy McGuinness shared best man duties with an old schoolfriend of Peter's, Michael Connell.

'I think he had five best men in the end,' says Toni Baker. 'He couldn't decide between them. Peter has five or six really close mates who have stuck with him throughout his whole life. His friends mean a lot to him.'

Peter has been loyal to his pals since making it in the entertainment industry, giving many of them work as script editors, extras and in the crew on *That Peter Kay Thing*, *Phoenix Nights* and *Max and Paddy's Road to Nowhere*; a couple of his pals from Salford University – Karl Lucas (who also appeared as one of the presenters of 'Armchair Superstore' in *Phoenix Nights*) and Gordon Isaacs – were employed to help out at live shows. He has said that his friends help him keep his feet on the ground: 'To them, I'm not Peter Kay or Brian Potter, I'm just Peter.'

Peter had wanted to DJ at the wedding reception himself (his old DJ-ing partner Michael Atherton being the other side of the world in Australia), but a few weeks before the wedding he told Brian Viner of the *Independent*: 'Susan won't let me.' 'We'll have a bit of eighties, a bit of nineties, some seventies dance music, a bit of Motown,' he told Viner. 'I know I should relax, but it's important, disco. There's nothing worse than some gobshite asking for something like "Eloise", the Damned, and they mither you until you put it on, then everyone sits down and they don't even dance themselves.'

In fact Peter had been planning the sequence of songs for his wedding since he was 14-years old, originally planning to use them when he married his first girlfriend, Catherine Hurst. 'They were called things like *Beginning of the Night, Vols I & II*. When it came to the big day, I hardly changed a thing: "Xanadu" by Olivia Newton-John, "Dancing Queen" by Abba ... and the first slow song was Tony Hatch's theme for *Mr & Mrs*.'

'Dancing Queen' was Peter and Susan's song and he made certain his wedding DJ had it by bringing along his own copy. For someone who had spent so long onstage discussing how people danced at weddings, what he played at his own was deadly important stuff. 'It's one song that everyone gets up and dances to,' he said. 'It were first song I danced to. You've got to. You can't be suicidal and play "Dancing Queen" without feeling a lot better. You just think, "Ohhhhh, never mind war, never mind death ..." '

As the evening wore on, Peter couldn't resist a spell on the decks and wrested control so he could play the theme tune from *Minder*. 'It were brilliant,' he told me. 'Everyone got up for that. But the thing is, it's so short by the time they got to the dancefloor it was over. So I played it again.'

After Peter and Susan returned from their honeymoon in Mexico, they had to live for a short while with Peter's mother – 'My life is like a sit-com,' he told visitors. Finally at the end of the year his *Mork and Mindy* tapes, Tony Christie albums and lifetime collection of old *Radio Times* were ready for their new home – the shed at the bottom of the garden.

'Susan said, "What do you have to keep those old *Radio Times* for? They've got little insects in them," ' Peter revealed to me. 'But you never know when you're going to have an argument over what time of night *Tenko Reunion* was on.'

On <peterkay.co.uk> Peter tells his fans that he's just 'cutting out all the effing and jeffing that tends to creep up from time to time' and then filming will be ready to begin on the next series of *Phoenix Nights*. 'I hope everybody who's reading this is well and happy,' he writes. 'If not, here's a little joke for you ... I was in the car the other day and a man asked me for a lift. I said, "Sure, the world's your oyster, go for it buddy!" I promise you that the series will be a lot funnier.'

In October 2001 Peter returned to St Gregory's Social Club in Farnworth. As before, the series had been co-written with Dave Spikey and Neil Fitzmaurice, but on top of his writing and acting duties this time he would be directing as well.

It is often remarked upon, often by people who haven't worked with him, that Peter Kay is hard to work with. He got this reputation on the sets of *That Peter Kay Thing* and the first series of *Phoenix Nights*, where his obsession with getting things exactly how he imagined them tested the patience of the film crew. 'I have heard that he became a bit difficult on *Phoenix Nights*,' says Iain Coyle. 'But I think that's the price you pay for working with a creative genius.'

'I'd like to be able to tell you about storms and diva tantrums, but I've only ever found him a pleasure to work with,' *Phoenix Nights* commissioning editor Iain Morris told the *Observer* in March 2005. 'But it's always easier to count the number of highly successful comics who are universally loved by their contemporaries than those who are resented.'

'I suppose the crew must have found me a constant annoyance,' said Peter in a 2001 website interview. 'But if the end result is something that they'll be proud of, then it's worth the hassle. Comedy is a very serious business. Everything you believe in is worth fighting for.'

Peter was annoyed by the budget constraints that hampered some of the filming in the first series. For the scene of Keith Lard giving his talk at the Banana Grove just ten extras had been booked. Unhappy that this wouldn't make the scenes realistic enough, he paid for some club regulars to turn up early and fill the seats.

Allegedly, in the making of *Phoenix Nights* series one Peter saw less than eye to eye with the experienced director Jonny Campbell. Although he has never discussed it on record, there have been hints that the pair didn't get along. In the summer of 2002, when he appeared on Toby Foster's BBC Radio Sheffield show they reminisced about Foster's time as Les the drummer in Phoenix Club house band Les Alanos.

Peter: 'It were bloody easy for you lot ... I had more grief on the first series than the second because I didn't get on with the director.'

Toby: 'What were his name, Jonny something?'

Peter: 'Don't say it, don't go stirring up trouble.'

Toby: 'You didn't like him, did you? I don't think he'd ever been this far north. He turned up on the first day of shooting and said [adopts posh accent]: "I love what you've done with this place, it's such a pastiche." We said, "No, this is how it is." '

With Phil McIntyre in his corner, Peter persuaded Channel 4 to let him direct a second series on his own. For McIntyre it was all part of the plan he had for all his clients, from Victoria Wood to Craig Cash – that they should have as much control over their work as possible. This approach was music to Peter Kay's ears; he told Brian Viner in the *Independent*: 'If you're an artist you don't just do outlines, do you, you colour it in as well.'

'Normally when that kind of thing happens there's a bit of a panic,' says former Channel 4 commissioning editor Robert Popper. 'They're a big star, they want to direct; you don't want to let them down. But you think, "Can they do it? Will they be able to act and direct; will they have enough distance from their stuff?" The stakes are incredibly high. I imagine the feeling was, "We've got to let him do it." But he pulled it off.'

Fortunately Peter's attention to detail and work ethic extended to the whole team behind *Phoenix Nights* series two.

After the first series ended with the club burning down after the evil Den Perry had dropped a lit cigar in the toilet waste basket, a disillusioned Brian Potter eventually had a flash of inspiration after visiting a friend in Blackpool who had packed in Clubland and opened a multi-purpose leisure facility on the Golden Mile – including 'lifts to all floors'. 'Lots of clubs around Bolton had turned into Italian or Chinese restaurants,' says Peter. 'The idea of the second series was to get that in. Dave brought back this article from a newspaper about a club in Blackpool that had everything under one roof – a solarium, bar, soft play centre for the kids – and so it all came from there, except with it being the Phoenix Club they'd be doing it with no money.'

After persuading the old team back to the burnt-down club – giving them a rousing 'If we build it they will come' speech to the soundtrack of the *Van Der Valk* theme tune – the stage is set for the second episode and one of the funniest scenes in British TV comedy history: 'The Phoenix Club Family Fun Day' with Jerry St Clair dressed as a giant red berry; Young Kenny with permanent tiger face – applied with a car paint spray; a portable toilet transformed into a children's play centre with a ball pond filled with a decades' worth of muddy footballs that had been kicked into Potter's back garden; and an obscene bouncy castle. As an example of the often bizarre pressures of being writer, actor and director, Peter Kay told me the full inside story of his penis. Well, not *his* penis.

'Ah, the 20-foot inflatable cock,' says Peter. 'The guy who made it, he were from Bury; all these other inflatable manufacturers had put the phone down on me. When he brought it to show it to us he was so proud of it, he says, "I'm in entertainment myself, you know", cos he makes bouncy castles. I first thought of it in about 1994. I just had this idea of this huge inflatable penis on the back of a lorry going down a back street and someone pegging their washing out and seeing it across the tops of the back walls.'

In the episode the inflatable is supplied by Eric, the man responsible for the Phoenix Club's regular deliveries of fruit machines that pay out in Deutschmarks and three-legged pool tables. Eric explains that he got it from a festival in Amsterdam, but Potter isn't impressed. 'There's kiddies around,' he says. 'They can't go jumping up and down on a ... love length.' When Eric persuades him it can be disguised as Sammy the Snake, he acquiesces, but disaster strikes when a couple of mischievous kids interfere with it and it begins expanding to gigantic proportions.

'Originally at this point we wanted the cock to fly off and float into the sky but we couldn't get it to work,' says Peter.

'It's really funny because you think of these things but three or four months later you're there with it. What happens is people get numbed to what you're doing. First of all everyone sees it and they all laugh, then the novelty wears off and you suddenly find you're in the rain, in December, at ten o'clock at night, freezing cold, with a 20-foot inflatable cock that's too big to go on the back of a lorry and you've not quite measured it right and everyone's getting really angry and the producer's shouting because the guy who's working the lighting generator has got to go at ten and he's screaming and he's shouting at someone else "Can we get a move on, can we get a move on" and I just had to stop to shout, "Stop, stop, look at what we're doing. It's a 20-foot cock we're all so serious about. Can you not realise what you're doing?" '

There's more!

'I wanted it to have pubic hair, and for Brian to disguise it with weeds, but Channel 4 wouldn't allow it,' he says. 'After giving up on the floating idea, we tried to see what it would look like with the cock exploding, so we had this guy trying to use all these different methods to blow this cock up, like. And we had some of the props people, who are quite prim and proper, ringing up and going [adopts posh woman's voice], "What's the situation with the cock?" and the assistant director going, "Well, the cock's arriving at two o clock", and you'd think, "Ha, you're talking about a cock, ha, ha." Some people are really prudish and it's like "the penis" ... anyway the guy who blows things up he always turns up with guns and explosives and pyrotechnics, he's a really funny guy – deaf as a post, mind. He was experimenting with all these different ways of filming it exploding for weeks and he'd come and see us with camcorder footage of him in his backyard exploding balloons. In the end we must have spent six thousand pounds just trying to blow it up.'

'Not since Austin Healey made his first clanking appearance in the Advanced Hair Studio's adverts on "Men and Motors" have I laughed so incontinently at the TV,' wrote Ally Ross in the *News of the World*. TV gold.

With the second series, *Phoenix Nights* became more and more Peter Kay's baby and less and less Dave and Neil's. Elements of his stand-up set started creeping in, too – at Le Grand Marche hypermarket in France (which was really Costco in Salford), Max and Paddy study a packet of Les Cadbury's Fingers, and Potter and co. take part in a *Crimewatch*-style reconstruction. Brian Potter even references Peter Kay's most famous catchphrase of all when he tells his doubtful troops the new reborn club will sell food.

'But not just any food, Jerry, proper food. Scampi, chicken Kievs, garlic bread.'

'Garlic bread?' asks Max.

'Garlic bread, that's right, Max, garlic bread. It's the future, I've tasted it.'

With *Phoenix Nights* painting a picture of clubland on the bones of its arse, the series had a very marked effect on reality. Encouraged by the show, takings went up in Bolton social clubs, who staged special *Phoenix Nights*-inspired cabaret evenings. There are some viewers who looked at *Phoenix Nights* and missed the comedy but loved the variety acts. Indeed, it was mooted at one point that Peter should take Talent Trek on the road to theatres across Britain. At the Farnworth club, which had been the set for the show, they suddenly found themselves opening their doors to a younger local clientele. Attempting to make the most of the club's fame, St Greg's manager Paul Barnwell dubbed his social club the Real Phoenix and started holding Sunday cabaret evenings, and with real life imitating art found himself playing host to various members of the cast who'd visit the club and meet fans.

'They are all really good people, I haven't got a bad word to say about any one of them,' he says, showing me a picture of him with his arm around Brian Potter. As a consequence of *Phoenix Nights* Barnwell has also found the club taking bookings for wedding receptions and stag dos. 'We had one bloke who had a party here and he hired a bucking bronco,' says Paul, who for a while found himself dubbed the Real Brian Potter. But visit St Gregory's on a wet Tuesday evening and it's an entirely different story. The handful of members in this formica-clad wonderland are closer in years to the Captain, who worked the door in the first couple of shows, shortly before dying in the middle of bingo, than to Young Kenny. Paul, though, is happy to show you the sights including the toilets where Den Perry dropped his cigar and the changing room to the side of the stage where Jerry popped his herbal tablets. The bar staff are lovely, the beer cheap and the pool tables empty.

'You should come on Sunday; it'll be buzzing then,' says the barwoman. 'We've got a Freddie Mercury look-alike on; he's very good.'

If people can go to Notting Hill to see a door or all the way to Scotland to see the set of *Balamory*, then why not this flat-roofed palace down a Bolton side street? Until the coach parties turn up Paul is waiting to hear if there is going to be a third series of *Phoenix Nights*. 'We'll be the last to know,' he grumbles.

'Two more lamb bhunas.'

Peter Kay, John Smith's advert

In April 2002 Peter made the switch to the big screen in *24 Hour Party People*, the tale of maverick Factory Records label boss Anthony Wilson, who split his time between discovering legendary Manchester bands such as Joy Division and presenting *The Wheel of Fortune* on Granada TV. Steve Coogan played Wilson – kind of Alan Partridge filtered through Brian Clough – while Peter played the small yet significant part of Don Tonay, the sideburned owner of the Russell Club, the venue of Factory-endorsed rock gigs in the early 1980s. Peter wasn't on screen for long, but they included his first ever sex scene, with a prostitute in the back of a van (what would his mum think?). He also managed to incorporate a few Potterisms into the dialogue.

'What sort of music is it?'

'Rock mainly, indie.'

'Indian?'

Garlic? Bread?

Peter and Steve Coogan had worked together once before, in a Comic Relief 2001 sketch. In it Coogan, as Alan Partridge, reluctantly travels to the north, or as he patronisingly puts it 't'North', to visit a boxing gym staging a 24-hour sparring session for Comic Relief, but ends up enraging the owner, Tony Maloney (played by Peter), by impersonating his accent.

Alan: ''Ey up.'

Tony: 'We're not Yorkshire, it's Manchester, flower.'

Alan: 'Just having some fun with the accent for Comic Relief.'

Tony: 'Dickhead.'

The sketch ends with Partridge in the ring with one of Maloney's boxers, none other than one Paddy McGuinness.

'With Steve Coogan,' says Peter, 'I always see it that he's in fifth year and I'm in third year, and third years don't knock about with fifth years! There's no animosity, but you do kind of look up to people like Steve in comedy, and you do sort of aspire to be them. When you do actually start to talk, you do realise they're not that different at all, you're very similar and you do get on, and you're just very very similar. I find that a lot, it's a bit disconcerting.'

24 Hour Party People wasn't Peter's first appearance in a movie. In 1999 he played a stuttering convict in *Going Off Big Time*, a Scouse gangland movie that had been written by Neil Fitzmaurice, and he'd made a cameo appearance in *Blow Dry*, a northern drama set in Keighley about a hairdressing contest that features the worst Yorkshire accent – imagine a camp Geoffrey Boycott – in movie history, courtesy of Alan Rickman.

With movie appearances, sell-out stand-up shows and his own sit-com, Peter Kay was stretching his empire to such an extent that no one would have been surprised if he'd announced he also did a spot of modelling on the side for Versace. His multi-tasking increased in the spring of 2002, when he signed up to become the new face of John Smith's beer in a £20 million ad campaign. The £20 million wasn't Peter's fee, incidentally, that's the estimated total amount they would spend placing the ads on TV. According to Peter, all he got was a life-size replica of his predecessor (a cardboard cut-out called Dave) and a tour of the brewery. With the exception of Dave, the cut-out Peter was following a great tradition of comic ads by John Smith's that had begun in the late 1970s with a flat-capped Yorkshireman who allows his terrier to sup on his pint. The dog is so overcome with glee at the taste of the beer that he jumps and does a cartwheel. Then in the 1990s, master of deadpan Jack Dee helped them launch John Smith's Extra Smooth with the help of some penguins.

Peter's adverts for the Yorkshire bitter begin airing in a well-picked slot halfway through the 2002 Champions League Final on ITV. A group of footballers at the side of the pitch are practising their impressive ball-juggling skills and catching the ball on the backs of their necks. When it comes to Peter's turn to impress, he boots the ball out of the park, where it bounces on the roof of a faraway greenhouse. "Ave it,' says Peter, shoving aside a tray of orange quarters and picking up a can of John Smith's instead. Come the start of the football season in September across the country, whenever a defender hoofed the ball into the stands for a throw-in vast sections of the crowd could be heard shouting, ''Ave it.'

A teetotaller advertising beer is a bit odd, but the 'No Nonsense' slogan and the commercials, all of which have the Peter Kay stamp, are a perfect fit. Kay's character is mean and bluff, but he doesn't know it; he's just a regular bloke who can't be dealing with pussyfooting around being nice. The other ads in the campaign are equally funny – chucking his mum out of her room because he wants to put a snooker table in it; taking two free boxes of washing powder from Danny Baker then slamming the door; telling his daughter on the phone from the curry house, 'There's no such thing as wardrobe monsters. It's burglars that break in through the window that you want to be worried about.'

Just as had happened with Leonard Rossiter's adverts for Cinzano with Joan Collins in the 1970s, and the Melanie Sykes-fronted spoofs for Boddington's in the 1990s, people talked about Peter's John Smith's ads more than the actual TV programmes between which they appeared. The campaign won awards and plaudits, but it was a genuine cultural phenomenon – sales of lamb bhuna increased, Engelbert Humperdinck made a comeback, and two divers who had won Golds at the Commonwealth Games said they'd 'like to give special thanks to Peter Kay for his top bombing'. Now in the Internet era people were emailing the ads to each other, especially when a 'banned' version of the curry scene appeared. In it Peter, while discussing how kids grow up faster these days, tells his wife that their four-year-old daughter had asked him where babies come from.

'What did you tell her?' she asks, a worried look descending over her.

'I said when a daddy loves a mummy very much he inserts his erect penis inside a woman's vagina, he ejaculates sperm, which travels through the womb, fertilising the egg, and it develops into a baby over nine months.'

Naturally not everyone found the ads hysterical; seasoned pontificator Peter York wrote in the *Independent on Sunday* that the only reason Peter Kay was chosen for the campaign was that the upper-middle-class media loveys behind it all 'love on-screen northerners because they think they're more real than themselves'. Ricky Gervais, from *The Office*, claimed he'd been offered a six-figure sum to do the ads before they asked Peter. Gervais went on to claim he'd been offered higher amounts from other advertisers, but had turned them down. 'I just don't think I should yet,' he said. 'If they ask now, they'll ask in a few years.'

Once decoded as the subtle oneupmanship of major comedy stars, the implication of Gervais's comments is: I don't need their money; you do.

Peter Kay has never been altruistic. In the early days he couldn't afford to be. As the breadwinner in the household after his dad had left, he juggled jobs as well as comedy gigs to pay his way at home with his mum (once when he was asked why he first went into comedy he joked 'crippling debt'). Then, when he started making money, it was always with the fear at the back of his mind that it would all end tomorrow, and he'd be back on the bins. Once he got the chance to earn larger sums of money he treated it with humour. In the *Live at the Top of the Tower* video there's a sketch before his stand-up set where he goes to talk to Paddy McGuinness, who is manning a makeshift merchandise stall in the foyer. The official stock looks as if it's been assembled by a three-year-old with a sticker-making set, and features Peter Kay mugs and a Peter Kay kettle that look as if they have been stolen from the Blackpool Tower staff room.

Just like his John Smith's character, when it comes to money Peter Kay doesn't mince his words: he wants it off you and more often than not he'll tell you why. He wants a car, a holiday, his own home, or he wants to pay for sister Julie's house to be rewired. Not only is it honest, it also turns the guilty situation of raking it in into a joke. It came as no surprise, then, that when the details of Peter's 2002 tour were announced it was called the 'Mum Wants a Bungalow' tour.

'Why?'

'Because she does.'

Chapter Nine
How Dare You

'Ten years ago a crack commando unit was sent to prison by a military court for a crime they did not commit. These men promptly escaped from a maximum-security stockade to the Los Angeles underground. Today, still wanted by the government, they survive as soldiers of fortune. If you have a problem and no one else can help, and if you can find them, maybe you can hire ... the A Team.'

The A Team, opening titles

'Here, as I watch the ships go by
I'm rooted to my shore'

The Kids from Fame, 'Starmaker'

On 30 August 2002, just as his 2002 'Mum Wants a Bungalow' tour was due to begin, the official website that had been started by a couple of his friends back in 1997 was taken offline. There was a message from Chris, the webmaster, telling fans that his services were no longer required; instead, a 'more official' site would shortly be taking its place. As Peter Kay's fame had grown, so had the amount of effort needed to run the website, and when Chris suggested they put ads on the site to fund their time Peter – who owned the domain name – decided to put it in the hands of his manager Phil McIntyre instead. Weeks later, in a scorched-earth policy, the personal messages from Peter had gone, the rants and jokes vanished, the episode guides were no more. In their place were pages and pages of merchandise – Garlic Bread T-shirts, mouse mats, calendars and mugs – but sadly no Peter Kay kettle.

Peter Kay plc was open for business. 'Maximising your brand potential' is what celebrities do in the twenty-first century. The canny stars realise that, putting art to one side, they are a commodity just like anything else. Blame 'Thatcher's Britain', as Peter's bearded doorman Max might say. Peter Kay was one of the first comedy acts to realise he was a brand and by 2003 Peter Kay calendars would be outselling Manchester United, Kylie and David Beckham at HMV stores across the country, and if they'd sold out, a visit to the website was always possible. Peter's way of coping with this mass burst of shameless consumerism was to treat it with the same disdain Les Dawson reserved for *Blankety Blank* chequebooks and pens – on some tour dates Paddy McGuinness would come out just before the interval and demonstrate some of the 'tat' (his word) available in the foyer. The tour was called 'Mum Wants a Bungalow', after all, so the more T-shirts and signed photos they sold the closer Peter was to his target of buying his mother's new home. Peter treated it like a one-man *Magpie* appeal for his mother, but the merchandising was no different from how rock bands operated (as a former tour manager, Phil McIntyre knew all about that), he was just being more up-front and honest about it – yet another illustration of Peter's no-nonsense attitude to business. Although, subsequently, Archie Kelly's request that Peter call his next tour 'The Cast of *Phoenix Nights* Want Bungalows Too' fell on deaf ears. They'd had enough money out of him.

While the tour blatantly seemed to be about making money, Kay was also openly concerned about not spending any. Appearing on Toby Foster's radio show on the eve of his Sheffield show, he asked the listeners if there was anyone who could lend him a Peugeot 208 because he was driving down to London and wanted to go in a nice car – recalling Brian Potter, from the first episode of *That Peter Kay Thing*, whose first thought when the Aquarius Club is sinking is to swim to the safe to collect the night's takings. One imagines him in a crisis situation saying, 'The theatre's burning down, you say? Quick, get the money from the T-shirt stall!'

The merchandising website has led many a commentator to whisper that Peter Kay is greedy, but it's not that. He's making a living; if people want to spend money on t'Internet mouse mats, let them. As stand-up comic and Kay fan Janey Godley says: 'Profit's not a dirty word! I wouldn't mind a bit more profit! What do these people think? Stand-up comedy's not a charity.'

'I'm not really surprised by his merchandising,' says Peter's old schoolfriend Michael Atherton. 'He always looks like he can't believe his luck, that somehow it isn't all real. And if his star does fade in the coming years, you can't blame a guy for grabbing what he can while it's there. It's not like he had much to start with.'

With his Internet site transformed overnight into a cyberworld-version car-boot sale, Peter began the 'Mum Wants a Bungalow' tour in earnest. Such was the snowballing success of these live shows that he could still be touring today if he had the energy and by the end he could have retitled it 'Mum Wants a Bungalow in Every Street in Bolton'. But he didn't know this when he started, playing warm-up dates at the Birmingham Glee Club, standing on a crate in front of 125 people; Leicester Arts Centre and Bury, Darlington, Maidenhead and Tynemouth followed.

He possibly didn't realise it at the time, but this was farewell to the world of fag smoke and dodgy Cher lookalikes. Instead, he was entering a new world of theatres and arenas. It was a case of goodbye Benson and Hedges, hello Maltesers and Skittles.

In Tynemouth there was almost tragedy when he ran across the stage mimicking a kid sliding across the floor on his knees at a wedding, and fell into the orchestra pit.

The warm-up dates gave him the chance to try out new material. A section he dubbed 'Surgery's open' was a chance for the audience to ask him questions, out of which popped stories (like going swimming as a kid and forgetting which locker was his in the changing room) he'd long forgotten. Jokes also came out of his attempts to ask people directions to the venues he was playing at – 'What is it about when people start giving you directions that you stop listening? They might as well be speaking Swahili.' And recalling taking his nan to see *Stuart Little* at the cinema – 'I told her it was a true story.'

In the Maidenhead show he got tongue-tied halfway through a joke about *Crimewatch* re-creations and mistakenly put one of his invented victims inside a burgled shop as the manager was opening up in the morning – 'What's Jean doing there?' he laughed. 'I'll have to change that.' In fact, because the mistake got a bigger laugh, he kept the error in, each night pretending he'd just made it.

Some may see this as a lie or a trick, but to others it is a mark of Peter Kay's genius; his ear for his own shortcomings is as finely tuned as it is to others'.

'I suppose that's the art of it,' he says, attempting not to sound too pretentious. 'Making people think you're making it up as you go along and you've just thought of these things. When in fact you've been polishing and polishing it every night.'

Thanks in no small measure to his website's promotion the first 50-plus dates of the original tour all sold out. Such was the demand that when he spied a pair of empty seats at the Hammersmith Apollo he said, 'What a waste, we could have had £600 between us on ebay for these!'

*

The 'Mum Wants a Bungalow' tour was not only his longest tour – previously his biggest was playing ten consecutive dates in 1999 just before his dad died – but also his first time on the road since *Phoenix Nights*. Not only did this give him a few new lines to throw back at hecklers – 'I'm not in a wheelchair now, son' – but also a chance to gauge the incredible popularity of the show. In Rhyl, Wales, he was delighted to see three blokes with tiger facepaint à la Young Kenny from the family fun day, and such is his godlike status in Bolton that coach parties from the town travelled as far as Edinburgh to see him.

The demand for tickets left him awestruck. On the eve of the first proper show at the Buxton Opera House on Monday, 16 September he told the *Bolton Evening News*, 'At the moment it's sold 101,000 tickets out of 111,000 and that's without any posters being printed. It's been absolutely incredible.'

It was about to get even more incredible, and as more and more dates were added to the end of the tour, which by now was stretching into the summer of 2003, he would end up playing to a staggering 380,000 people in a 180-date marathon that would eat up 11 months of his life. It was the biggest comedy tour this country had ever seen and rough estimates put the gross figure of total ticket sales at £5 million. At Bolton house prices, this was enough to buy his mother the entire suburb and turn it into a golf course, with a bit left over to buy her a Sodastream.

Despite this popularity, some critics still didn't seem to get it. Reviewing his London Palace Theatre show in the *Guardian*, journalist Brian Logan wrote, 'He is a confident and companionable stand-up, but his particular skills – a killer eye for character, and for tone of voice – seem more suited to the deadpan comedies with which, on telly, he's so swiftly made his name.' Sarah Barrell, reviewing his Edinburgh Assembly Rooms date, called him a 'cosy performer' and concluded 'Royal Variety Show, here he comes' – ignoring the fact that he'd already played the Royal Variety show four years previously.

Most of the remaining 379,998 members of the audience disagreed with these assessments and left theatres happier than when they'd entered them a few hours earlier – which is the point of going out, after all, something many critics seem to forget – stopping on the way out to buy an apron emblazoned with the legend 'Garlic Bread?' Ker-ching!

As with his rival comedians, who bemoaned the similarities between their act and his, newspaper critics have always tended to label Peter Kay as 'hackneyed' and unoriginal. The truth is that, as long as something is funny, these things don't enter an audience's head; it's about entertainment. And for Peter Kay any criticism is drowned out by ringing tills. One is reminded of Brian Potter heckling an alternative comedian and the Phoenix Club's ill-fated Funny Farm evening – 'Tell us a joke we know.' On the 'Mum Wants a Bungalow' tour he only has to mention the words 'garlic bread' and the crowd roars its approval.

The 'Mum Wants a Bungalow' tour was so popular that even famous people couldn't get in. At the Manchester Lowry Theatre the requests of several Manchester United players for free tickets were turned down. The typically forthright response from the Kay camp – 'They can buy their own.' Although this snippet has the ring of an invented newspaper story, the public voiced its approval.

In Halifax, midway through the tour, Peter's old friend from his garage days, now a writer for Manchester's *City Life* magazine, Marc Rowlands, caught up with him. Kay was frazzled – 'I haven't seen *Emmerdale* for months' – but as friendly as ever.

'Do you get bored by people coming out with "garlic bread"?' asks Rowlands.

'Well, you can't moan about catchphrases, because it's your own fault,' replies Peter. 'It's flattery really, until they won't shut up. But then we've got a couple of lads that drag 'em out by their hair.'

In his *City Life* article, Rowlands nailed Peter Kay's appeal better than any other journalist when he wrote that the genius of Peter Kay is that he 'exposes the ridiculous things we don't see in everyday life because we've become accustomed to living with them'.

'He highlights the traits in his own family that we thought were so individual as to be exclusive to our own,' added Rowlands. 'It's almost like he's grown up in your house, drinking the same drinks, shopping at the same places, reminding us of the ludicrous '70s TV programmes we'd forgotten that we used to watch together. People think they know him, because they believe that when he's talking, he's talking just to them.'

At times on the 'Mum Wants a Bungalow' tour, as you looked around at an audience equally split between young and old, it was tempting to surmise that Peter Kay is not 'Marmite' comedy – you either like it or you don't – it's 'Gravy' comedy that you either like more or less than everybody else. Prior to 'Mum Wants a Bungalow' people made the assumption that because his comedy was about working-class life, only working-class people would find it amusing – this too was debunked. Unless you're some son of a rock star or a member of the royal family, it all rings true. Maybe even Princes Harry and William got to bring Connect 4 into school on the last day of term, who knows?

The tour was supposed to end in Bolton at the Albert Halls on 3 April but such was the rolling nature of the bookings that an extra date at the vast 18,000 MEN Arena in

Manchester – where Peter once showed people to their seats and confiscated bottles of Bacardi – was added. Rather than a glorious homecoming, the Bolton gig – his first in the town since he played a benefit show at the Octagon Theatre in 1999 – ended on a sour note when his dressing room was burgled and his video camera and mobile phone stolen. If it had happened anywhere it would have been upsetting, but in Bolton?

'I am furious that someone could stoop so low,' he told the *Sun*. 'I feel like I bend over backwards to do my town proud. I love Bolton and was looking forward to playing here. Then this happens.'

He still stormed it, and with his mum, nana, Susan, *Coronation Street* stars, Bolton Wanderers footballers and loads of old schoolfriends in the audience, he recorded one of the shows for a future DVD.

The MEN Arena show, which was on his 30th birthday – 2 July – was also (rightly) captured for prosperity. Apart from Baddiel and Newman, who played a one-off show at Wembley Arena, at the height of their *Mary Whitehouse Experience* success in the 1990s (which unlike Peter's show was only half-full), it was the biggest stand-up comedy show ever in the UK. Even the enormous size of the venue seemed to have little effect on Kay's ability to connect with his audience. It was little short of astounding.

And then he went home, watched *Emmerdale Omnibus* and fell asleep for six years.

Well, not quite: the next day he was at Bolton Hospice on New Chorley Road, where he is a vice-president, telling the elderly residents that for the next few months his only plans were to grow a beard.

Not that he became a hermit. Next, he announced that Susan (who was still working in Boots in Bolton town centre) was pregnant with their first child, helped choose his mother's bungalow in Ladybridge, helped his nan emulsion her front room and even went to a football match.

Whether the newspaper story about the Manchester United players being turned down for guest-list tickets for the Lowry show is true or not, Gary Neville and co. appeared to have forgiven him. At half-time during a match between United and Fulham in October 2003, he told the 67,727 Old Trafford crowd a few jokes and looked on as a Norwegian teenager showed off his ball-juggling skills. 'Twenty-six, twenty-seven,' he counted before delighting everyone with his trademark ''Ave it!' as the kid booted the ball into the stands. 'Brian Potter can do that,' he told them as he left the pitch.

There was also validation from Michael Parkinson, for whom he once worked as a warm-up man, who called him 'Britain's best-loved young comedian'. In return Peter told him that his nan was a fan of Parkinson's. 'You know that compilation CD you've got out?' he said to Parky. 'The other day my nan says, "Ooh, he's got a copulation out." '

Nana Kay, it seems, is as prolific with the malapropism as Brian Potter. Peter told Parkinson about her criticising her grandson's handling of his car, saying, 'Your driving's a bit erotic.'

Just before Christmas 2003, Channel 4 released a DVD (or as Peter's nan put it 'a VD') of *That Peter Kay Thing*. It had been released before on video but the popular new DVD format meant that he could add out-takes, deleted scenes and an audio commentary. In the first week alone it sold a staggering 145,000 copies, dislodging the *Star Wars* trilogy and Disney's *Aladdin* off the top of the charts. A year previously, the first series of *Phoenix Nights* had sold similarly quickly, competing to top the million sales of *The Office* over Christmas. The DVD boom means that programmes can enjoy an afterlife long after they've aired, and for many people – because of the bad original scheduling and because of his rise in popularity with *Phoenix Nights* – this was the first chance they'd had to meet Leonard and Mr Softy. 'For whatever reason, and I don't know why, some people just don't watch Channel 4,' says former commissioning editor Robert Popper.

Maybe the fourth button on British remote controls is always faulty, maybe people got put off the channel when Damon Grant used the word 'pissing' in *Brookside* all those years ago (everyone's pissing these days though); who knows but this strange phenomenon was to be Peter Kay's gain. In due course the astronomical sales of his TV shows would be matched by his *Live at the Bolton Albert Halls* DVD, whose total sales of 1.3 million are double those of the previous bestselling live DVD. But it was the success of *That Peter Kay Thing* that pleased him most. Even more so when the channel gave him a breakdown of the sales figures and he saw that it was selling much more in the south of England than in the north.

'Mind you,' he said during a fan question-and-answer session on the *Live at the Top of the Tower* DVD, 'they prob- ably get all their copies from car boot sales in the north.'

Despite his denials, it had been a fallacy concerning his career that only northerners got his humour. He even denied it during the 'Mum Wants a Bungalow' tour when he told Toby Foster on BBC Sheffield that 'people from the north live in London too, so it's OK'. But this stark evidence seemed conclusive. Although maybe there is something in Andrew Collins's argument that *Phoenix Nights* 'represents a kind of lost world to most people in the south'. Lancastrians have a chip on their shoulder about their southern neighbours – often for sound economic reasons (it's easier to close a factory in St Helens than in south London) but sometimes due to the south's perceived snobbery. As Sylvia Lovat Corbridge wrote in her book *It's an Old Lancashire Custom*: 'It is a

Lancashire custom to be on the defensive. We anticipate jokes about rain, "by gum" and Wigan; we expect people to peer at us through the thin layer of smoke they fancy they see around our heads.'

Which maybe explains why, when he reprised the role of Max the doorman a couple of years later, Kay wore a 'London is Shit' baseball cap.

At the end of 2002 Peter Kay stopped doing interviews with the press. He found them exhausting and he was fed up with their lies and the way they always made him try to slag off other shows. But most of all he was pissed off by the way they patronised him. Flicking through his clippings, it's not hard to see how he became so resentful. In the *Sunday Mirror* in January 2001 an interview with Peter begins 'It's just gone midday according to Peter Kay's watch, and his stomach agrees. "Ey oop, time for me dinner," he says. "I'm fair famished and if I don't get me dinner on t'dot I'll be good fer nothing, for t'rest of t'afternoon." '

'It's like the f***ing *Goodies* or something,' he told Toby Foster.

Worse, the *Daily Mail* once wrote, 'I know Channel 4 has to cater for minorities, but if it chooses to glorify Boltonians, subtitles might help the rest of us.'

'Once you become famous you become public property,' he told Foster. 'You can't go around moaning "I want a private life" ... go and be a plumber then, but in interviews they just want sleaze.'

As they do with many celebrities, the British tabloid press have a difficult relationship with Peter Kay. They know their readers love him, but they can't get to him. If Peter Kay can make it in showbusiness without ever leaving Bolton, he can continue to make it in showbusiness without the help of the tabloids. Like all celebrities he is sensitive about the things that are written about him – he can read a hundred great reviews but the one bad one will outweigh them all. In their frustration in recent times the tabloids have run stories like the one in the *Sun* about Peter's father. There were also pictures of Susan in the *People* still turning up for work at Boots in her 'white uniform jacket and sensible shoes' despite being married to the second richest man in British comedy (in 2005 the *Mail on Sunday* estimated his wealth to be £4.5 million).

His fame and wealth have attracted female celebrity admirers – Pamela Anderson tried to set up a dinner date with him in 2005, claiming she 'totally got his humour', and Gillian Porter confessed to a longstanding crush. He's unlikely to be impressed. As he told a woman who shouted out 'I love you' during the 'Mum Wants a Bungalow' tour, 'No you don't. Say I didn't do what I do, say I was just a bloke and I looked like this, would you love me then?'

In these celebrity-obsessed times it seems incredible to many that you can be so rich and so popular and refuse to play the fame game, but incredibly Peter and Susan appear to have achieved it. In reality it's pretty easy not to be hounded by the paparazzi – you just don't go to the Groucho Club or hang out with the 3 A.M. girls. If making it big is like winning the lottery, then the Kays haven't gone wild with their cash – they are more like the Lotto winners who say that it won't change them. This, among other reasons, is why Peter Kay demands more respect from the public than he does from people within the media. Even though he is not 'one of us', it feels like it.

In the records at Companies House, Susan is listed as a director of Peter's production company Goodnight Vienna, her profession listed as pharmacist. She worked in the store right up until the birth of their son Charlie Michael, who was born weighing 7lb 3oz at 9.01 p.m. on 12 January 2004. This project put all others on hold and, wanting to spend time with his wife and son, Peter decided to put back filming of the *Phoenix Nights* spin-off series he had written with Paddy McGuinness during the 'Mum Wants a Bungalow' tour. The decision to write a series based around the two doormen surprised some, but in series two of *Phoenix Nights* their bungled attempt at being hired killers (with a broom handle World War II Broomhandle Mauser no less) is the main story arc.

As Peter told me, 'There's something about Max that really fascinates me.' Although, here too he is annoyed by a slight continuity error. The first time we meet Max he is describing what sounds like a violent fight – ' ... quick scissor kick to the temple. Goodnight, my friend.' At this Paddy looks at his colleague and tells him, 'You see, that's why I don't go to parents' evenings, they get me angry.' Later storylines reveal that Max is a Dad.

For Paddy McGuinness the wait between *Phoenix Nights* and the new series was filled by his first rudimentary attempts at stand-up. Like a Bolton version of the Rat Pack, alongside other members of the *Phoenix Nights* team – Archie Kelly, Janice Connolly and Steve Edge – McGuinness toured venues in the north west of England on the honestly titled 'Jumping on the Bandwagon' tour. Typically, there was a suggestion in stand-up comedy land that Peter wasn't best happy with this development, but it turned out to be false and he even visited a couple of shows, joshing with his friend Paddy: 'You haven't got an act, have you? Well, I say that you have got an act, only it's mine.'

Before he disappeared into a world of Pampers and Farley's rusks, there was one piece of Peter Kay magic for us to enjoy, when on 10 January 2004 he made a welcome return to the troubled streets of Weatherfield. Peter and *Coronation Street* actress Sally Lindsay had been firm friends ever since she had been cast as Tracy Burns, the woman Ray Von was supposed to have murdered in the first series of *Phoenix Nights*. It was only a matter of time before she would manage to cajole him to appear in the ITV soap with her. Not that he needed much persuading.

'I've always been a huge fan of the *Street*. I think it's hard to live in the north west and not be,' he said. 'I've been brought up with it all my life and it still amazes me that everything stops when you hear that famous theme music at 7.30.'

He was a bit worried about continuity, having appeared in the soap seven years previously as a shopfitter – 'I'm still getting royalties from Chinese TV,' he'd tell friends: '£2.81.' The solution was a rather unflattering bowl-cut wig and some false teeth, so that he could transform himself into Eric the drayman – he couldn't have been less attractive if he were the secret love child of Albert Tatlock and Ena Sharples.

Corrie bosses first asked him to play a probation officer who would take off Les Battersby's security tag. Then he suggested the Shelly storyline because he thought she needed a date to cheer her up after her split from love rat Peter Barlow.

Despite looking like the last person in the world the Rovers Return landlady is ever likely to fancy, Eric persuades her to go out on a date with him. Their scenes together are some of the sweetest and most squirmishly embarrassing in *Coronation Street* history – from the moment he meets Shelly's mum, Bev, and says, 'You look too young to be her mother … oh, apart from your neck' to their awkward scenes in a posh *nouvelle cuisine* restaurant – 'You don't get much, do you?'

'I'm surprised he's not asked to do more acting,' says TV producer Iain Coyle. 'He was amazing in *Coronation Street*. I know people who work on it and the speed at which they turn that round is incredible. There's no two takes, they just do it.'

Better still – and almost turning *Corrie* into a *Phoenix Nights* special – was the fact that Janice Connolly (aka Holy

Mary) played Eric's mother and surprised him by being at home when he returned with Shelly. 'Oh,' says Eric, caving in with despondency, 'I thought you were at jazzercise.'

Peter watched at home with Susan and baby Charlie – he didn't want to watch it on tape, he wanted to see it as everybody else did, running in from the kitchen with a cup of coffee (milk and two sugars) when he hears the theme tune.

He's a hands-on dad, is Peter, changing nappies – 'I went right off that Frankie Dettori when I found out he didn't do nappies' – and getting up at 5.30 a.m. when Charlie cries, like every other new father. He enjoys the whole new set of life's little mysteries that being a parent opens up, such as 'Why does everyone cheer when a child burps?' But there was some evidence that he got bored being at home so much, when he made an impromptu visit to Michelle Mullane's 'Michelle Around Midnight' radio show on BBC GMR and told them that he'd recently phoned the station to enter a competition. 'I knew the answer, "Timewarp", so I came running out of the bath to find the phone,' he told Mullane. 'Susan said, "What are you doing?" I said, "Entering a competition." She says, "What's the prize?" and I said, "Two tickets to Comedy Store", and she said, "What do you want them for?" I said, "That's not the point, I know the answer." So I got through and they answered and I said, " 'Timewarp' ", and they said, "Who's this?" I said, "Peter Kay", and they put the phone down. I'd never got through to a phone-in before ... well, except *Going Live* when Five Star were on.'

Ah, so it *was* him!

'Sponging for a living
Checking out the women
Driving on the road to nowhere.'
       Max and Paddy's Road to Nowhere theme tune

Who needs the newspapers when you've got Jonathan Ross? On bonfire night 2004 Peter Kay starred in one of the most hilarious editions of *The Jonathan Ross Show* there has ever been or is ever likely to be. During the interview, mockingly referring to the chaos he had caused, he told Ross, 'It's TV gold, this.' But the thing is, it was true. First we were treated to the surreal sight of seeing him in the dressing room next to singer Gwen Stefani and her exotically dressed female Japanese bouncers – Peter called them 'the cast of *The Man with the Golden Gun*' – especially funny, as ex-James Bond actor Pierce Brosnan was there too. Then when he emerged from the green room, he went completely off script, turned away from the sofa he was walking towards and went to join Ross's house band Four Poofs and a Piano, with whom he performed a stirring rendition of 'Starmaker' from the *Kids from Fame* soundtrack. 'Come on Jonathan, let's play about with the format,' he said, ushering his highly reluctant and dazed host over to join him. Once they eventually sat down, after a couple of verses of '(Is This the Way to) Amarillo', Peter upset Ross's star guest by saying, 'Last week I thought she were a fella.' 'I think you look spectacular,' Ross covered. 'You would, you're having a mid-life crisis.' He also gave Jonathan a Parkin Loaf, purchased for 69p from Dutson's the Family Bakers on Bury Road, Bolton. 'Not that you'd go that far north,' he told him. 'You'd need a tetanus.'

'It was a masterful act of on-air hijacking,' wrote Alex Games in the *Independent on Sunday* a day later. 'It also showed someone utterly at home in a studio, knowing which camera to face, denouncing and deconstructing the system even as he posed and mugged for it. Another, more crafty by-product of all the high jinks was that he had to answer comparatively few questions about himself.' Peter did talk briefly about his 'Mum Wants a Bungalow' tour; about Charlie, who is named after his dad; and about his new series, *Max and Paddy's Road to Nowhere*, which he described as a spin-off 'like *George and Mildred* from *Man About The House*'. 'I'm only here for the clips; roll 'em,' he said, taking even Ross aback with his sheer cheek.

When the first episode of *Max and Paddy's Road to Nowhere* aired the following Friday, it was not seen as an unqualified success by the press, and was generally deemed as a step down from the high quality of *Phoenix Nights*. Damningly, Jim Shelley in the *Mirror* wrote: 'Aptly-titled *Road to Nowhere*, it's like watching Channel Five trying to do its own imitation of *Phoenix Nights*.'

Garry Bushell at the *People* was more enthusiastic. 'The humour is cartoony – Joe breaks a leg but doesn't seem to mind. The sight gags are terrific – like the laugh-out-loud *Dirty Dancing* spoof as Paddy teaches Max to strut his stuff, to the horror of a passing family. Neat lines and new slang abound. I liked Cherry Bakewells for boobs.' But even he had his doubts and wondered: 'Are Max and Paddy strong enough to carry the show alone?'

The answer is most definitely yes – although more than one knockabout series seems unlikely. *Max and Paddy's Road to Nowhere* turned out to be a grower, with each episode funnier and better than the last – this was reflected in the ratings for the show, which began at 3.6 million, slid to 2.6 million, then climbed back up beyond 3 million again. Episode 5, where our heroes had to share their motorised home with a flatulent pig, was the funniest TV moment of the year by far – unless you counted Peter Andre 'making up' a song he'd already released in *I'm a Celebrity Get Me Out of Here*.

Meanwhile, back in Bolton, sales of Parkin Loaf at Dutson's on Bury Road went through the roof. 'We see him in here about once a week and he never plays the big star,' said Helen Dutson about their celebrity customer. 'He just orders a corned beef salad and mayonnaise bap and has a pie while he's waiting.' Yes, that's a pie while he's waiting.

Max and Paddy's Road to Nowhere picked up where *Phoenix Nights* left off, with club doormen Max and Paddy driving off into the sunset to live a new life travelling the British Isles in a motorised home. The show gave the illusion that our friends were travelling around England, but as ever most of the locations allowed Peter to be able to drive home for his tea. Much of the humour came from their discomfort at having to live with each other in such close quarters, as for example when Paddy questions Max's hygienic standards. Max: 'How dare you. How dare you. I have a good stand-up wash in that sink once a week.' Paddy: 'Once a week! Stray dogs wash more than that. And what's wrong with deodorant? It's not the work of the devil, Max, give it a whirl some time.'

The jokes were more ribald than before and the best ones came from their opposite personalities – Paddy a bit of a stud, Max a bit of a loser, Paddy an unreconstructed lad, Max struggling to be a politically correct new man. The journey was, as much as anything, a voyage of sexual discovery for Max with Paddy as his Mr Miyagi, motivating him into living *la vida loca*.

'Women love a man in a uniform,' Paddy tells his friend.

'Do they?' questions Max. 'Let's go out dressed as a couple of Nazis and see how far we get.'

There was a surprise, though: Max is actually a father. This revelation is received with incredulity by Paddy – 'You've had sex?' The mother? A girl who was 'a kind of midget'. 'Isn't that a song by Queen?' asks Paddy.

'I didn't like that storyline so much,' says sit-com writer Graham Linehan. 'I thought it was a bit too much having your cake and eating it, telling all those short jokes. But it did show another side to Peter Kay, that he wants to pull at people's heart strings.'

Peter also gave us a new catchphrase – 'How dare you'; we learned about two gents who 'operate outside the law' called Magnet and Steel (Max's idea for a TV cop show) and found out that Max's full name is Maxwell Bygraves. Best of all, there was a flashback to Bolton in the mid-1980s with Max working as a bouncer at the Aquarius Club – before the flood – and we got to see Brian Potter running, a marvellous sight.

Cross-referencing *Phoenix Nights* aside, the jokes were a bit more spelled out and obvious than Peter's previous work – in the ignoble history of spin-off shows it was closer to Ronnie Barker's *Going Straight* than Kelsey Grammer's *Frasier* – and Potter notwithstanding, there is none of the multi-character roles we'd previously enjoyed. Still, it was all good fun and Max and Paddy were a charming couple of oafs anyone would enjoy sharing a pint with.

Never one to miss out on an opportunity to sing ('Write the theme tune, sing the theme tune,' as *Little Britain*'s miniature Dennis Waterman might have it), there were also a couple of chances for Peter to belt out a 1980s standard. At the 40th birthday party of his old schoolmate, the Wolfster, he finds himself singing Elton John's 'I Guess That's Why They Call It the Blues' accompanied by Paddy on the jazz harp. It was actually pretty good. Playing keyboards in the backing band, dressed as George Michael from Wham!, was Toni Baker, who continued to write the music for all of Peter's shows. He wasn't the only one to have followed our friends from the Phoenix Club. In Episode 4, when Max and Paddy find themselves in prison, Brian Potter wheels himself to their rescue with his Free the Phoenix Two campaign. Later we see a news report of a benefit show live from Bolton, with Marc Park singing a cover of Take That's 'Back for Good' – 'Whatever they said, whatever they did, they didn't mean it …' Holy Mary, Kenny Snr and Young Kenny also appear in the episode, but pointedly not Jerry St

Clair – even though at the end we see a banner draped over the club wall reading 'Happy Sixtieth Birthday Jerry'.

The joke didn't go unnoticed by Dave Spikey, still in his early fifties, who called it 'a bit cheeky'. In an interview on <www.chortle.co.uk>, when asked what he thought of Max and Paddy he replied: 'Not my cup of tea, I'm afraid. Hate to say it, but pretty obvious, blatant, unsophisticated comedy for me. But, hey, what do I know?'

The fall-out had been rumbling for quite some time; as far back as the 1999 British Comedy Awards Spikey had been miffed that he hadn't joined Peter onstage and he felt he hadn't got the credit his contribution deserved. In the following years he told interviewers: 'That's all blown over now. We're friends, we text each other a lot these days. It's cheaper.' Any chance of a reconciliation seemed completely blown by 2004, however, when he wrote on his website on 10 April: 'Talking of writing, I was watching the British Book Awards on TV yesterday and was shocked and stunned when *Phoenix Nights* by Peter Kay was nominated in the category of "Best TV-related books of the year". I can only presume that they took all the bits that Neil and I wrote out, but then that begs the question as to why it's still such a thick book.'

A very strange sort of rivalry seems to have developed between Dave Spikey and Peter Kay since *Phoenix Nights* and while it may well be coincidence it does seem rather odd that the man previously known as 'The Saint' is a patron of Chorley FM (the real community radio station that just happens to share a name with the not-real radio station where the listener comes first) and is the new host of *Bullseye* – a game show Peter Kay did much to bring back to public awareness during the 'Mum Wants a Bungalow' tour. Or maybe we're imagining things.

For his part, Neil Fitzmaurice has kept his own counsel, although he too has not been invited back into the Peter Kay fold and recently said that reports of a third *Phoenix Nights* series were 'just paper talk'. Furthermore, it doesn't seem to have escaped Peter's attention that Neil Fitzmaurice recently appeared in a sit-com called *Eyes Down* set in a northern bingo hall co-starring Beatrice Kelley, not to be confused with the *That Peter Kay Thing* episode also called 'Eyes Down' and also set in a northern bingo hall that also co-starred Beatrice Kelley. Peter mentions it on the DVD commentary of the second series of *Phoenix Nights* – a recording both Spikey and Fitzmaurice don't appear to have been invited to. However, Fitzmaurice is not given the treatment afforded Daniel Kitson in the commentary: every time he appears on screen, playing Spencer the mumbling barman, Peter gives him a two-word sobriquet: 'the bastard'.

The reason? Comments Daniel Kitson made to Plymouth's *Evening Herald* in February 2003, while he was on a nation-wide tour. When asked about *Phoenix Nights*, Kitson said that he wasn't happy with his work on the show. 'I didn't like *Phoenix Nights*. 'I didn't think it was absolute rubbish, but I didn't think it was the work of genius that some people lauded it as. I thought it was racist and lazy. I won't do something like that again.'

Sadly, he wasn't asked to justify his racist barb – requests to discuss it for this book were not replied to – but it can only have been intended as a comment on Ant and Dec, the Chinese asylum seekers who end up working in the Phoenix Club kitchens. 'It didn't seem to bother him at the time,' says Peter. 'The bastard.'

The rift between the pair – while comical – is such that when Channel 4 screened some *Phoenix Nights* out-takes as part of a special 'Peter Kay Night' in April 2006, Kitson's face was pixellated out in some scenes, *à la Crimewatch*. One senses that if he could erase him from *Phoenix Nights* completely, he would. He has been loyal to the same band of comics for years and helped them all, but at the same time the thought of someone profiting from him while also betraying him sends him spinning into a rage.

Like Daniel 'The Bastard' Kitson, who won the 2002 Perrier Award at Edinburgh, Dave Spikey and Neil Fitzmaurice have done well since appearing in *Phoenix Nights*. Dave Spikey finally got to make his sit-com set in a regional newspaper office (not the *Bolton Independent Leader*), *Dead Man Weds*, which was very funny but badly scheduled opposite *Desperate Housewives*, and has shone in the quiz show *8 Out of 10 Cats*. Neil Fitzmaurice managed to appear in the other great sit-com of our generation, *The Office*, as well as enjoying starring roles in T*he Bill, Holby City, Peep Show* and *Doctors*. But then everyone seems to have benefited from the afterglow of the Phoenix Club – Ted Robbins (Den Perry), Toby Foster (Les) and Justin Moorhouse (Young Kenny) all host popular regional radio shows. Archie Kelly (Kenny Snr) played Waggy, the second-hand car salesman in *Shameless* who touches up Veronica's breasts, and Steve Edge was the assistant boss in *Mike Bassett: England Manager* and ran naked across Brentford FC's pitch in an advert for the ITV Sports Channel. While some of the diminutive Bolton Wanderers fans ('How far away are they?') who caused Max and Paddy so much bother in Episode 5 could be seen in *Snow White* at the Civic Theatre in Darlington.

And Paddy McGuinness? Well, Paddy McGuinness is the new Peter Kay.

In 2006, mirroring Peter's 2002/03 'Mum Wants a Bungalow' dates, Paddy is playing to a seemingly endless number of full houses across Britain. Not wishing to appear as if he is riding the coat tails of his friend's success, he tells audiences that he's a very different proposition. 'Peter tells you about the wedding night, I tell you about the honeymoon.' Wink, wink.

Appropriately, his tour is called 'The Dark Side', and as he tells audiences a sequence of jokes about wanking, visiting an STD clinic and his lovemaking prowess (not necessarily in that order) it's not hard to see why. He does, however, reprise his act as Lord Love Rocket from the ladies' night in *Phoenix Nights* for the encore and even cajoles everyone into a sing-along of the *Minder* theme tune. It's funny, but if Peter Kay is Arthur Daley to Paddy's young Terry, then he's sorely missed. Wanna buy a mouse mat? There's loads in the warehouse.

Chapter Ten
Weeping Like a Willow

'I don't want to achieve immortality through my work. I want to achieve it through not dying.'

Woody Allen

'It's a funny thing this celebrity. If you don't wave back you're a miserable bugger, if you do wave back you're a big-headed bugger. I don't know.'

Fred Dibnah

It is often said in football that the sign of a successful team is that they keep winning even when they play badly. The celebrity equivalent of this is when you get more and more famous despite not actually doing anything. This was certainly the case with Peter Kay in 2005: despite the fact that he wasn't writing or appearing in his own TV series or live tour for the first time since 1998, his Celebdaq stock rose far and away beyond that of any other British comedian. He most definitely has become the 'megastar' stand-up comic Adam Bloom predicted he'd become all those Edinburgh Festivals ago.

Peter's rising fame was partially due to the John Smith's adverts, which had made him an omnipresent face on TV. But it was also thanks, in no small measure, to a song that had been following him around since he was seven years old, one his mum and dad would play over and over again on the living-room stereo.

The year began with what could have been seen as a Prince Philip-style gaffe when he was quoted as saying, 'I don't know why they call it Comic Relief. They should just call it Relief cos there's nothing funny about it.' With the tabloid and stand-up fraternity sharpening their swords, he stopped them in their tracks when it transpired that he was to play a major part in the fundraising marathon. Just as had happened with his Jill Dando joke in 1999, the remark was quickly forgotten.

As had been shown up by Ricky Gervais's ape dance in *The Office*, while Comic Relief is an excellent charitable cause it is also imbued with telethon naffness – of wacky accountants going mad for the day and bathing in Big Bob's Baked Beans, of kids paying 10p to wear their own clothes to school and of stiff building society branch managers carrying gigantic over-sized cheques (all too aware that this rewards their employers with more publicity than the amount they are donating could pay for in advertising). But Peter Kay entered into the spirit of the event with unfettered gusto and on *The Parkinson Show* in early March showed his one-time boss a music video that was the focal point of the 2005 Comic Relief effort. In it, Peter, dressed like a 1980s Mr Byrite model in purple suit and gaudy Hawaiian shirt (an outfit not too dissimilar to the one he wore as a dancing bear in *Max and Paddy's Road to Nowhere*), is seen marching down a corridor cheerily miming as he is joined by a riotously eclectic selection of showbiz personalities from Bernie Clifton and Keith Harris (with feathered friends) to Michael Parkinson himself. The song is '(Is This the Way to) Amarillo', as previously heard sung by Max and Paddy as they drive the Asian elders to a mosque at the start of the second series of *Phoenix Nights* and before every night of the 'Mum Wants a Bungalow' tour, where he'd sing it in the aisles with his tour manager Gordon Isaccs on backing vocals. Of course anyone who had known Peter from his schooldays would have known the song had even greater significance for him. Long before showbusiness and fame called, he used it on the soundtrack to the video of his hallowed *The Wizard of Oz* appearance. '(Is This the Way to) Amarillo' was, as he had continued to do throughout his career, Peter Kay cross-referencing Peter Kay, and Tony Christie – the 1970s crooner he was miming along to – was just along for the ride. It should also come as no surprise to learn that Peter's talismanic lion suit, which he wore in the *Wizard of Oz*, features too – worn by his friend Danny Baker as he strides down the yellow brick road to nowhere with Peter and Heather McCartney as Dorothy.

On his chat show, Michael Parkinson was beside himself with enthusiasm, especially when they showed the scene where Ronnie Corbett is seen tumbling over. It was later revealed that the pairs of celebs joining Peter in his march to see 'sweet Marie' were walking on treadmills in front of a blue screen.

On Comic Relief night, Jonathan Ross was no less effusive and the video got replayed three times – with callers offering to donate more cash in return for repeat showings. Each time it was shown, the giant cheque-holding audience cheered when their favourite celebrity appeared on the screen. Somewhat hysterically, the Sooty Appreciation Society claimed that Sooty and Sweep got the biggest response, but there was no doubting who the real star was.

The '(Is This the Way to) Amarillo' Comic Relief video is a brilliant piece of fun. It reminds us that with all the sophisticated, intelligent and complex humour there is on our TV screens nothing beats sheer outright, uncomplicated entertainment. Well, apart from a fart gag. Originally there were no plans to release '(Is This the Way to) Amarillo' as a single, but public demand was such that Christie's song – which had only got to no. 18 in 1971 – was rush-released. Oddly, the cover proclaimed that it was 'Featuring Peter Kay' despite the fact that he did not appear on the version released on CD. No matter. It sold thousands, staying on top of the charts for seven weeks – a stay in this position that hadn't been seen since Wet Wet Wet were in their pomp.

There was a price to pay for its success, though, as Peter revealed when he joked, 'It's ruined a good song, that.' Now, with the whole nation singing along and an army squadron doing a mock video spoof called '(Is This the Way to) Armadillo', the song that had soundtracked Peter's life was lost to the nation.

Thanks to the now ubiquitous nature of his fame, there was also the inevitable accompanying backlash. The bigger you get, the bigger target you become. Predictable, then, that in his *Daily Mirror* column, offended by Kay's grandstanding on *The Parkinson Show*, Tony Parsons took a wild shot at the nation's number-one comedian. In the article, headlined 'Please Stop Singing … O-Kay?', the populist author bemoaned his 'charidee chortles' and wrote: 'Peter Kay is an old-school, 16-stone light entertainer of a kind that 30 years ago would have been telling crap jokes about Chinkies, Pakis and West Indians called Chalkie. For some reason (possibly because they learn their trade performing in front of pissed audiences who are stupid enough when they're sober), that type always think they can sing as well as tell jokes.'

Parsons – an excellent and enjoyable columnist who loves playing devil's advocate with popular culture – did a great disservice to his wit with his comments, and the paper printed a small selection of the offended responses. However, as wildly inaccurate as his accusations were, there *was* a growing sense of discontent with everybody's favourite Boltonian. Jim Shelly in the *Mirror*, noting the 'Spazzy Paddy' jokes in *Road to Nowhere*, asked, 'Surely these days are long gone?' But the main difference this time was that the disquiet came not from the press or a closed circle of southern comedians crying into their shandy about some gig in 1996 but from the public. When Peter released his *Live at the Manchester Arena* DVD there were cheers as his fans rushed to buy it, but then, when they discovered that he was performing the same set as on the *Live at Bolton Albert Halls* DVD they had purchased the previous year, there were groans of consumer unrest. In the customer reviews on <amazon.co.uk> the words 'con' and 'rip-off' featured prominently. The thoughts of a 'viewer from Halifax, West Yorkshire' far from unique: 'I have watched both the Blackpool show and the *Live at Bolton Albert Halls* DVD and loved them both. When *Peter Kay: Live at the Manchester Arena* came out I was excited to watch it. I have just seen it and was not impressed, to say the least: every single part of it was repeated from the two previous DVDs.' While a London Amazon customer said, 'I am outraged that I paid full whack for this and Peter should be ashamed.'

If anything, the mistake of the *Live at the Manchester Arena* DVD was one of bad marketing. If it had been sold as a 'Mum Wants a Bungalow' documentary, nobody would have complained; in fact they would have applauded that they'd got a bonus live set. Instead, the behind-the-scenes film was tucked away as an extra, along with the '(Is This the Way to) Amarillo' video the whole nation had already seen more times than their own front doors, and Peter Kay ended up looking like a cheap suit-wearing double glazing salesman on *Watchdog*.

With all the criticism in the air surely it was time for Peter Kay's loyal fans to stand up for their man and, mimicking Brian Potter's *Spartacus* moment when Jerry is assaulted by a heckler in *Phoenix Nights*, pronounce as one, 'You push him, you push me.' Their chance would come, but first there was more substantial evidence that proved that, rather than falling out of love with Peter, the British public loved him more than ever. Such was his Midas touch that he was held responsible for a sudden surge in sales of meat and potato pies; even replicas of the Pakistan cricket shirt he wore as Max sold out across the land. He was voted Britain's Best Loved Comedian, a gay icon by the readers of *Bent Magazine*, the man most of us would like to share a bag of chips with and, according to a poll conducted by the Co-operative Bank, the voice we'd most like to tell us directions on an in-car satellite navigation device. How about from Peter Kay's house to, er, the Co-operative Bank? There was, though, one poll that Peter would have preferred not to top in 2005: he headed <chortle.co.uk>'s list of the most over-rated comics in Britain (narrowly beating Jim Davidson). Maybe only Tony Parsons voted. It seemed very unfair.

Thankfully, incandescent with rage, Peter Kay fans bombarded the website with emails to put them right on their error: 'Your poll stinks. Peter Kay rocks,' wrote Dean Ramsey; 'You are a big load of bollocks,' scrawled someone called piroadmark, who continued: 'You load of scrotums.' While one fan simply asked the chortle editors: 'Are you on drugs?'

Chortle probably found the inarticulate nature of these emails amusing, but there is no denying that they got it very wrong. Considering his enormous popularity and the relatively small number of awards he has won, there is a stronger case to make that he is the most underrated British comedian.

'The same website did a survey last year, where Peter was named the funniest man on the planet,' voice of reason Paddy McGuinness told Teletext (a great place to find cheap holidays, by the way) after the Chortle announcement. 'Whoever is successful finds the same media that build them up like to knock them down. I don't think Peter will be bothered one bit.'

As ever, Peter's response was hidden within his work. In April 2006, as part of the special 'Peter Kay Night', he and Paddy McGuinness filmed the links between the shows in character as Max and Paddy. Reading from a TV magazine that the *Live from Manchester* show is on next, Max says, 'He's just brought this out on DVD last Christmas, the money-grabbing bastard.'

Turning negativity into humour has been Peter's way of dealing with it his whole life. At school, when his teacher Paul Abbott told him, 'Life's just a joke to you, Kay', he turned it into a catchphrase, repeating it under his breath whenever he was in trouble. In 2006 he's taken to calling himself a 'roly poly funnyman', turning a comment about him in the *Daily Star* into a gag.

Of course, the one thing that would shut everybody up would be if Peter did a stand-up tour again. However, the chances of that are Ryvita-slim. Exhausted by the marathon 'Mum Wants a Bungalow' tour, he revealed in November 2004 that he was considering quitting stand-up comedy because he feared it would damage his health. 'I don't want to be dropping dead of a heart attack,' he told the *Radio Times*. 'You look at the people you love, like Les Dawson and Eric Morecambe, and you think, "Why did they do that to themselves?" They didn't have the confidence to say no.'

It is an incredible admission for a man in his early thirties to make, but a fear that Eric Morecambe's son, Gary, can sympathise with: 'Peter Kay is the same as my father,' he says. 'I don't think being funny is his job, I just think it's something he is. If he was told tomorrow he'd never be paid again to be a comedian he'd still entertain people. My father said no to nothing and it badly affected his health in the end. Even when he got things on a lot better level and was doing less, he couldn't resist climbing on that treadmill. I think Peter has been looking at people like my dad and like Les Dawson and he's learning from it.'

Indeed the secretaries at Phil McIntyre's office probably spend more time turning down offers for Peter Kay than anything else. True to his word, apart from the occasional charity show Peter has not performed stand-up since 2003 – not that you'd know it from the number of times his live shows are repeated on TV. When it was first shown on Channel 4 in August 2004, his 'Live at the Bolton Albert Halls' show was watched by 6.7 million viewers – the highest ratings ever for a stand-up show.

One rare live performance came when he hosted a charity evening for the Teenage Cancer Trust at the London Royal Albert Hall on Thursday, 7 April 2005. Peter appeared as himself and as Brian Potter, even singing 'The Wind Beneath My Wheels' (his subtly altered version of Bette Midler's 'Wind Beneath My Wings'). But the most remarked-upon moment of the evening came when *Mighty Boosh* star Noel Fielding suffered a hail of unsophisticated four-lettered heckles during his set and, losing his train of thought, disintegrated into incomprehensible mumbling, leaving the stage to cries of 'Taxi' from one audience member.

Rather than sympathise with the distraught surrealist, Peter told the audience that it wasn't his cup of tea at all and that it all went over his head. Stoking the flames, the *Mirror*'s 3 A.M. Girls painted a picture of riotous scenes backstage at the end of the show, with Peter Kay locked in his dressing room as the young Rod Stewart look-alike seethed at the after-show party. Later, Noel Fielding and his *Mighty Boosh* partner Julian Barrett prolonged the feud in the pages of gentlemen's journal *Zoo* (a great magazine for zookeepers). Referring to Peter, Fielding told the publication: 'There are some people who like that sort of thing. We sort of hate that shit really.' Barrett was no less forthcoming: 'My mum loves him. Whenever I go home it's just Peter Kay, Peter Kay all day long – I'm like, "Yeah, all right!" '

Organisers reminded people that the event raised a lot of money for the Teenage Cancer Trust and, wisely, Peter refused to comment.

Enjoying his semi-retirement, back in Bolton with Susan and Charlie, Peter was spotted at a *Balamory* live show, and carrying his young son around town in a portable car seat. Despite Peter's incredible fame and wealth, the family enjoy an ordinary life. And while Peter may no longer visit the café in Bolton Market for his regular meal of baked potato with tuna mayonnaise and baked beans, he is regularly seen around town and at Asda in Astley Bridge, where he once filmed the 'Black Bin Bags' song with Dave Spikey. As a rule, the people of Bolton leave him alone as he does his weekly big shop, but if disturbed he will inform them of his love for Weight Watchers banoffee pies ('just one and a half points').

Inspired by becoming a father, he has made moves to enter into a new part of his career that, once he's old enough to use the DVD player properly, his son might enjoy. In partnership with Chapman Entertainment – the company behind such global tots' TV hits as *Fifi* and *Bob the Builder* – he is set to become the voice of Roary the Racing Car. The 52-part series, set for 2007, follows the adventures of a young racing car that bears an uncanny resemblance to Peter Kay. And if you think the market is flooded with Peter Kay merchandise, wait till you see the number of products (from bath foam to skateboards) Roary's makers have in store for us. First, though, Charlie got to hear his father's voice coming out of a handlebar moustache-sporting playdough policeman as PC Mackintosh in *Wallace and Gromit: The Curse of the Were-*

Rabbit. Peter's finest moment come when he warned villagers of falling giant rabbit droppings.

In his premature dotage, Peter also goes to loads and loads of concerts, including his favourite new artist, Michael Bublé, at the Manchester MEN Arena. Bublé, a favourite with the lasses, tells the men in the audience, dragged to the show by their wives: 'Fellas, I just put air in the tyres. You get to ride the bike all night long.' Peter also makes a habit of introducing live bands onstage when they come to town – Keane, Elton John and Doves were all ushered from the wings by Peter Kay. It became such a habit that it was absolutely no surprise at all to find him at the biggest event of the year, Live 8. Sally Lindsay's boyfriend, session drummer Steve White, plays with the Who, so it was decided that Peter would introduce them onstage. However, things didn't go quite as planned. As is the chaotic nature of such enormous events, Live 8 was running massively behind schedule once it was time for Peter to perform his task for the day. As the technical crew attempted to equip the stage for Townshend and Daltry's performance, Peter was prodded onstage and told to 'fill'. He didn't know how long he was supposed to do this for; he thought he was meant just to be telling the exhausted white rubber-braceleted mass ' … and here's the Who'. Instead, seconds seemed like hours as he paced the stage apologising for 'not being Robbie'. Mark Sutherland, who was covering the event for BBC radio, watched from what became dubbed the golden circle – the section of the audience at the front of Hyde Park filled with competition winners, the press and VIPs. 'We stood there thinking this can't be on telly, surely,' says Mark. 'He started singing "Amarillo" but then sort of wandered off, but you could still see him on the big screen talking to people and then he came back on and tried to do the song again. Then these roadies kept walking past and he kept accosting them, asking what was going on. He didn't tell any gags or anything. He said something about wanting to be on the motorway. We were all stood there saying, "What's going on here?" It looked like no one had told him what to do and he was just winging it, and he had to wing it for a lot longer than he expected to. After Mariah Carey, it was the most embarrassing moment of the day.'

Not everyone agreed, and despite witnessing Paul McCartney with U2, Coldplay, Pink Floyd and Madonna, for many people at the event, dancing around at the back of the park to Peter Kay singing '(Is This the Way to) Amarillo' was their happiest moment of a strenuous day. Not one to be put off by such a setback, Peter even returned to Hyde Park a few weeks later and appeared onstage with his childhood favourites, Queen. In fact the whole of 2005 felt like this, like he'd been let out of school early. He didn't have to turn up on *The Paul O'Grady Show* dressed as a Christmas tree – he just wanted to. He didn't have to walk off the street and into the offices of Century FM and go on air completely unannounced to tell a couple of jokes, he'd just been in the area and had felt like it. And his DJ set at gay Manchester night club Homie Sexual helped him get out of the house for a bit.

Then in December 2005 there was news that this fallow period in Peter's career was coming to a close when newspapers – prompted by a BBC press release – started reporting that not only was a third series of *Phoenix Nights* due, but also a movie. The only downside was that 'we'll have to kill off some of the characters'.

The source of this information was an interview Peter had done for BBC 6 Music with DJ Vic McGlynn. Alongside popular indie bands the Foo Fighters, Franz Ferdinand and the Kaiser Chiefs, who had recorded similar shows, Peter Kay had been invited on to the station as controller for the day for their regular special event called 6 Music Selector. It was a huge coup for the station – which despite being one of the most critically acclaimed of the BBC's national radio stations attracts the smallest number of listeners. In early December, Peter recorded the interview and chose his music. Although there was some disquiet that his taste – Billy Joel, George Benson, the Flying Pickets' cover of 'Psycho Killer' – didn't exactly match the station's profile, the interview was great and was seized upon by the press office. However, what they neglected to tell us was that Peter's comments were originally very heavily laced with humour and accompanying 'maybe's, all of which would have been made clear once the show was broadcast, but it never was. Angered by the leak, Peter refused to sign a release form and the tapes were locked away in a vault. So will there ever be a third series of *Phoenix Nights* or even a movie?

As Peter told Radio One's Edith Bowman just before Christmas 2005: 'I think there's more chance of them bringing back hanging.' Laughing, he did give *Phoenix Nights* fans some hope. 'Yeah, it'll be back some day. You always need something to fall back on. Hitler were a house painter. It'll be back one day … I love Brian Potter.'

Indeed Brian has made several appearances of late – he's even in Max and Paddy's spin-off exercise DVD (a spoof too far that would have made a funny sketch). On Monday, 16 January 2006 Brian Potter even got to co-host an edition of *Top of the Pops* singing Dead or Alive's 'You Spin Me Round' as co-host Fearne Cotton gave his wheelchair a whirl around. It was the first time people talked about the ailing pop show at work the next day for years. On it Brian gave us his verdict on some of the movers and shakers in the charts – James Blunt is 'a modern-day Gilbert O'Sullivan', Morton Harket from A-ha 'is ageing backwards', the Kooks 'need a haircut' and 50 Cent is 'a load of rubbish'. There was also a plug for the Phoenix Club: 'Junction 5 of the M61, just past Balti Towers, coach parties welcome'.

As well as Potter, we've even seen Marc Park again – reincarnated in Peter's pop video for Texas, with Sharleen Spiteri taking the place of Cheryl Avenue as the object of Marc's creative vision. Rather brilliantly, the video references *An Officer and a Gentleman* and Lionel Richie's 'Hello' video and was filmed at Farnworth Veterans Club in Bolton, the set of the first *That Peter Kay Thing* episode, 'In the Club'.

In June he made an appearance in *Doctor Who* (insert Dalek Bread gag here!) as vulgar villain Victor Kennedy, proving yet again that he has the acting chops on top of all his other skills – but then, as he has shown in *Linda Green*, *Blackpool* and *The Catherine Tate Show*, he is no less impressive performing other people's material than he is his own. His desire to play straight roles suggests that, having proved himself as a comedian, he still has a desire to prove himself an actor.

Peter Kay is contracted to one more show for his long-time supporters at Channel 4, but the real question is what he does next. According to reports, ITV have been knocking, offering a substantial pay rise and the chance to take his pick of new dramas. Some industry insiders predict that he may be tempted to Sky. The biggest surprise of all would be if he remained at Channel 4. But if it ain't broke, why fix it? Indeed it shouldn't be ruled out that he will at some point return to the characters in *That Peter Kay Thing* at one stage he suggested that he would like to mimic Granada's *7 Up* series and return to them seven years later to see how their lives had advanced. From the Texas video we know what's happened to Marc Park – he's a security guard dreaming of the good old days – but what of the others? Is Leonard still carrying his giant cross around Bolton, preaching the Lord's word and still failing to get a laugh from his boy-making-a-noise-like-a-frog joke? Or did he meet an unsavoury end at the hands of his mass-murderer pen pal, Walter? Was Mr Softy more successful with porn than with ice-cream? And did Mathew Kelly at the Arena ever get to wear a name tag with his real name on it? Meanwhile, somewhere in a box at the BBC, Peter's uncompleted series *Seaside Stories* is hiding.

Peter's steps into children's TV and the more accessible *Max and Paddy's Road to Nowhere* indicate that his blaspheming days are behind him and that prime-time TV awaits. As he told the owner of the Frog and Bucket, the Manchester comedy club where he cut his teeth as a new stand-up, he is destined for Saturday night at 7.30 p.m. Gary Morecambe feels this is Peter Kay's natural home. 'You do feel that what is missing on television is just wholesome family entertainment,' he says. 'It could be that he's the one that comes in and replaces the Morecambe and Wises and Mike Yarwoods.'

'His next move could be a chat show,' says author and sitcom writer Andrew Collins. 'He's so old-fashioned he could single-handedly take television back to the glory days of the 1970s, wearing a cummerbund and hosting a variety show in a big top. Game shows are his for the taking, too. There is no irony to what Peter Kay does, so at least if he did turn up on the twenty-first-century equivalent of *Bullseye* he'd do it with sincerity, and not with the knowing wink of Ant and Dec or Johnny Vaughn or Graham Norton.' Incidentally, only one of those celebrities Andrew mentions has ever been to Bury.

For those upset by the vision of Peter Kay in a cummerbund, *Father Ted* co-writer Graham Linehan offers a more visionary career path. 'I have a feeling he will make a very successful British film at some point. He's one of the people who's capable of doing it.' Furthermore, Linehan strongly believes that our man from Bolton can succeed where Morecambe and Wise, Tony Hancock and Steve Coogan have stumbled and make an impact beyond the cosy confines of pastie and pea suppers. 'I don't think you can get the audience he gets for his live DVDs and it to just stop once it hits the coast,' he says. 'There is something about him that's touching something more than regional humour; he's touching something that's human, and that's what you need when you're writing films. I don't think he should make any concessions to an international market, I just think he should make a film that feels right to him and I think an international audience will just follow along if he sticks to his guns. Morecambe and Wise were very much a pair of stand-ups messing about in front of the camera, and Steve Coogan is a very fine comedian and actor, but Peter Kay's an actor, director, writer, and the people to compare him to, the people he should be emulating, are people like Woody Allen.'

As Peter himself once said on the set of *That Peter Kay Thing* in his home town, 'There are a million stories in Bolton, behind all those doors.' His tongue was in his cheek, but maybe he's right, and maybe he'll carry on making them and Bolton will become some mythical British mecca for people in America and beyond. It's possible.

If anything, 2005 and 2006 have proved that Peter Kay will stay famous long after *Phoenix Nights* and 'The Services' and even *Max and Paddy's Road to Nowhere* become fading memories. Once people forget about garlic bread, Rola Cola and the way mums dance at weddings, he'll still be around. He will achieve it all without compromise and without leaving Bolton. The best is still to come and, as Brian Potter might say, 'The world's your lobster.'

'You know, he always imagined having a biography written about him,' says Michael Atherton, remembering Peter Kay age 16. 'He even had a title – *When the Laughter Stops* – and a mental picture of the cover, a close-up picture of his face with a wistful expression. Honestly, that's true!'

To be continued ...

The Little Book of Mis-kay-lany

AS HEARD ON CHORLEY FM

Paul Owen – 'My Favourite Waste of Time' (1986)

Tiffany – 'I Think We're Alone Now' (1988)

Johnny Nash – 'I Can See Clearly Now' (1972)

Ryan Paris – 'Dolce Vita' (1983)

Aneka – 'Japanese Boy' (1981)

Mr Mister – 'Kyrie' (1986)

Rock Steady Crew – '(Hey You) the Rock Steady Crew' (1983)

Transvision Vamp – 'Baby I Don't Care' (1989)

Culture Club – 'Church of the Poison Mind' (1983)

Bananarama – 'Robert De Niro's Waiting' (1984)

Wham! – 'I'm Your Man' (1985)

Cheryl Avenue – 'I Will Survive' (1999)

Yazz and the Plastic Population – 'The Only Way is Up' (1988)

Cockney Rebel – 'Make Me Smile (Come Up and See Me)' (1975)

Waterboys – 'The Whole of the Moon' (1985)

Dennis Waterman – 'I Could be so Good for You' (1979)

Tony Christie – '(Is This the Way to) Amarillo' (1971)

Blue – 'Keep On Movin'' (1999)

Bill Withers – 'Lovely Day' (1978)

TRACKLISTING TO JERRY ST CLAIR'S SOLO ALBUM *YOUNG AT HEART*

'Sexbomb'

'She Bangs, She Bangs'

'Drugs Don't Work'

'Gangsta's Paradise'

'Martika's Kitchen'

'Lythium'
'Alphabet Street, Batdance/Get Off' (medley)
'Rock Me Amadeus' (in German)
'Belfast Child'
'Brimful of Asha'

FOR SALE ON LADIES' NITE

The Developer
Thai Beads
Female Climax Cream
Blow Job Action Couple
Mini G Spot
Man to Lamb
Oro-Stimulator
Perfect Pleasures
Sex Lube
Choc Chip Dick Lick
Love Eggs

SIGNS YOU MAY HAVE MISSED

Batteries Available at the Bar (Dildos not Included)

Banana Grove Presents ... Deidra Kay

Hidden Tiger! Crouching Dragon! Peking Duck! Available here!

Big Jo's, Kings of the Road: 'Trailers for sale or rent'

Scrawled on side of van: 'If you think I'm dirty you wanna meet the wife!'

Items available from the Potter's Platter menu: Farmyard Special, Bold Yankee and Northern Beef

PHOTO OPPORTUNITIES TO USE UP HOLIDAY FILM

Mum on patio
Dad looking baffled
Dog in front of radio
Self-portrait

PADDY'S CHAT-UP LINES

Evening girls, wanna have a look into my crystal balls?

Lordy, Lordy, I wouldn't mind hanging out of that.

Here's 10p, phone your mum and tell her you won't be coming home tonight.

Pick a number between one and ten ... You lose, take your tops off.

Nice legs. What time do they open?

STARS OF THE '(IS THIS THE WAY TO) AMARILLO' COMIC RELIEF VIDEO IN ORDER OF APPEARANCE

Peter Kay (Lee Lard look-alike)

William Roache (Ken Barlow)

Anne Kilbride (Deirdre Barlow)

Keith Harris with Orville (blue comedian and non-flying bird)

Bernie Clifton plus ostrich (*Crackerjack* legend, non-flying beast)

Max and Paddy (a couple of doormen)

Shelly Lindsay (Rovers Return landlady)

Jimmy Savile (Mr Fix It)

Albert Wilkinson, Trevor Jones, Craig Salisbury, Big Mick and Nick Read (Bolton Wanderers hooligan firm)

Jim Bowen (Bully's special prize)

Mr Blobby (unemployed pink rubbery lifeform from Crinkly Bottom)

Danny Baker (Daz salesman)

Heather Mills-McCartney (Macca's wife)

Geoffrey Hayes and Bungle (*Rainbow* presenters)

Michael Parkinson (chat show king)

Ronnie Corbett (One Ronnie)

Tony Christie (singer, uncertain of route to Amarillo)

Lee Lard (Peter Kay look-alike)

Shaun Ryder and Bez (Happy Mondays fellas)

Roger Taylor and Brian May (a pair of Queens)

Sweep and Sooty (argumentative glove puppets)

Ramakant Shah (Mahatma Gandhi look-alike)

Trevor Payne (thinks he's Cliff Richard)

Shakin' Stevens (singer, knows what's behind green door)

ALTERNATIVE NAMES FOR BRIAN POTTER

Ironside

Davros

Phantom of the Optics

Dr Strangelove

THAT PETER KAY THING CO-STARRING 'TV'S OWN' BOB CAROLGEES AND SPIT THE DOG

'The Services' – Due to pop in on Bolton First Services on way back from hairdresser's.

'In the Club' – Brian Potter claims to have discovered Bob Carolgees, Spit the Dog, the Krankies, T'Pau and Tom O'Connor.

'The Ice Cream Man Cometh' – Disbelieving policeman says, 'Oh yeah and my name's Bob Carolgees.'

'The Arena' – Steward Mathew Kelly is co-starring in *Oliver!* with Lulu, Lennie Bennett and Bob Carolgees

'Leonard' – Special guest presenting Leonard with his reward.

'Lonely at the Top' – As Marc's career spirals downwards he learns that he has been replaced on 'Night Fever' by Carolgees. 'What's he got that I haven't got,' he asks, 'apart from a spitting dog?'

Phoenix Nights Series One – Endorsing colon care on a leaflet Jerry is reading while on the toilet.

Phoenix Nights Series Two – Hosting daytime chat show on teenage pregnancy being watched by Brian Potter.

Max and Paddy's Road to Nowhere – Paddy is tuning in the radio when he briefly pauses on a radio announcer saying 'and Bob Carolgees'.

YOU LOOK FAMILIAR

Deirdre Kay – Peter's mum enjoys Alfred Hitchcock parts in all Peter's shows. Featured on poster on wall of Den Perry's Banana Grove club.

Susan Kay – Peter's wife appears in many crowd shots and played Clinton Baptiste victim Sonia in *Phoenix Nights*. Last seen grooving to a couple of dancing bears.

Dougie – If there's any phoning to be done in Peter Kay-land, you'll need to phone Dougie.

Cowardly Lion suit – Peter's *The Wizard of Oz* suit appears in 'The Services', *Live at the Top of the Tower* and '(Is This the Way to) Amarillo'.

WEATHERFIELD GAZETTE: LATEST NEWS

'It's people like Jim McDonald that keep me going' – Brian Potter finds hope in *Corrie* survivor.

'I've got narrow veins like Jack Duckworth, but it doesn't stop me' – just one of Leonard's ailments.

'In memory of Alan – Died 8th Dec '89' – flowers tied to Blackpool lamp-post in honour of Alan Bradley.

'It worked for Deirdre Rashid' – Brian Potter launches his Free the Phoenix Two campaign.

I'M NOT FEELING MYSELF

Waitress in 'Leonard' has been off with the runs, which were 'very loose'.

Harry Haroon can't make it to Leonard's award night because his wife's not feeling so good; 'her foot's come back'.

Tom Dale in 'Eyes Down' hasn't taken a day off in 14 years. Even when the doctor suspected he had meningitis – 'put that on your film'.

'Adeena's phoned in with a water infection' so she can't work at 'The Services'.

Jerry St Clair thinks he's 'ruptured an artery'.

The words 'Stranraer' cause sudden angina symptoms in Brian Potter.

I ♥ '80S MOVIES – TEN FILMS PETER KAY HAS PARODIED

Mannequin

Karate Kid

Cannonball Run

Taxi Driver

Dirty Dancing

Midnight Cowboy

Ghostbusters

ET

An Officer and a Gentleman

Ghost

Dirty Harry

Shawshank Redemption

FIVE PEOPLE WHO LOOK LIKE PETER KAY

Joe Royle (football manager)

Alf Roberts (*Coronation Street* grocer, deceased)

John O'Shea (Manchester United defender)

Mungo (canine in *Mary, Mungo and Midge*)

Billy the Fish (goalkeeper)

CITY LIFE COMEDIAN OF THE YEAR WINNERS

1990 – Sister Mary Immaculate (Caroline Aherne)

1991 – Dave Spikey

1992 – Shared by Steve Vernon and Paul Glasswell

1993 – Tony Mills

1994 – Dave Rothnie

1995 – Chris Addison

1996 – Peter Kay

1997 – Shared by Neil Anthony (aka Neil Fitzmaurice) and Dom Carroll

1998 – Steve Harris

1999 – Jason Manford

2000 – Justin Moorhouse

2001 – John Bishop

2002 – Phil Walker

2003 – Seymour Mace

2004 – John Warburton

2005 – Andy Watson

THINGS THAT ANNOY PETER KAY

People who point at their wrist while asking for the time.

People who say, 'Oh you just want to have your cake and eat it too.'

When people say, 'It's always the last place you look.'

When people say, while watching a film, 'Did you see that?'

People who ask, 'Can I ask you a question?'

Rich Tea biscuits.

When something is 'new and improved!'

When people say, 'Life is short.'

When you are waiting for the bus and someone asks, 'Has the bus come yet?'

GREAT DOUBLE ACTS

Maxwell Bygraves and Paddy O'Shea (the Maxster and Padster)

Mary and Joseph (Holy Mary's kids)

Les and Dennis (Mick Bustin's two lads)

Ben Dover and Phil McCracken (what now?)

Rose and Theresa (bingo groupies)

Trigger and Minnie Ha Ha (Cowboy and Native American bride)

Tippit Twins (lesbians before it was popular)

TOP FIVE *THAT PETER KAY THING* MOMENTS

Paul LeRoy's girlfriend saying 'Stop looking at her tits' in the Talent Trek 99 Final.

Alan McLarty drunk on the hard shoulder of the M61.

Keith Lard's fire safety speech.

'I don't care whose it is. I don't care what it is. It's floating.' Pearl, 'The Services'

'She's took it out off me this morning, she's thirsty, she'd 80 gallon for breakfast.' Utah, 'The Services'

Marc Park's speech about being a ladies' man: 'I used to have them hanging off my cock. I was like a human cup tree, I'm not deformed or anything like that ...'

LEONARD'S FRIENDS

The Duke

Turkey George

Carl Who Waves at Cars

3-2-1 Tommy

Jackie Busher

POTTERISMS

'Are my eyes dreaming, Jerry, or have you got two of my builders singing acapulco?'

'The world's your lobster.'

'You're a bloody hypodermic Jerry.'
'We're in a catch-21 situation.'
'Like a bull to a red rag.'
'We've got to grab the cow by the horns and pull together.'
'I want everything shit-shaped and Bristol fashion.'
'Rubber burns? Isn't he a Scottish poet?'
'Jerry St Clair. Licensee and my left foot.'
'Like St Paul, the road to Domestos.'

TEN COMEDIANS WHO HAVE INFLUENCED PETER KAY

Eric Morecambe
Steve Martin
Steve Coogan
Victoria Wood
Caroline Aherne
Les Dawson
James H. Reeves
Ronnie Barker
Leonard Rossiter
Robin Williams

'OL' TOILET MOUTH!' SOME ALTERNATIVE SWEARING

Sweet baby Jesus and the orphans!
Shine a light!
Shut up you girl
Jesus H
You're twisting my melons man
Sweet Jesus and the Mary Chain
Get bent

ITEMS FOUND IN KEITH LARD'S BAG

A ball with a bell on
A muzzle

Dog chews

Chloroform

THE TAO OF LEONARD

1. Don't die with any fun in the bank. You're a long time dead, live your life, cockers.
2. Do all the good you can by all the means you can in all the ways you can in all the places you can at all the times you can so long as you ever can.
3. Tell a lie, lose an eye.
4. Live life to the max.
5. Life's an adventure.
6. A home without a Bible is like leaving the door ajar for the devil to call.
7. Many a good tune can be played on an old fiddle providing the strings don't break.
8. How can you get bored of life when you don't know what's coming next?
9. Life is like a motorway. Sometimes it might seem like you've chosen the wrong lane, it might not be a smooth ride, but keep driving. Sometimes it might feel like you're going too fast. Slow down, pull into services and have a toasted tea cake.
10. If you fancy a jar, forget the car.

BULLSEYE PRIZES

In 1 – Sodastream

In 2 – library video cases

In 3 – Ferguson Videostar

In 4 – George Formby grill

Special prize – a speedboat

'DANCING QUEEN' (ALTERNATIVE VERSION)

'Dancing Queen young string bean only seventeen / Dancing queen feel the meat on a tangerine/ Dancing queen eating Chinese with Mr Bean oh yeah / You can dance in your underpants.'

WISDOM OF POTTER

Dancers are not drinkers.

The higher a monkey climbs the more you can see its arse.

Clubland will never die.

It's amazing what you can do with a computer and access to t'Internet.

The secret to running a successful club is to cater for the family. Nothing offensive, nothing blue …

Would you suck a 10-year-old banana? No. Exactly.

Battery acid is a good remover.

TOP FIVE *PHOENIX NIGHTS* SERIES 1 MOMENTS

The horse mating the Bucking Bronco.

Brian asking Jerry for romantic advice while in the toilets, then the whole of his answer inaudible due to hand-dryer noise, except the end of his tale '… covered in piss'.

Clinton Baptiste turning the Phoenix Club audience into an angry mob … 'Now I'm getting the word nonce.'

Max and Paddy being attacked by a gang of seven three-foot-tall Bolton Wanderers fans.

The Robot Wars when they dispense with technical wizardry and start axing the other robots by hand.

JUST OUT ON LIMITED EDITION VIDEO

Beverly Hills Cock

Shaving Private Ryan

Forest Dump

Willy Wanker and the Chocolate Factory

Party Pissing

Look Who's Porking

Charlie's Anals

Phantom Penis

TOP FIVE DUNKERS

Hob Nobs

Ginger Nuts

Malted Milk

Digestives

Bourbons

SONG LYRICS IN DIALOGUE

'Well my heart definitely belongs here, in First Services Bolton. She's my first, my last, my everything.' Pearl, in 'The Services'

'She's a grafter, she's my bridge over troubled water, that's what I always tell her. She's my night in white satin and she drives the van.' Marc Park, in *That Peter Kay Thing*

'I always thought that love was true in fairytales. Meant for someone else but not for me.' Brian Potter, in *Phoenix Nights* Series 1

'One god and one love, let's get together and feel all right. Bob Marley.' Leonard De Thompkinson, in *That Peter Kay Thing*

'Burn baby burn, disco inferno. Burn baby down, burn that mother down, another child orphaned.' Keith Lard, in *That Peter Kay Thing*

'This old heart of mine, been broke a thousand times.' Brian Potter in *Phoenix Nights* Series 1

'You'll find a girl, if you want you'll get married: look at me, I'm old but I'm happy.' Max, in *Max and Paddy's Road to Nowhere*

'Come on Billy, don't be a hero.' Max, in *Max and Paddy's Road to Nowhere*

'Ooh, it's bootylicious.' Brian Potter, in *Phoenix Nights* Series 2

CAN BRIAN POTTER WALK?

The case against:

Seen standing as the Neptune Club burns.

Sells shopmobile for Cadillac.

Car is clamped outside a gym.

Clinton Baptiste says, 'You can walk.'

The case for:

Cannot feel Beverly playing footsie with him under the table.

Uses vase instead of glass.

Says: 'I'd like to moonwalk but life's a shithouse.'

Soils himself while trapped on stair lift.

Clinton Baptiste says, 'You can walk.'

TOP FIVE *PHOENIX NIGHTS* SERIES 2 MOMENTS

When Brian Potter first sees the inflatable cock and balls.

Brian running into Jerry singing about black bin bags in Asda.

The fortune cookie incident at the grand opening of the Golden Phoenix.

Brian stuck on his stair lift and asking, 'What would Thora Hird do?'

When confused members of the audience do actually 'stand up' when Jerry sings, 'I'm the Real Slim Shady please stand up' as Eminem during the 'Stars in Your Eyes' show.

THINGS WORTH REMEMBERING

You only get a bucket and a half.

Laugh or burn, it's up to you.

Where there's tragedy there's trade.

Life is for the living.

Slippers make you run faster.

Take the C off chips and what have you got?

Never trust a man in Farah.

There's no maternity leave in showbusiness.

PETER KAY'S FAVOURITE TV SHOWS AGED 12

'Allo 'Allo

Porridge

Gentle Touch

Only Fools and Horses

Coronation Street

No Limits

Bullseye

3-2-1

Minder

Mork and Mindy

BOLTON INDEPENDENT LEADER COMMUNITY AWARDS 1999 BEST LOLLIPOP LADY NOMINEES

Doreen Gash

Heather

Diane Purdy
Rita Chalk

THINGS PETER'S NAN SAYS

'Your driving's a bit erotic.'
'Have you got Harry Potter on VD?'
'When you going t'Egypt?'
'Donnie Osmond is a Moomin.'
'I've got a smashing copulation CD.'
'Don't put those bloody cameras on me!'
'See them George Formby grills?'

PETER KAY'S FAVOURITE FOOD

Pear drops
Weight Watchers banoffee pie desserts
Chicken in black bean sauce
Baked potato with tuna and baked beans
Fish and chips
Holland's meat and potato pie
Cauliflower grills
Hob nobs
Parkin loaf
Tuna bap
Häagen-Dazs Bailey's ice cream

TRUE FACTS ABOUT THE PHOENIX CLUB'S KENNY SNR

Used to bag dead bodies in Vietnam
Has slept with Bonnie Langford
Is very friendly with the SAS
Absolutely hammered Robert De Niro at swingball
His surname is Dalglish
Homebrew has won awards
Has seen the Lord's face in a pepperoni pizza
Knows what horse shit tastes like
Main supplier of wood chip to Chuck Norris
Can blow up a bouncy castle with his mouth

FILMS IN WHICH SEAN CONNERY WEARS A WIG (ACCORDING TO MAX AND PADDY)

The Rock
Never Say Never Again
Highlander
Highlander II: The Quickening
Zardoz
The Hunt for Red October
The Avengers

NOT AVAILABLE IN THE SHOPS: SOME ITEMS FROM KAY'S CATALOGUE

Piagra (helping gentlemen last all night long. Available in aniseed, spearmint and linament flavour)

Tantasy (the tanning aid that's not a fantasy)

Invader 2000 (get back you bastard)

Spray Maine (full Sean Connery-style hair thickness)

Umbrella hats (they're umbrellas and they're hats)

Les Cadbury's Fingers (taste exactly the same as Cadbury's Fingers. It's incredible)

Rola Cola (4p for 30 litres)

Kamikaze lager (lifetime supply available now)

Gaspeén (mineral water bottled in the mountains of Afghanistan)

One Dips (our new name for Rich Tea biscuits)

Big Bob's Baked Beans (also known as Big Bob's Bastard Beans)

Snake Eye Pie (actually just chicken and mushroom)

Camerilla Biscuit-Flavoured Condoms (sadly past sell-by date)

Millennium Cone (now with seven flakes)

Hoverboards (available from 2015)

CONTENTS OF MAX'S POCKETS

A pound-coin holder (empty)
An afro comb
I've Stroked a Beaver at Drayton Manor keyring

CONTENTS OF PADDY'S POCKETS

Pornographic magazine (*The Finger Club*)

One pack of condoms (ribbed for the ladies' pleasure)

SPOT-ON PETER KAY OBSERVATIONS

The first item on an airport carousel is always a pram.

Answer machines and old people are not a good combination.

When you're drunk at a wedding you think those white bits of card from the bottom of Party Poppers are pound coins.

When someone tells you directions you go deaf.

When somebody's giving you a phone number you always use a pen that doesn't work.

Mums call you by everyone else's name in the family before they get to yours.

TEN MOVIES PETER KAY BOUGHT ON VIDEO

It's a Wonderful Life

Airplane!

The Man with the Golden Gun

Finding Forrester

Blazing Saddles

The Producers

The Odd Couple

Dr No

Escape to Victory

The Wizard of Oz

THE WAY TO AMARILLO ... FROM BOLTON

Train: Bolton Station to Manchester Airport

Plane No. 1: Manchester to Las Vegas McCarran International Airport

Plane No. 2: Las Vegas to Dallas Fort Worth Airport

Plane No. 3: Dallas to Amarillo International Airport

Taxi: Airport to Amarillo

RAY VON'S FINEST MOMENT

'Fun is the key, but keep seated at all times or you may die.'

TOP FIVE *MAX AND PADDY'S ROAD TO NOWHERE* MOMENTS

Max showing Paddy his notebook filled with childish pictures of two
   detectives he's created called Magnet and Steel.

The TV theme tune face-off.

The cow flying through the air when they run into it.

Brian Potter being sprayed down outside the Phoenix Club shouting 'I
   am Brian Chelsea Potter and I am not the Taliban.'

When the pig they are transporting to market starts farting and Max
   resorts to wearing swimming goggles to stop his eyes burning.

NOT REAL SHOPS

Kebabylon

Tantastic

Porn Again

Plaice Your Orders

Sweet Truck Haul Ltd

Balti Towers

Only Foals and Horses

You Can Call Me Halal

UTAH THE COACH DRIVER'S RULES

1. If you're going to be sick you mop it up yourselves.

2. No solids in the toilets.

3. Only a leg stretch at services, no food.

4. No bottles.

5. No buggering about with the emergency exits.

MAX AND PADDY'S ROAD TO NOWHERE LOCATIONS: ALL ROADS LEAD TO BOLTON

Episode One: White Cliffs Shopping Centre is Crompton Place Shopping
   Centre in Bolton

Episode Two: Safeways supermarket (now a Morrisons) in Breightmet, Bolton; Mick Bustin's Garage is Radcliffe Tyre Centre in Radcliffe, Bolton

Epiiode Three: The Wolfster's 40th birthday party in London is Dobbies Sports and Social Club on Bradley Fold Road, Bradley Fold, Bolton

Episode Four: Magistrates Court is Swinton Civic Centre on Chorley Road, Swinton

Episode Five: The Beadle's Arms pub is the Farmer's Arms on Manchester Road, Swinton

Episode Six: Newcastle is Lower Market Street, Farnworth, Bolton; service station is Bolton West

GAMES SANS FRONTIÈRES (SUPPLIERS OF QUALITY TAT TO THE LICENSED TRADE)

Pool tables with one short leg

Das Boot fruit machine

Flavoured condom machines (six months out of date)

Foxy boxing

Indoor golf

Mechanical bulls

Six-feet-high-Kerplunk

Inflatable Sammy the Snake, fun for all the family

LITTLE THINGS YOU MAY HAVE MISSED

When Holy Mary's mobile goes off while she's in church the ringtone is 'Hot Stuff', as heard on *The Full Monty* soundtrack.

In Brian Potter's address book (seen while he's calling round his staff) there are some curious entries – 'Big Julie, afternoons only, ramp fitted', 'Sluts R Us' and 'Rubber Pants', No. 1 Leakers Road.

In *Peter Kay Live at the Bolton Albert Halls* we see him driven to the venue in a car marked BS Taxis – the cab company owned by Marc Park's manager in *That Peter Kay Thing*.

When Max and Paddy emerge from the Phoenix Club 'Sarolium' they are wearing white gowns embroidered with Le. Ponderosa – the name of the hotel complex in Blackpool that Brian visits.

Brian's doorbell chime is 'Tears of a Clown'.

When Jerry is having his sigmoidoscopy the song playing on the radio is 'The Whole of the Moon' by the Waterboys.

One of the salesmen on the fictional Armchair shopping channel is called John Lennon.

When Marc Park goes back to being a greengrocer he keeps his 'personalised' number plate – MEMPC2.

The road recovery van attending to Alan's broken-down truck is marked ARC (Alan McLarty from *That Peter Kay Thing*'s alternative to RAC).

Holy Mary's son, Joseph, is 'doing a BTEC in joinery down the college'.

The green Ford Cortina in the Phoenix Club car park gets vandalised further with every episode.

In *Max and Paddy's Road to Nowhere* the registration plate of their motor home is BOL 10X.

CHEAP POP THAT'S WORSE THAN ROLA COLA

Suncharm

Panda Pop

Quattro

Hey Brothers

Quenchie Cups

PETER KAY'S FAVOURITE THEME TUNES

1. *Minder*

'*Minder*'s a brilliant theme, I've always loved *Minder*. It's a great one for singing along in the car. *Minder* always reminds me of Wednesday nights at nine o'clock, Benny Hill would be on at eight. I'd go to bed at 8.30 and I'd always hear *Minder* through the floor, then I'd hear the front door close and my dad going out and I knew where he'd be going. He'd send us to bed and then go and get fish and chips and he'd come back and I'd always come down and go, "I can't sleep … ooooh fish and chips" and he'd go, "All right, you can have a butty", and I'd stay and watch a bit of *Minder*.'

2. *Mork and Mindy*

'Lovely theme. Boulder, Colorado. I saw it recently and the theme came on and I had this rush of being a child and I remember my dad just laughing and laughing at it so much. I loved *Mork and Mindy*.'

3. *Fall Guy*

'*Fall Guy*'s a cracking theme. [Sings]: "I never spent much time in school, but I taught ladies plenty" … bit saucy there, cos it's Lee Majors singing you know. [Sings]: "When I wind up in the hay it's only hay, hey, hey". I thought yeah, you were up all night writing that one, Lee. He was a stuntman, a bounty hunter who kind of operated outside the law and he went off and did his own thing. That was a sing-along one that. That were Friday nights, half seven to half eight, then *Gaffer* were on or *That's My Boy*, then at nine o'clock it were either *Shine On Harvey Moon* or *Gentle Touch* or *Flambards*, with *Winner Takes All* at seven.'

4. *This is Your Life*

'Oh yeah, *This is Your Life* is a really great theme. Someone once told me *This is Your Life* is the best format for a programme in the world – there's suspense, surprise, tears, it will never die, it will always be on, always. Everyone flicks it on and says, "Just see whose life it is."

5. *Sportsnight*

'That was another one you heard through the floorboards. I was always hearing *Robin's Nest*. *Sportsnight* was like a vivid waking-up dream. They had *Closedown* after *Sportsnight*.'

6. *Hill Street Blues*

'Ah, all Mike Post's themes are good, but this one's best.'

7. *The A Team*

'Everyone loves *The A Team*. They were Vietnam vets and you hired them for free; if you were in trouble you'd call the A Team and they'd come and help you. Why? *The Equaliser* was very similar. Where he got his money from I'll never know. He had a New York apartment, massive apartment with a panic room; the rent on that alone must have crippled him, plus he did it all for free … you'd come and find the Equaliser and he'd come and balance the odds. I remember thinking, "How can he run this?" '

8. *The South Bank Show*

'My favourite show of all time, *Porridge*, didn't even have a theme, just loads of gates and doors slamming and "Norman Stanley Fletcher, you have been found guilty …" – very serious. *Two Ronnies* was always a good theme. *South Bank Show*'s a classic, it's great: you get all excited and then Melvyn Bragg comes on: "Blah blah, Czechoslovakian poet". Flick that shit off ... but the theme comes on, here we go!'

9. *Superstars*

'Thursday eight o'clock that were on; 7.30 *Top of the Pops*, eight o'clock *Superstars*. It's bizarre cos I must have been about four, but I remember *Superstars* like it was yesterday.

10. *The Pink Panther*

'This is a great theme tune. It reminds me of Saturday nights; we used to have breakfast at night-time. That was my dad's day to cook and that was all he could make, so we'd have full English for tea. We'd have tea watching *Pink Panther* and *Dr Who* then my mum and dad would go and my grandad would baby-sit and we'd watch *3-2-1* or a film. I remember watching *American Werewolf in London* with my grandad. I knew that scene with Jenny Agutter were coming up and I had to leave the room. I couldn't watch muck with my grandad. Besides, I'd already seen it about eight times. I'd come back and my sister would be reading back of tissue box: "Are they two-ply, these tissues?" '

'Peter Kay's Favourite Theme Tunes' were originally published in *The Guardian* in an interview with Johnny Dee.

Acknowledgements

That Peter Kay Book includes a substantial amount of exclusive material, including an unpublished transcript of my own two-hour interview with Peter Kay. Many people spoke to me off the record – you know who you are, cheers – and many kind people agreed to talk openly about Peter, over the course of numerous meetings, emails and phone calls. I would like to give very special thanks to Peter's old school pals Michael Atherton and Karen Peel, who gave up a great deal of time to help with the book.

This book would not have been possible without the help of three very special people: Chris, Jacqui and Dorrie. I thank you for appearing like angels at my hour of need. I am very fortunate to know people as thoughtful as you. Also to Kathy, Holly and Annie – sorry for becoming a Peter Kay-obsessed lunatic! Dad and Jo – much love to you. You can phone me now, it's OK, I've finished.

The generosity of Jon Wilde was most crucial. Jon, go and take your dog for a walk. Much gratitude also to the lady at Bolton Library who I had running up and down stairs fetching books like a madwoman – you are doing a great job looking after those crazy family tree folk. A multitude of high fives to Ian Gittins and Miranda West.

Thanks, in no particular order, to: Gary Morecambe, Andrew Collins, Graham Linehan, Sonia Hurst, Adam Bloom, Doreen Gash, Billy Bedlam, Lisa White, Dawn Panton, Iain Coyle, Cheryl Avenue, John Marshall, Lloyd Peters, Mathew Kelly, Paul Barnwell, Steve Alcock, Toni Baker, Robert Popper, Janey Godley and Marc Rowlands.

Finally, thank you for the music, the songs I'm singing. Thanks for all the joy they're bringing. Who can live without it? I ask in all honesty. What would life be? Without a song or a dance what are we?

Oh, and thank you to Peter Kay.

Bibliography

BOOKS

Allen, Woody *Without Feathers,* Ballantine
Cook, William *The Comedy Store – the Club That Changed British Comedy*, Little, Brown
Corbridge, Sylvia Lovat *It's an Old Lancashire Custom,* Dennis Dobson
Double, Oliver *Stand-Up,* Methuen
Margolis, Jonathan *Bernard Manning: A Biography,* Orion
Nevin, Charles *Lancashire, Where Women Die of Love,* Mainstream
Peter Kay's Phoenix Nights: The Scripts Series 1 and 2 (4 books)
Thompson, Ben *Sunshine on Putty*, Harper

VIDEO/DVD

Peter Kay, Live at the Top of the Tower
That Peter Kay Thing
Blow Dry
Going Off Big Time
24 Hour Party People
Ted Robbins, Live and Large in Blackpool
Phoenix Nights Series One and Two
Peter Kay, Live at Bolton Albert Halls
Peter Kay, Driven to Distraction
Max and Paddy's Road to Nowhere
Peter Kay Live in Manchester
Max and Paddy's The Power of Two
Wallace and Gromit: The Curse of the Were-Rabbit

INTERNET SOURCES

<peterkayonline.com>
<peterkay.co.uk>
<davespikey.co.uk>
<chortle.co.uk>
<offthetelly.co.uk>
<bbc.co.uk>

<channel4.com>
<theguardian.co.uk>
<billybedlam.co.uk>
<peterkayforum.com>
<thecustard.tv>
<ruscoe.net/maxandpaddy>
<peterkayfan.co.uk>
<www.northstarproductions.co.uk>
<thisislancashire.co.uk>
<thisisbolton.co.uk>
<manchesteronline.co.uk>
<hoscar.demon.co.uk>

CREDITED ARTICLES

Banks, Martin: 'Peter Kay, Glee Club' (2000), *Birmingham Evening Mail*; Jackson, Nick: 'Funny Man Peter In The Big Time' (1997), Ackerley, Chris: 'Peter's Show Is a Record Breaker' (2002), Savage, Ian: 'Peter's Tour de Force' (2002), all *Bolton Evening News*; Bennett, Steve: 'Review' (2002), *chortle.co.uk*; Burgess, Marissa: 'Contrast and Compere' (2003), Rowlands, Marc: 'Those Peter Kay Things' (2003), 'Once Upon a Time In The North' (2003), all *City Life*; Paterson, Peter: 'Animals Before Humans' (2001), *Daily Mail*; Fulton, Rick: 'Peter Kay's Phoenix Nights' (2001), 'Paddy Power' (2006), Morgan, Kathleen: 'Quickfire Peter' (1998), Robertson, Cameron: 'I Don't Want To Die Laughing' (2004), all *Daily Record*; Jefferies, Mark: 'Ricky Turned Down TV Beer Deal' (2003), Jefferies, Mark: 'Peter Chaos' (2004), Morgan, Gareth: 'Humour? I'm Working On It' (2001), all *Daily Star*; Spikey, Dave: 'That Peter Kay Connection' (1999), 'News' (1999-2006), 'Dave On Chain letters' (1999), all *davespikey.co.uk*; Roberts, Wendy: 'Telly Stardom Won't Drag Peter Away From Home' (1999), *Derby Evening Telegraph*; Atherton, Ben: 'Comedian Kay Comes Clean on Sick Jill Joke' (1999), Somerville, Colin: 'Cereal Filler' (1998), all *Edinburgh Evening News*; Lee, Veronica: 'It's Another Kay Thing' (2001), *Evening Standard*; Beacom, Brian: 'Peter's a Sound Bloke' (2001), *Glasgow Evening Times*; Donohue, Simon: 'Cool Venue' (1996), *Lancashire Evening Telegraph*; Gould, Phil: 'The Rise and Rise of...' (2002), *Liverpool Daily Post*; Viner, Brian: 'Motorway Services With an Ironic Smile' (1998), *Mail On Sunday*; Barnes, Anthony: 'Laidback Liam Sits it Out' (2001), Donohue, Simon: 'The Rise and Rise Of Peter Kay' (2003), all *Manchester Evening News*; Neild, Andy: 'Comic Peter's Shock at Award' (2000), *Newsquest*; Walliams, David: 'Noel Gallagher Interview' (2005), *Observer Music Monthly*; Lyons, James: 'Anger Over Dando Joke' (1999), *PA News*; Freeman, Martin: 'Comedian is Funny

Peculiar' (2003), *Plymouth Evening Herald*; Jinks, Peter: 'Fringe Comics Go Channel Hopping' (1997), *Scotland On Sunday*; Jagasia, Mark 'Bolton - The New Showbiz Capital of the World' (2000), *Sunday Express*: Laws, Roz: 'Living On The Edge' (2005), *Sunday Mercury*; Donnelly, Claire: 'How Peter Kay Became the King of Comedy' (2004), Ellam, Dennis: 'I Owe It All To Bolton...' (2001), Hewett, Rick: 'Man U Can 'Ave It' (2002), Hyland, Ian: 'Royle Ructions' (1999), all *Sunday Mirror*; Davies, Mike: 'Northern Magic Is a Kay Thing' (2000), *The Birmingham Post*; Born, Matt: '£10,000 Damages For Fire Officer' (2001), Lee, Veronica: 'The Comedian With 16 Faces' (2000), all *The Daily Telegraph*; Gibson, Janine: 'Four Seasons Its Schedules' (1999), Logan, Brian: 'Peter Kay' (2002), Margolis, Jonathan: 'Shut Up, Dad' (1999), McLean, Gareth: 'Peter Kay Profile' (2004), Moore, Emily: 'My Inspiration' (2000), van der Zee, Bibi: 'He Could Have Been a Bingo Caller' (2000), Walsh, Collette: 'Funny Ha Ha' (1997), all *The Guardian*; Barrell, Sarah: 'Assembly Rooms' (2002), Byrne, Claire: 'Chorley FM Under Fire' (2005), Lee, Veronica: 'Meet The New Les Dawson' (1998), 'Something Funny's Going On' (1998), 'Have You Heard The One About the Warm-up Act' (2002), 'Laugh - By Order Of The Committee' (2000), Rampton, James: 'Edinburgh Festival '98' (1998), Rudebeck, Clare: 'Graduate Careers: How I Got Here' (2002), Viner, Brian: 'Podgy Peter Pulls It Off' (2000), 'The Gag With The £10,000 Punchline' (2001), 'Viva Johnny Vegas' (2003), all *The Independent*; Games, Alex: 'Funny Bones' (2004), York, Peter: 'John Smith's Bitter' (2004), all *The Independent On Sunday*; Carroll, Sue: 'The Funny Thing About Bolton' (2000), Catchpole, Charlie: 'Britcoms Have The Last Laugh' (2000), 'Potter's Stairlift To Heaven' (2001), Parsons, Tony: 'Please Stop Singing... O-Kay?' (2005), Purnell, Tony: 'Peter's Too Much of a Good Thing' (2000), Ridley, Jane: 'Family Night Out' (2002), Robertson, Cameron: 'Coronation Pete', Shelley, Jim: 'Shelleyvision' (2004), all *The Mirror*; Flett, Kathryn: 'Don't Turn Your Noses Up' (2000), Woodcraft, Molloy: 'Wednesday TV Review' (2000), Merritt, Stephanie: 'Special Kay' (2005), all *The Observer*; Bletchley, Rachael: 'Don't Give Up The Kay Job' (2005), Bushell, Garry: 'Peter Hits Bullseye' (2004), 'Phoenix Nights Is Working Class Act' (2002), all *The People*; Smith, Aidan: 'This'll Make You Laugh' (1998), Synnot, Siobhan: 'Flight Of The Phoenix' (2004), all *The Scotsman*; Dowell, Ben: 'That Thing He Does' (2000), *The Stage*; Brockway, Sally: 'Chat's Showbiz' (2002), Compton, Louise, 'Bizarre Workout DVD' (2006), Hockney, Karen: 'I'd Sooner Give It Up Than Move To London' (2002), Patrick, Guy: 'TV Peter's Theft Fury' (2003), Yates, Charles: 'Peter Kay Buys His Mum That Bungalow' (2005), 'Peter Kay's Secret Heartache' (2005), all *The Sun*; Phelan, Stephen: 'Perrier? Who Needs It?' (2003), *The Sunday Herald*; Fanshawe, Simon: 'Pride Of The North' (1998), Nicol, Patricia: 'The

Surreally Useful' (1998), all *The Sunday Times*; Oliver Wilson, Chris: 'Smash Wit' (1999), *The Times*.

UNCREDITED ARTICLES

The majority of the quotes in this book are from my own transcripts and sources. When this is not the case, where possible I have credited the writer and/or publication. However, some of the articles researched on the Internet did not have complete credits, plus many news stories do not name the journalist. My heartfelt apologies to anyone I miss out in the following list of research material.

'Comic Kay boosts Baker's profits' (2005), 'Comedian's dressing room burgled' (2003): <bbc.co.uk>; 'Bolton comic scoops top award' (1996), 'Comic Peter slammed over Dando joke' (1999), 'Comic to make his directing debut' (2001), 'Comic's a real wag' (1996), 'Corrie Cameo' (2004), 'Film fans honour movie buff Leslie' (1996), 'Fire adviser hands over TV cash' (2001), 'For Pete's sake have a laugh' (1998), 'Funnyman bids for fringe benefit' (1998), 'Funnyman Peter is big news back home' (1999), 'Funnyman Peter misses the fun to help Omagh fund' (1998), 'It all adds up to comic Peter' (2005), 'Laugh? I nearly choked to death' (1999), 'Life's a bundle of laughs ...' (1998), 'Peter announces Bolton shows' (2002), 'Peter becomes master of mirth' (1996), 'Peter friends up for Comic Relief' (2001), 'Peter Kay' (2002), 'Peter Kay to be a dad' (2003), 'Peter Kay's joy ...' (1998), 'Peter's big mistake' (1999), 'Peter's friends' (1999), 'Peter the Great' (1997), 'Peter's top billing on Parkinson' (1998), 'Peter's voice is key to success' (1999), 'Spikey's a real wag' (1996), 'Spitting image' (2000), 'Star turns down new offers ...' (2002), 'The big breakthrough' (1998), 'Welcome to the Wild West – Houghton that is' (1998), 'Young folk set the scene' (1996): all *Bolton Evening News*; 'That Peter Kay Thing' (1999), <channel4.com>; 'A Bitter Man' (2005), 'Dave Spikey' (2002), 'Dave Spikey' (2003): all <chortle.co.uk>; 'Comedian horrifies guests with Jill joke' (1999), *Coventry Evening Telegraph*; 'Wicked whispers' (2005), *Daily Mail*; 'Say sausages' (2005), *Glasgow Evening Times*; 'Rock-Kay mountain high' (2000), 'Laughing all the way to London' (1999): *Lancashire Evening Telegraph*; 'Pride of Manchester' (2002), *Manchester Evening News*; 'Peter cheers up sad Reds' (2003), *Stockport Express*; 'Phoenix jail nights' (2004), 'Krackers from Kay' (2002): *Sunday Mirror*; 'Fancy a pint?' (2003), 'Producer's Choice' (2003): *Televisual*; 'Home entertainment' (2000), *Guardian*; 'Phoenix will not rise again' (2005), *Independent*; 'Gagged by model mum' (1997), *Mirror*; 'The new faces of TV comedy' (1999), *Observer*; 'Bolton wanderer' (2005), *Sunday Herald*; 'Peter Kay special' (2004), *Zoo*.